The

History

of

Money

ALSO BY JACK WEATHERFORD

Tribes on the Hill
Porn Row
Narcóticos en Bolivia y los Estados Unidos
Indian Givers
Native Roots
Savages and Civilization

The
History
of
Money

From Sandstone to Cyberspace

JACK WEATHERFORD

 THREE RIVERS PRESS • NEW YORK

Published by Three Rivers Press,
New York, New York.
Member of the Crown Publishing Group.

Random House, Inc. New York, Toronto, London, Sydney, Auckland
www.randomhouse.com

THREE RIVERS PRESS is a registered trademark and the
Three Rivers Press colophon is a trademark of Random House, Inc.

Originally published in hardcover by Crown Publishers in 1997.

Printed in the United States of America

Design by Leonard Henderson

Library of Congress Cataloging-in-Publication Data
Weatherford, J. McIver.
    The history of money / by Jack Weatherford.
    Includes bibliographical references and index.
    1. Money—History.   I. Title.
  HG231.W4   1997   332.4'9—dc21   96–49432

ISBN 0-609-80172-4

10 9

For
Walker Pearce

CONTENTS

III. ELECTRONIC MONEY

FOREWORD

> *Money is one of the shatteringly*
> *simplifying ideas of all time*
> *. . . it creates its own revolution.*
> —PAUL J. BOHANNAN

THE DOLLAR IS DYING; SO TOO ARE THE YEN, THE mark, and the other national currencies of the modern world. Our global money system is infected with a deadly virus, and, already severely weakened, it is now only a matter of time before it succumbs. The dollar, mark, and yen will join the ducat, cowrie shells, and the guinea in the scrap box of history, as items of interest primarily to antiquarians and eccentrics.

Just at the moment in history when money dominates the whole of our society, it faces some strange and ominous challenges. In the last decades of the twentieth century, the global money system began to cough and sputter, to jerk and stumble. The currencies of several weaker nations unexpectedly sickened and died in a paroxysm of inflation, while the exchange rates of the strongest and healthiest currencies wobbled and lunged uncontrollably one way and then another. After reigning as the world's major financial institutions since the Renaissance, banks teetered and fell under billion-dollar losses that seemed to occur inexplicably overnight. The United States continued to nurse a rising national debt, growing trade imbalances, episodic bouts of inflation, and a long-term decline in the value of the dollar. Despite rather awkward but extensive intervention at many levels, no government seems able to control its own currency, and new financial institutions now stretch across the globe in a network of interconnected businesses with a power never before known in history. Supposedly global agencies such as the International Monetary Fund, the United Nations, and the World Bank seem largely irrelevant to the finances of any but the weakest players already on the international dole.

Despite the alarming monetary situation, the demise of the present monetary order will mark neither the end of commerce nor the death of money. Even as the old system staggers hesitantly into its grave, we can discern the new system rising on the horizon to replace it. We can see a flickering image of that new system in the soft glow of the computer screen, and we can smell its acrid scent among the electric cables on the floor of any international currency exchange. We can hear it in the electronic whir of encoded chips on plastic cards passing through the electronic readers that are already replacing the old cash registers. In the realms of cyberspace, money is now being reinvented as a free-floating force that can appear instantaneously anywhere in the world in any amount. No longer tethered to the fortunes of one government or a single country, the new money is emerging in a large variety of new forms. The new money is raw power.

The new technology is already changing the way we earn and use money, and it will create a whole new class system of rich and poor. The new money system will transform the way we distribute goods and the way we finance civic life. It will rearrange the political map of the world and create whole new local and global entities that are difficult to imagine today. The newly emerging system will change the very meaning of money.

The present revolutionary change in the nature and uses of money constitutes the third great mutation in money. The first generation began with the invention of coins in Lydia nearly three thousand years ago and resulted in the first system of open and free markets. The invention and dissemination of coins and the accompanying market created a whole new cultural system—the classical civilizations of the Mediterranean. The new monetary and market system ultimately spread around the world and gradually destroyed the great tributary empires of history.

The second generation of money dominated from the beginning of the Renaissance through the industrial revolution, and it resulted in the creation of the modern world capitalist system. It originated in the banks of Italy, and it eventually created the system of national banks and the paper money that they issued for use in daily commerce. The invention of banking and the paper money system destroyed feudalism, changed the basis of organization from heredity to money, and it changed the basis of economic power from owning land to owning stocks, bonds, and corporations.

Each of the two initial types of money created its own unique culture that differed markedly from all earlier ones. Now, at the opening of the twenty-first century, the world is entering the third stage of its monetary history—the era of electronic money and the virtual economy. The rise of electronic money will produce changes in society as radical and far-reaching as the two earlier monetary revolutions caused in their own eras. The new money will make sweeping changes in the political systems, in the organization of commercial enterprises, and in the nature of class organization. Virtual money promises to make its own version of civilization that will be as different from the modern world as from the world of the Aztecs or the Vikings.

ACKNOWLEDGMENTS

I WOULD LIKE TO ACKNOWLEDGE SPECIAL INSPIRA-tion during the writing of this book from Voltaire's comment that "it is easier to write on money than to obtain it, and those who gain it, jest much at those who only know how to write about it."

I also acknowledge the many contributions of my Macalester College colleagues: Ellis Dye, Arjun Guneratne, David McCurdy, Anna Meigs, Emily Schultz, and Anne Sutherland. I thank the staff of the DeWitt Wallace Library, as well as my wonderful students for their comments, suggestions, and criticisms.

I greatly appreciate the help of my agent Lois Wallace, my campus editor Mary Vincent Franco, and my Crown editors, Karen Rinaldi and James O. Wade. For their professional advice and expertise, I thank Edward DeCarbo, Dan Getsch, Kathy Hyduke, Edward M. Kadletz, and Carolyn Ybarra. I owe a special debt to George McCandless of the Economics Department of San Andres University in Buenos Aires, Argentina. Working with him frequently reminded me of the admonition that Georg Simmel wrote to his readers in *The Philosophy of Money* that "not a single line of these investigations is meant to be a statement about economics."

For special support along the way, I thank Cindy Hermann, Peter Johnson, Rochelle Jones, Kirk Frederick, and my family.

No government or foundation money was used in the research, writing, or publication of this book.

INTRODUCTION
The World Market

> *The thing that differentiates man*
> *from animals is money.*
> —GERTRUDE STEIN

A YOUNG MOTHER, BAREFOOT AND BARE-BREASTED, hurries out of a mud hut with her nursing baby tied loosely at her side in a cloth sling and with six eggs floating in a bowl of milk balanced delicately on her head. Even though the sun has not yet broken over the horizon, sweat ripples across her face and drips from the gold ring piercing the middle of her lower lip. From the ring, the sweat drips down her chest and rolls across the decorative scars that glisten on her stomach.

One morning in every five, she arises before dawn to begin the eleven-mile trek from her village of Kani Kombole in the West African country of Mali to the town of Bandiagara, where a market is held every five days. She hurries out of the family compound to join her sisters, her female cousins, and the other village women who have already begun the slow climb up the cliff that contains the tombs of their ancestors and that forms part of the Bandiagara Escarpment, a rise of some 1,500 feet to the plateau above.

As the panting women slowly climb the rocky face of the escarpment, the mud and thatch huts gradually recede from view until they appear to be nothing more than sand castles on a beach. In the heat, the two- and three-story huts, the rickety corncribs, and the goat pens seem to melt in the first rays of the penetrating tropical sun. The women march for nearly three hours. They carry their nursing infants with them, but must leave behind the heavier children who

are too young to make the arduous journey on their own. On her head
or back, each woman carries something to sell in the marketplace—
a bag of tomatoes, a bunch of small onions, a bowl of chilies, or a sack
of sweet potatoes. Flies buzz around them constantly, attracted by the
moving feast of fresh foods. Occasionally, the women stop to rest on
some large rocks in the shade of a lonely and misshapen baobab tree
in an otherwise austere landscape. They take small sips from the
milk bowl, but they cannot rest for long. Pestered by the growing
swarm of insects and always in a hurry to get to market before their
customers arrive and before the heat of the sun peaks, the women
push solemnly ahead.

A short distance ahead of the women, a small caravan of men
marches with donkeys piled so high with millet that they look like
parading haystacks. Even though all of the travelers come from the
same village and often from the same families, the men and women
travel in separate groups on their separate missions.

On the other side of the world in an apartment building on the
Upper West Side of Manhattan, a young man clutching a new leather
briefcase given to him as a graduation gift waits for an elevator.
Dressed in a gray suit, gym shoes, and a raincoat, but without a tie,
he steps into the elevator, which is already crowded. With a silent
nod, the young man puts the briefcase between his knees and awkwardly ties his floral-print silk tie without elbowing his neighbors. As
he leaves the building and moves onto the sidewalk, he joins a rapidly
moving column of people from adjoining buildings headed for the
subway where they join even more people pressed together in the cars
that carry them south to the Financial District at the southern tip of
the island. After emerging from the subway, the man pauses to buy
a sesame bagel, which he plunges into his pocket, and a paper cup
filled with fresh-roasted Ethiopian-blend coffee, which he sips
through a hole in the plastic lid. Five days a week he makes the
same commute from his apartment building to the New York
Stock Exchange, situated among some of the tallest skyscrapers in
the world.

The town of Bandiagara, Mali, lies in the Sahel, the borderland between the southern Sahara and the thick rain forest along the West African coast. Once in the market, the women of Kani Kombole go their separate ways. One takes her onions to the onion truck where the buyer will transport them to the city. Those with tomatoes spread out their sashes on the ground and arrange their produce on them, protecting their goods from the sun under small canopies of thinly plaited straw on gnarly sticks. The woman who had balanced the milk and eggs on her head takes her load to the dairy area, where she displays the eggs in a small gourd next to the larger bowl of milk. Once she has sold her goods to townspeople or traveling wholesalers, the village woman might buy a plastic pail, some tobacco, a block of salt, a few cups of sugar, or some other luxury goods to take home with her. The food, however, is for the townspeople to buy, not her. The few overripe bananas from the coast, the dried dates brought in from an oasis in the Sahara, and the expensive oranges from the coastal farms cost more than the whole load of vegetables or milk that she was able to bring to market.

Except in the Muslim communities where almost all public activities fall into the domain of males, women operate and manage the markets throughout West Africa. The women carry the produce to and from the market, and they negotiate the buying and selling. Most of the people who come to the market as buyers or sellers are women. Although men may wander through on a specific mission, the interactive style of the market is female and based largely around enduring ties of kinship, friendship, and personal knowledge of one another.

Despite their illiteracy and complete lack of formal education, most of the women in the marketplace at Bandiagara can negotiate, buy, and sell with great facility. They barter produce for produce, will accept payment in coins and paper money—often in several different currencies—and can make change. Even though they cannot read the words on the money, they recognize the value of the different bills primarily by their color, shape, size, and the images on them. Because transactions are made publicly in front of a line of other attentive women, the marketplace abounds in advice and help in each transaction to make sure that it proceeds according to tradition. Women bargain and barter often without even sharing a common language. All they need is a couple of words and a set of hand gestures to signify the numbers. A clenched fist means five; a hand clap signifies ten.

The milk seller's primary competitors in Bandiagara are not other women like her in the neighborhood; they are the dairy farmers of Wisconsin, New Zealand, and the Netherlands. The imported milk is condensed, canned, and distributed free in the poor countries of Africa. Although clearly marked "not for sale" in English, it persistently shows up for sale in the stall immediately next to the young mother from Kani Kombole. The amount of canned milk for sale depends in part on economic conditions in North America, Europe, and the South Pacific. It depends on how much milk Nestlé, Hershey, or Kraft buys for their annual production and on the fluctuating value of the American dollar, the Dutch guilder, and the New Zealand dollar relative to the French franc, to which the West African franc of Mali is tied. It depends on how hot the summer is and how much ice cream people eat; it depends on the world's annual yield of soybeans, one of the major competitors of milk products. The amount of canned milk for sale in Bandiagara in any given month also depends on the dairy subsidies and the foreign aid appropriations made by the U.S. Congress in Washington, D.C.; the food policies of the United Nations high commissioner for refugees in Geneva and the European Common Market headquartered in Brussels; and the mercurial aid programs of religious and other private charitable organizations around the world.

When there is an abundance of donated milk on the Bandiagara market, the young mother is less likely to sell her fresh milk. When the cans of milk disappear, she will earn more money and will be able to take home more goods that day. Her eggs provide a small financial cushion that help to stabilize her income somewhat, since foreign food programs frequently donate milk products but rarely send eggs abroad. She can usually sell the eggs, even on days when she and her family drink the bowl of unsold milk rather than carry it all the way back to Kani Kombole.

The Money Net

The floor of the New York Stock Exchange seems as littered as the ground in the market of Bandiagara. Instead of peanut shells, corn husks, and banana leaves, however, the floor is covered with multi-colored slips of paper from financial transactions. Any experienced trader can instantly determine the volume of activity and the areas where it has transpired by the number of white and yellow slips of paper piled up around a hot zone like pottery shards around a kiln.

Aside from the messy floor of the exchange, the cavernous hall looks deceptively like a high-tech automobile assembly line with banks of electronic equipment, miles of blue computer wires, and monitors hanging down on flexible arms like the robotic equipment used to put cars together. The green letters on the electronic boards cast an ethereal glow into the antiseptic atmosphere of the large cavern. Despite the apparent chaos on the floor, activity is carefully regulated by a system of colors. The monitors give out the latest financial information in an eerie computer light; each worker has his own particular jacket color and type of plastic identification badge; and the bright yellow telephones are easy to spot. Workers on the floor chat idly about sports, chew gum, or munch snacks in casual groups that suddenly spring to life as frenzied huddles of would-be buyers and sellers jump, shout, and gesture furiously whenever the stock of a particular company comes into play.

Although women are allowed to work on the floor of the stock exchange, it remains largely a male domain with a decidedly masculine style of interaction that is loud and intense. Traders on the floor haggle and transact business for people and institutions throughout the world. In the space-age booths on the floor, they receive requests for purchases or sales from their home office, located somewhere nearby in the Financial District, which, in turn, have received orders from branches and customers around the world. Depending on the time zones, they can connect with virtually any financial nexus on the globe, through a few telephone calls and computer transmissions.

Every stage of the procedure can be executed electronically until the final moment when buyer meets seller in the form of two traders standing face-to-face on the exchange floor to negotiate the details.

It does not matter that one is trading for a Belgian in Osaka and the other for retired teachers in Omaha. They may not even know where Osaka—or even Omaha—is, but at the last moment all of these transactions from around the world are finalized in a personal encounter between a trader trying to sell for the highest price and a trader who wants to buy at the lowest price; both are acting on behalf of people whom they will probably never know or even see. The same communication lines that brought the requests will, in turn, instantly transmit information about the sale to computer monitors around the world and thus influence other players in their decision to enter or to avoid the market at this particular moment.

When the sun sinks lower in the sky and the scorching noon heat subsides, the young mother gathers up her baby, the empty milk bowl, and the three kola nuts that she purchased with her earnings. She then joins the long line of women marching out of town toward their villages and the evening chores that await them at home. Without the heavy milk on her head, her feet move more lightly, and she scurries along toward the family compound in Kani Kombole, where she will help to milk the family goats before losing the light of day.

At the end of a long day on the stock exchange, the young man loosens his tie and joins friends for a beer and some rumor-swapping mixed with an extended analysis of what happened on that day's markets and speculation on where the market is headed in the days to follow. On the way home he picks up some take-out Italian food for himself and his roommate, who turns out not to be home; so he shares his dinner with his roommate's dog as they watch a basketball game on television. After eating, he clicks on his portable computer, updates the values of his own investments, and sorts through the advertisements and bills that arrived in the mail.

The young mother in the marketplace in Mali and the young stock trader in New York do not live in the same country or even on the same continent. They will probably never meet or even know of each other's existence. He is an Irish Catholic living in one of the most technologically advanced, affluent, and crowded cities in the world; she belongs to the animistic Dogon tribe and lives in a small village without running water or electricity. He uses the most advanced communications technology in the world, while she can neither read nor write and must bargain with hand signals. They speak different languages, live in different worlds, and despite the modern modes of communication and transportation, each of them might have great trouble understanding the values and lifestyle of the other.

Yet they are united in one network, in a single grid of interlocking institutions that spans the globe connecting the stock markets of Hong Kong, San Francisco, and New York to Amsterdam, London, and Lima as well as to all the small towns, villages, and farms scattered around the globe. The same market connects every country, every language, and every religious and ethnic group. Many independent markets once operated throughout the world. Some sold milk and beans; others sold stocks and bonds. Some sold insurance or agricultural futures; others sold mortgages or cars. Today electronic communications efficiently connect all of these markets into a single, international market, uniting all parts of the globe and, just as importantly, all parts of the market.

They are united by one thing: money. No matter whether they call their money dollars, rubles, yen, marks, francs, pounds, pesos, bahts, ringits, kroners, kwansas, levs, escudos, liras, biplwelles, rials, drachmas, shekels, yuans, quetzals, pa'angas, ngultrums, ouguiyas, rupees, schillings, or afghanis, they all operate in essentially the same way as smaller parts of an international monetary system that reaches every farm, island, and village on the globe. No matter where and no matter what the local currency, the modern system permits the easy and quick flow of money from one market to another.

If one could strip away the clattering machines, electronic beepers, video monitors, cellular telephones, computer keyboards, and miles of blue cable, the stock exchange would look much like market day in Bandiagara when the merchants huddle in their miniature stalls persistently offering their meager wares for sale. Whether the transaction is for bolts of cloth, bags of spice, slabs of salt, rolls of tanned skins, bowls of fresh milk, or ownership of a small portion of a large corporation, the fundamental activities of the market differ very little.

Money has created a unified world economy that includes the price of milk and eggs in the market at Bandiagara as well as the price of stock in Sara Lee Foods or PepsiCo on the New York Stock Exchange. Although fluctuations in politics, religion, technology, and even the weather can play a role in any of these endeavors, money constitutes the basis of the entire system and forms the crucial link in establishing value, facilitating exchange, and creating commerce. Money unites them all together into a single global system. It is the tie that binds us all.

One hundred years from now, the market women of Africa will still be doing a thriving business, but the stock exchange will probably have disappeared. People will always need to make personal contact to procure the daily necessities of life, but they do not need it for financial transactions. The electronic market is rapidly replacing the face-to-face market of the stock exchange in a way that it can probably never do with food.

CASH CONFIGURATION

Even though the young American man in New York and the young Dogon woman of Mali live in an economically united world and work in similar markets, there are many obvious yet important differences between their cultures and lives. At the heart of these differences is the fundamental role played by money in the lives of the people of Dogon compared with the part it plays in the lives of Americans. The Dogon woman uses money only once every five days when she goes to market; the man in New York uses money every day and nearly every waking hour.

Money constitutes a minute part of the Dogon woman's life away from her village and is rarely used inside the village, where interactions center on her kin and her husband. Money is a part of virtually every interaction of the American's day, however, from work and meals to fiddling with his computer at home; money penetrates the heart of his life. The American man and the Dogon woman live in cultures with different core values and focal points.

Every culture organizes life around a few simple principles, activities, and beliefs. The other institutions and activities of the society hang from that core like branches from a tree trunk. These central acts, institutions, and values form what Ruth Benedict—arguably the most perceptive American anthropologist of the twentieth century—called a "cultural configuration."

Dogon culture configures itself around a core of art, ritual, and myth. Around the world, museums feature the unique sculptures, masks, and headdresses of Dogon artisans. In addition to these arts, the people decorate their mud huts, clothing, and bodies, and they spend much of their time in a cycle of ceremonial dances and rituals intimately tied to their unique cosmology and myths. Ritual and art become the central forms of expression around which and through which they organize their political, economic, and social life.

The Dogon emphasis on the arts is unusual in the inventory of world culture, but it is certainly not unique. The Balinese of Indonesia, the traditional Hopi and Pueblo people of the United States, and a few other cultures in the world share their focus on art, myth, and ritual. Most cultures, however, have far more mundane cultural configurations than these artistic ones.

In East Africa, the cultures and social systems of the nomadic tribes focus on cattle. In his classic study of the Nuer people of Sudan, British anthropologist E. E. Evans-Pritchard described them as obsessed with their cattle. Boys take the name of their favorite bull and write love songs about their cattle. Women call themselves cows and their men bulls. Marriages become official only through the transfer of cows to the wife's family, and homicides have to be redressed and expiated by providing cows for the victim's family. Cattle are more than a store of wealth or value; cows constitute the social idiom of Nuer life.

The Bedouins of Arabia and North Africa focused on camels. The Navajo and the ancient Hebrews focused on sheep. The Plains Indians of North America, the gauchos of South America, and the Mongols and Turks of Asia focused on horses. The culture and social system of the Saami, or Lapps, of northern Scandinavia focused on the reindeer, and the Cree of Canada focused on the caribou. This focus was more than just a passionate interest, like the American interest in cars or the Japanese fascination with electronic devices;

rather, these animals became the focal point around which the entire culture configured itself.

Ancient Egyptians focused on the authority of a powerful state bureaucracy centered on a death-and-burial cult. Laborers spent decades building the pyramids and the other tombs of their pharaohs, and the economic organization of the whole country focused on supplying and completing these great projects. In contrast to the monetary cultures in which gold served as a medium of exchange and economic organization, in ancient Egypt it served as an object for burial. The Egyptians buried more gold and other precious commodities in the earth than any other known civilization in history.

The cultural focus is not always an animal or object. The culture of Tibet, for example, focuses on the rituals, rites, and meditations of that nation's unique variety of Buddhism. The Tibetans' largest buildings were temples and monasteries that served as centers of politics and economics as well as religion and learning. Prior to Tibet's subjugation by the Chinese, monks ruled the country and about a quarter of the male population entered the priesthood.

Many of the tribal societies of New Guinea and Melanesia were organized around the political competitions of their so-called Big Men who arranged marriages, cultivated yams, and distributed pigs. Among the Papuan people, these Big Men negotiated marriages in order to form good alliances and to get wives who could grow yams and raise fat pigs with which the Big Man could then make more alliances for himself and for his children who, in turn, helped him produce more yams and pigs. The cycle culminated in *mokas*, a great celebration of feasting, dancing, and oratory during which the Big Man gave away as many pigs and as much food as he could in order to make yet more economic and political alliances and thereby begin a new round of marriages, yams, pigs, and *mokas*.

Human sacrifice served as the central organizing principle of the Aztec Empire of ancient Mexico. In the early years the Aztecs sacrificed war captives, but once they had defeated all of their neighbors, they faced a shortage of sacrificial victims. They solved the problem by waging ceremonial wars, or flower wars, which they enacted with their subject peoples solely for the purpose of capturing young men for sacrifice. They erected massive pyramids for conducting these rituals, and they organized their wars and even their ball games around the core rituals that expressed the main beliefs of their culture.

It is difficult for us to understand how the Dogon could have organized their lives around art and ritual, the Nuer around cows, the ancient Egyptians around death, the Aztecs around human sacrifice, and the Papuans around marriages, yams, and pigs, but each of these offered a focus for conducting the essential activities of life.

It would probably be just as difficult for them to understand our world, organized as it is around this odd abstraction we call money. Papuans recognize that yams and pigs can be eaten. Marriage brings sexual gratification and the production of children. The Dogon recognize that art is beautiful to behold, and rituals can be enjoyable activities and pastimes. By contrast with these forms of aesthetic and biological satisfaction, money lacks immediacy; yet in modern society, money serves as the master key that unlocks nearly all pleasures—as well as many pains.

Money constitutes the focal point of modern world culture. Money defines relationships among people, not just between customer and merchant in the marketplace or employer and laborer in the workplace. Increasingly in modern society, money defines relationships between parent and child, among friends, between politicians and constituents, among neighbors, and between clergy and parishioners. Money forms the central institutions of the modern market and economy, and around it are grouped the ancillary institutions of kinship, religion, and politics. Money is the very language of commerce for the modern world.

A LANGUAGE ALL NATIONS UNDERSTAND
Aphra Behn, a seventeenth-century dramatist who grew up in Surinam, wrote in her play *The Rover* in 1677, "Money speaks sense in a language all nations understand." Money not only speaks sense, it also imposes that sense on whatever society it conquers, and it does so in a way that subjugates all other institutions and systems. From virtually the moment of its invention, money became ever more important in Western society and eventually overwhelmed the feudal

system and the aristocratic hierarchies of earlier civilizations. As money swept through history and across societies, its impact seemed surprisingly similar from ancient Greece and Rome to modern Japan and Germany.

The tendency of money to replace family values appeared very early in Japan in the works of seventeenth-century writer Saikaku Ihara. He wrote at the same time as Aphra Behn, but on the other side of the world; nevertheless, his observations on life seem quite familiar: "Birth and lineage mean nothing: money is the only family tree for a townsman. . . . Though mothers and fathers give us life, it is money alone which preserves it."[1] What he wrote in the seventeenth century is echoed in 1936 by Gertrude Stein, who said that "the thing that differentiates man from animals is money."

Even though little else unites their cultures, money has produced similar sentiments in a twentieth-century poet, a second-century Roman philosopher, and a seventeenth-century Japanese business writer. Their comments show how money was evolving into the key element in a new and complex type of society so very different from that of the Dogon, the Hopi, or the Nuer.

Money has had a greater impact on the life of the American man working on the floor of the New York Stock Exchange than on the life of the Dogon woman in the Bandiagara market, but the difference is one of degree and not of kind. The difference is more quantitative than qualitative because the Dogon have also headed down the same path as the monetary cultures of the world. The Dogon are walking a little slower than the rest of us, but our economic way of life may be about to disappear just as quickly as it came into being.

The young man working on the floor of the New York Stock Exchange will soon seem as quaint and old-fashioned as the woman carrying milk and eggs on her head. They both work in market systems that are rapidly becoming obsolete as money mutates into a new form that demands new kinds of markets, new ways of making financial transactions, and new kinds of businesses.

Phase I

CLASSIC CASH

Money alone sets all the world in motion.
—*PUBLILIUS SYRUS*

1

Cannibals, Chocolate, and Cash

> The last conflict is at hand in which
> Civilization receives its conclusive form—
> the conflict between money and blood.
> —OSWALD SPENGLER

IN THE CENTER OF THE AZTEC IMPERIAL CAPITAL OF Tenochtitlán, the priests performed their daily sacrifices. They marched the victim up the steep stairway to the top of the pyramid, where four priests grabbed his limbs and spread him out on his back on a large stone altar. One of the fearsome and blood-spattered priests raised an obsidian knife above his head and then plunged it into the heaving chest of the victim held down on the altar before him. Quickly yet delicately, he slit open the chest and thrust his probing fingers between the ribs in search of the victim's heart. The priest pulled out the still pulsing heart and tossed it onto a flaming brazier— an offering to Hutzilopchtli. The sacrifice could be performed in as little as twenty seconds; yet the heart could continue throbbing on the burning brazier for as long as five minutes.[1]

For Aztec merchants, the climax of the liturgical year of Aztec sacrifices came during the midwinter festival of Panquetzaliztli, the Raising of the Banners, when they could show off their success and wealth by sponsoring one of these human sacrifices. Unlike warriors who personally captured enemy soldiers on the battlefield for eventual sacrifice on the altar, the merchants had to buy their sacrificial victims at a price of up to forty woven cloaks.[2] After paying for his victim, a merchant had to feed, clothe, and care for him in lavish style over many months as he was being prepared for the grand spectacle. In order to sponsor the sacrifice, the merchant had to host four lavish banquets and celebrations for other merchants and military leaders. Each banquet required new costumes, jewelry, and regalia for the merchant and his sacrificial victim. After procuring the lavish goods especially for the banquets, the merchant had to offer them as gifts to the guests in appreciation for their participation in the celebration. Only after all the appropriate ceremonies had been performed, the banquets hosted, and the expensive gifts presented did the merchant finally escort his victim up the long flight of stairs to the altar where the priests ripped out his heart. After the sacrifice, the merchant took the mutilated body home, where the women cleaned it and cooked it. The merchant then served it in yet another ritual meal with corn and salt but without the customary chilies. Everyone was free to enjoy the flesh except the merchant himself, for whom the sacrificial victim was something like a son.

Under the guidance of the high priest, called the *tlenamacac* or firegiver, the Aztecs orchestrated a series of sacrifices throughout the year. In preparation for these rituals, the priests pierced various parts of their own bodies, including the tongue and genitals, with maguey thorns as an offering of their own blood to the gods. An appropriately pious priest always had small open wounds on his temples from which blood oozed down the sides of his head. His hair grew long and matted with the blood, providing him with a frightening appearance and a horrendous odor that clearly set him apart from others in the Aztec world.

Each god and each commemorative place in the complex Aztec calendar called for its own kind of sacrifice. In the early spring, for example, people fasted for rain and sacrificed tamales and small children to Tlaloque and Chalchiuhtlicue. Later in the spring, they performed more rain ceremonies to Xipe Totec, the fertility deity, in the form of gladiatorial sacrifices. The priests tied the victim to a stone and armed him with a stick studded with feathers in place of blades. With this ritual weapon, he had to fight warriors with real weapons of sharp obsidian blades. The warriors strove to cut the victim only slightly so that he might be cut many times and thus bleed as much and as slowly as possible to prolong the power and spectacle of the sacrifice. The priests seized less cooperative victims who refused to play the role of ritual gladiator, bound them with ropes, and offered them to the fire god by slowly roasting them alive.

In subsequent ceremonies during the ritual year, priests flayed men and tortured children to death so that their tears might induce the gods to send more rain. The gods supposedly had a special fondness for babies born with a double cowlick; priests seized such babies from their mothers at birth and kept them in a special nursery until time for their ritual sacrifice. Throughout the year, special victims impersonated the gods. An impersonator of the god Tezcatlipoca had to be a handsome young man without a blemish. For a year, he lived as the god, participating in rituals, singing, dancing, and playing his flute throughout the city. People regaled him with gifts and flowers. He had four beautiful wives, but at the end of the year, he had to leave them and climb the pyramid, where his heart was ripped out and his head severed.

The most dramatic sacrifice came during a dance when priests seized the impersonator of Xipe Totec and quickly flayed him. A priest then put on the skin of the dead person and continued the ceremony. In a female version of the same ceremony, a woman was sacrificed and her skin worn by a priest of the goddess Toci.

Although the sacrifices sponsored by the merchants ended up on the dining table of a special banquet, most sacrificial victims had a more mercantile end. After the sacrifice, the priests rolled the heartless body back down the steep stairs that the victim had ascended only minutes before. At the bottom of the pyramid, attendants severed the head and placed it on a trophy rack containing the slowly rotting heads of previous victims. They disemboweled the corpse and sent the choicest cuts of meat to the *tianquiztli*, the city market, where they were sold for chocolate.

CHOCOLATE CASH

The Aztecs used chocolate for money, or, more precisely, they used the cacao seeds, usually called beans. With these cacao seeds, one could buy fruits and vegetables such as corn, tomatoes, chilies, squash, chayotes, and peanuts; jewelry made of gold, silver, jade, and turquoise; manufactured goods such as sandals, clothing, feathered capes, cotton padded armor, weapons, pottery, and baskets; meats such as fish, venison, duck; and specialty goods such as alcohol and slaves.[3]

The Aztec marketplaces usually stood adjacent to the main government buildings so that the exchange of goods could take place under the close supervision of government officials. Markets like the one in central Tenochtitlán occupied a great area, but the government prohibited any buying or selling outside the officially prescribed trading zone. Government officials regulated prices and sales, and they stood at the ready to punish and even execute anyone violating the law of the market. The government also sponsored a hereditary caste of long-distance merchants, the *pochteca*, who had an important official status within the state and had their own god, Yahcateuctli. In addition to the *pochteca*, the Aztecs sent out official tribute collectors, or *calpixque*, to all parts of the empire to bring back goods for the central administration in the highland valley of Mexico.

The empire operated primarily on the basis of tribute, the markets functioned as subsidiary parts of the political structure, and many different standardized commodities served as forms of near-money. Several tribute lists have survived and show the amount due from various provinces in the form of corn, amaranth, beans, cotton armor, obsidian knives, copper bells, jade, gold, sandals, shields, feathered capes, cacao, shells, feathers, and other practical and ornamental goods. The vast bulk of goods that passed through the Aztec Empire moved primarily as tribute from the peripheral parts of the empire to its capital. In this regard, the Aztec Empire was like virtually all other empires in the era before the spread of money. Ancient Egypt, Peru, Persia, and China all functioned as tributary systems rather than market systems.

Within this tributary system, the local markets played a minor role in distributing goods, but cacao had a major role within that smaller sphere of activity. Of all the forms of Aztec money, cacao proved to be the most commonly available and the easiest to use. The cacao tree produces large greenish-yellow pods that look something like cantaloupes. When ripe, the fruit has a fleshy white pulp that is quite delicious, though it tastes nothing like chocolate. When preserved by drying and toasting, the beans can last for many months before being ground up to make chocolate.

Cacao grew mostly in southern Mexico in what are now the states of Oaxaca, Chiapas, Tabasco, and Veracruz, and in the Central American nations. From these areas it was traded and sent as tribute throughout the Aztec Empire, particularly to the capital, Tenochtitlán, the site of modern Mexico City. Cacao became so important as a means of exchange that it produced its own counterfeiting industry. Criminals would take the small husk of the cacao bean, empty it, and replace it with mud. They then sealed the husk and mixed the fake cacao beans with real ones to further obscure them.

Commodity money like cacao operated in a system based more on barter than on purchase. An Aztec would exchange an iguana for a load of firewood or a basket of corn for a rope of chilies, and if the goods did not have precisely the same value, the traders used cacao to even it out. The cacao bean served as a way to calculate value and to round out the exchange, but it did not serve as the exclusive means of exchange. The seller who wanted to exchange a nopal (cactus) worth five cacao beans for an ear of corn worth six cacao beans, for instance, would turn over the nopal and then add one cacao bean to even out the trade.

For large purchases, merchants calculated values in terms of bags of approximately 24,000 beans, but such quantities proved too cumbersome for use in daily transactions. As in many primitive systems where commerce focused on certain important commodities, the Aztecs used more than one commodity to standardize exchanges. In addition to cacao beans, they used *quachtli*, cotton cloaks, the value of which varied from 60 to 300 cacao beans. The *quachtli* served for larger financial transfers such as the purchase of slaves or sacrificial victims, for which the bags of cacao beans would be too bulky.[4] Other standardized exchange commodities included beads, shells, and copper bells, which were traded as far north as the modern state of Arizona.

Commodity money has the great advantage of being an item of

consumption as well as a means of exchange. The Aztecs could easily grind their cacao money into chocolate paste, then beat it vigorously into a container of water to make a delicious drink that they greatly prized. Unlike paper money and cheap coins that can easily lose their face value, commodity money has a value in and of itself and thus can always be consumed no matter what the status of the market.

Chocolate, like all other types of money, has no inherent value outside of a cultural context. In order for it to have value, people have to want it and know how to use it. The Mesoamerican love of chocolate as a food and as a means of exchange contrasted greatly with the values of the first European pirates to seize a ship loaded with cacao beans: the pirates mistook the cacao beans for rabbit dung and dumped the entire cargo into the sea.

The Aztec Empire of Mexico illustrates how complicated the economic and political relationships can become even in the absence of money. Their distribution system reached as complex a level as an empire and a protomarket system could reach within the confines of a tributary empire and primitive or commodity money. Through the use of particular commodities, they came almost to the point of creating a modern monetary system, but they never quite crossed the line.

COMMODITY MONEY

Throughout the world, commodities from salt to tobacco, from logs to dried fish, and from rice to cloth have been used as money at various times in history. Natives in parts of India used almonds. Guatemalans used corn; the ancient Babylonians and Assyrians used barley. Natives of the Nicobar Islands used coconuts, and the Mongolians prized bricks of tea. For the people of the Philippines, Japan, Burma, and other parts of Southeast Asia, standardized measures of rice traditionally served as commodity money.

Norwegians used butter as money, and in the medieval era, they used dried cod that could be easily converted into other goods or into coins by trading with the Hanseatic merchants living in Bergen. They, in turn, sold the fish in southern Europe where there was great demand for it on Fridays, during Lent, and at other times when the Catholic church proscribed the eating of meat.

In China, North Africa, and the Mediterranean, people used salt as commodity money. At great risk in some of the hottest places on earth, tribesmen of the central Sahara mined large slabs of salt three feet long and several inches thick. The Sahara contains some of the purest salt in the world, and a caravan of passing salt merchants might at first sight be misperceived to be transporting slabs of white marble tied to the sides of their camels. Because of its purity, the salt can be easily cut into a number of standardized sizes. Merchants usually wrapped the smaller denominations of salt in a protective reed covering in order to reduce the danger of the salt chipping and prevent people from scraping off parts of it between trades.

The modern English word *salary* and the Italian, Spanish, and Portuguese word *salario* are derived from the Latin word *sal*, meaning "salt" or, more precisely, from *salrius*, meaning "of salt." It is thought that the Roman soldiers were paid in salt or that they received money for the purpose of buying salt to flavor their otherwise bland food.

Pastoral people often used live animals as a type of money in which the value of everything else was calculated. The Siberian tribes used reindeer, the people of Borneo used buffaloes, the ancient Hittites measured value in sheep, and the Greeks of Homer's time used oxen. Wherever people have had cattle, they have tended to use the cattle as a form of commodity money. Pastoralists calculate and pay virtually everything—from slaves and wives to fines for adultery and murder—in cows.

Cattle played an equally important role in the economy of many ancient European peoples from Ireland to Greece and throughout the Indian subcontinent. The cattle complex survives in modern times in eastern and southern Africa among tribes such as the Masai, Samburu, Dinka, and Nuer.

The traditional importance of cattle survives indirectly in several modern European languages. The word *pecuniary*, which means "related to money," is derived from the Latin *pecuniarius*, meaning "wealth in cattle." The *as*, a Roman coin, represented a value equivalent to one-hundredth of a cow. Related English words include *pecunious*, an obsolete term meaning "wealthy," and the more commonly used *impecunious*, meaning "poor."

The importance of the bovine idiom in European culture is further illustrated by the word *cattle*, which is derived from the same Latin roots that gave us *capital*, another broader term for money. *Chattel*—any item of movable personal property such as a slave—is derived from the same source. Thus modern names for two of the most important economic systems in European history, capitalism and feudalism, can both be traced back to systems based on cattle.

Even human beings have served as a measure of money. In ancient Ireland, slave girls became the common value against which items such as cows, boats, land, and houses were measured. Viking raiders and merchants sold the young women to slave traders in the Mediterranean, where they were highly valued because of their red or blond hair. Irish males had far less value as slaves.

In parts of equatorial Africa, by contrast, male slaves had a higher value than females and children, who would be measured as mere fractions of the value of a male. Of all the forms of money, slaves proved one of the least reliable because of their high mortality rate and their tendency to escape.

MODERN COMMODITIES

The use of commodity money has never disappeared, and it rises again whenever the normal flow of commerce and economic life is interrupted. Cigarettes, chocolate, and chewing gum filled temporary monetary gaps throughout Europe at the end of the Second World War. Not since the fall of the Aztec Empire had chocolate had such a high purchasing power as when the American soldiers arrived in Europe.

During the tyrannical reign of President Nicolae Ceauşescu in Romania, the country had an ample supply of paper money and aluminum coins, but the money had virtually no value because the dictator and his wife exported almost everything produced in the country. They rationed food, allowing fewer than two thousand calories a day for each of the common people, and the temperature in their homes and offices was not allowed to rise above 55 degrees. Under such an austere regime, cigarettes—particularly Kents—

functioned as the real currency of the nation. Anything could be bought for cigarettes—food, electronic goods, sex, or alcohol. Cartons of cigarettes had the advantage of being easily broken up into ten packs per carton, each of which could in turn be broken up into twenty cigarettes.

Consumable commodities such as tobacco and chocolate serve as adequate means of exchange, but they cannot perform all the functions of money. For example, they make a poor store of value. Anyone who had to accumulate sacks of grain or a load of tobacco as a way of amassing wealth would soon find that the grain rotted or was eaten by insects and rats, and the tobacco would slowly lose its flavor and begin to fall apart. In order to store their wealth for use in the future, people need more durable items such as cloth, furs, feathers, whale teeth, boar tusks, or shells. These commodities last longer than food; yet they too eventually deteriorate and lose their value. Food items might function adequately for the exchange of goods, but they are not good stores of value.

Animal skins and furs proved extremely useful in Russia, Siberia, and North America, but they had little practical use in the warmer markets of the Caribbean, Africa, South America, and southern Asia. The Canadians used the thick, luxurious beaver pelts that their large country produced and that were so popular with European hatters and clothiers. Farther south in the British colonies, the settlers used the skin of the North American deer, which achieved great importance in trade. Each skin was known as a *buck*, a word that has survived as a slang term for the dollar.

Throughout history, commodities and valued articles sometimes created an economic system that superficially resembled a money system, but such systems were invariably limited in scope and utility. Primitive money works best in a tribal community or in a heavily regulated market. At one end of the political and economic spectrum, empires such as that of the Incas of Peru organized their entire realm without the use of any markets or any money. At the other end, the Aztec capital, Tenochtitlán, built a tributary state allowing the limited use of money with a protomarket system largely controlled by a ruling military class.

Whale teeth served as items of great value in Fiji and a few sur-

rounding islands, where they still play an important role in the ceremonial life and the prestige system of the people. Whale teeth,
however, did not prove very effective in trade with other people, who
simply had no interest in them. Similarly, dog teeth were valued as
a medium of exchange in the Admiralty Islands, but outsiders frequently found them disgusting and did not want to trade for them.

The desire for rare and valuable objects often induced entrepreneurial individuals to make risky journeys high into the mountains,
deep into the jungle, or far out to sea. The items became important
as gifts, particularly at important moments in the life cycle such as
birth, puberty, marriage, or death. They also became important as gifts
between friends or as a part of the making and breaking of alliances
among villages or particular groups of people.

Durable commodities such as shells, stone, and teeth provide a
long-term store of value, but because they occur naturally, their size,
texture, color, and quality varies, and that fact keeps them from being
entirely fungible. One whale tooth will not precisely equal another
in value, and thus it becomes difficult to use the teeth interchangeably in a commercial system. Some items such as shells may be so
abundant in coastal areas that they are too common to serve as
money, and yet in a mountainous area they can be too rare to serve
as general money.

Even the cowrie shell, which had enormous popularity across
much of Africa and other areas bordering the Indian Ocean, was of
no use to most people in the world. They did not see its value, and
therefore the shells always had limited circulation in specific areas.
With items such as shells, however, tribal people came very close to
developing real cash economies. Shells departed from the merely
decorative aspect of culture and became a way of accumulating and
storing wealth as well as a mechanism of trade.

Money never exists in a cultural or social vacuum. It is not a mere
lifeless object but a social institution.[5] To function completely as
money, a material cannot exist simply as an object; it requires a particular social and cultural system. Once the system is in place, many
different objects can serve as money. Often these uses arise from
within the political or prestige sphere of social life rather than the

commercial or subsistence spheres. Such items may be used to buy titles, to mark deaths, to negotiate marriages, to claim the right to use magic spells, or to acquire ritually powerful songs. More rarely, they have been used in the exchange of land, cattle, and other major goods, but even these exchanges often came about as subsidiary parts of a larger political or marriage negotiation rather than as merely commercial activities.

THE LOVE OF GOLD

Next to food, humans seem to value metal as one of the most popular commodities in exchange. Of all the substances that can be used to make money, metal has more practical applications and has held its value over a longer time and a wider distance than any other. Because it is long-lasting, it serves as a good store of value. Because it can be made into smaller and larger pieces, it serves as a good means of exchange. It is not as bulky as the logs used by the Hondurans, nor is it as cumbersome as the bags of corn used by the Guatemalans. Unlike food commodities, which disappear when used, metal can be converted into something useful at any time and yet retain its value. It can be jewelry or a spear tip on one day and serve as money the next.

From Scandinavia to equatorial Africa, people have used particular standardized objects made of iron as money. The Sudanese made iron into hoes. The Chinese used a slightly differently shaped hoe made of bronze as well as miniature knives of the same material. Ancient Egyptians used copper, while the people of southern Europe preferred bronze. The people of Burma used lead, and the people of the Malayan Peninsula used the tin that abounds there.

In West Africa, people used copper rings known as manillas as a specialized form of currency. Throughout Liberia and other parts of West Africa, people used long strips of iron flattened on both ends and known as Kissi pennies, after the Kissi tribe that manufactured them. The tribes of the Congo used brass rods, and in East Africa, many tribes manufactured metal objects in a distinctive shape for use only in their own society. The shape of their iron money was as much a form of identification for the people as their language.

As technology developed, the type of desired object became more sophisticated and made great advances with the discovery of different metals. Of all the metals, gold has been the most universally valued. Gold has relatively few practical uses outside of decoration and some sophisticated modern technological applications; yet people throughout the world have been attracted to it. Even if it lacks utility, empirical evidence shows that humans everywhere have wanted to touch it, wear it, play with it, and possess it. Unlike copper, which turns green; iron, which rusts; and silver, which tarnishes, pure gold remains pure and unchanged.

People around the world have closely associated gold and silver with magic and divinity. Sometimes the list of divine substances included other precious goods such as silk cloth in India, vicuña cloth in ancient Peru, olive oil in Judea, and butter in Tibet, but people almost everywhere regarded gold and silver as sacred substances. In most cultures, the gods valued offerings of precious metals more than flowers, food, animals, or even human beings.

The Maya of the Yucatán sacrificed gold, silver, and jade objects to their gods in their sacred cenotes, deep pools of water formed in the peninsula's limestone base. In one of the highland communities of Colombia before the arrival of the Europeans, the Chibcha Indians performed an annual ritual in which they covered their chief with gold dust. When he dived into the sacred lake, the water washed off the gold, becoming a gift to the gods. The chief was known to the Spaniards as El Dorado, the Golden One, and his wealth became the object of the greatest search in world history.

In particular, gold was considered a divine substance.[6] People around the world noted the resemblance of its color to the sun, a coincidence to which they ascribed a deeper meaning. The ancient Egyptians believed that gold was sacred to Ra, the sun god, and they buried great quantities of it with the corpses of their divine pharaohs. Among the Incas of South America, gold and silver represented the sweat of the sun and the moon, and they covered the walls of their temples with these precious metals. Even after conquest, when the Spaniards took the Indian gold and silver, the natives decorated their new Christian temples with foil paper to imitate the sacred substances, and they tossed gold- and silver-colored confetti into the air in place of gold dust. The ancient people of India considered gold the sacred semen of Agni, the fire god; therefore they donated gold for any service performed by Agni's priests.

PROTOMONEY

As early as the end of the third millennium B.C., the people of Mesopotamia began using ingots of precious metals in exchange for goods. Mesopotamian clay tablets inscribed in cuneiform in 2500 B.C. mention the use of silver as a form of payment. People called these uniform weights of gold and silver minas, shekels, or talents. An entire warehouse of olive oil, beer, or wheat could be reduced in value to an easily transported ingot of gold or silver. This system proved effective for merchants accustomed to dealing with a whole shipload or warehouse of goods, but gold remained too scarce and valuable for the average person wanting to sell a basket of wheat or buy a goatskin of wine. Such people had no access to this system of gold and silver ingots.

Once human technology and social organization developed to the point of using standardized amounts of gold and silver in exchange, it became only a matter of time before smaller coins appeared. The technological and cultural leap from primitive coins constituted the first money revolution in history, and to the best of numismatic knowledge, it happened only once. It took place in western Asia in what is today Turkey, and from there it spread around the world to become the global money system and the ancestor of the system in which we live and work today.

Money does not occur in nature, and no version or analog of it exists among any other members of the animal kingdom. Money, like language, is uniquely human. Money constituted a new way of thinking and acting that changed the world immediately. Only now, after nearly three thousand years, is the full power of money becoming apparent in human affairs, as it supplants or dominates many of the traditional social bonds based on family, tribe, community, and nation.

2

The Fifth Element

*Money ranks as one of the primary materials with
which mankind builds the architecture of civilization.*
— LEWIS LAPHAM

T HE OLDEST RECORDED WORD IN EUROPEAN LIT-
ature is the ancient Greek word for rage at the beginning of
Homer's *Iliad*. In English, we usually translate his first line as "Sing,
O Muse, of the rage of great Achilles," but the original text begins
with the word that means "rage," "wrath," or "anger," and that emo-
tion becomes the primary one in Homer's account of the Trojan War,
ten years of conflict during which Greeks sacrificed, killed, tortured,
raped, maimed, and enslaved one another. These rage-driven men
lived in what modern scholars call the heroic, or Homeric, age on
the edges of the great ancient empires of the time. Their world would
have remained in the shadows of historical darkness had it not been
for the two great Greek epics, the *Iliad* and the *Odyssey* by Homer,
which comprise an overture to civilization's recording of its own
fateful unfolding. The Greeks portrayed to us in Homer's work were
people of combat, not people of commerce. The heroes pursued lives
of war, raiding their neighbors and defending their family honor.
Homer described in vivid detail the weapons of his heroes, the armor
they wore, the designs on their breastplates, and every implement
they used in battle. He described the beauty of their ships, but he also
grimly related where the spear entered the warrior's head, where it
exited, and how long the slain warrior's mother and wife cried at his
funeral.

Money had no place in the epic poems of Homer, just as it had no place in the lives of his heroes. In the words of Voltaire, "Agamemnon might have had a treasure, but certainly no money." Commerce did not appear in Homer's poetry in which men pursued honor, not wealth; they imposed their will upon others at any cost. They did not negotiate, compromise, or argue over the value of worldly goods. The strongest demanded that goods be given to them as tribute for use in their campaigns; they did not deign to haggle with shopkeepers.

Fortified palaces, like that of Agamemnon in Mycenae and Priam in Troy, formed the center of the Greek communal life in the Homeric age, and markets did not figure as places of importance. Each town tried to produce as many of its own goods as possible so that it would have to trade as little as possible with other towns. In their spare time, the Homeric heroes hunted, feasted, and played ritual war games.

Homer gives no hint of thought or self-reflection among his heroes. Their ideas and impulses came either from a deep-seated desire to increase their own personal honor or as inspiration whispered into their ears by the gods. The heroes of Homer were men of passion rather than the men of moderation so admired in classical Greece. The phrase *gnothi seauton* (know thyself), which later became the motto of the classical Greeks of the Golden Age of Athens, would have been virtually meaningless to Achilles, Odysseus, Paris, Hector, Agamemnon, Priam, and the other Homeric heroes, who were men of action, not reflection.

How could we imagine Odysseus coming home from his ten years of wandering to establish a pottery workshop, oversee a farm, or open a wine shop? Like the other Homeric heroes, Odysseus cavorted with divine beings, fought dreadful monsters, drank heavily, seduced women (both mortal and divine), and lived among other heroes in an eternal game of defending and increasing honor. Commerce had little meaning for Odysseus and his comrades because they lived in a world that did not yet know money.

Despite their lack of knowledge of money, it was very near the walls of Troy that money was born. It was here in the little-known kingdom of Lydia that humans first produced coins, and it was here that the first great revolution began. This revolution was destined to have a far greater impact on our world than all the heroes of ancient Greece.

As Rich as Croesus

Through the millennia, a succession of kingdoms arose, flourished, and withered along the Ionian coast and adjacent islands. Each one left something that its neighbors and successors later adopted into their own culture. Of the many great civilizations that flourished and withered in ancient Anatolia, the Lydian does not rank among the best known. The Lydians spoke a European language and lived in Anatolia after about 2000 B.C. They formed a small kingdom under the Mermnadae dynasty beginning in the seventh century B.C., but at its height, the Lydian kingdom was little more than an overgrown city-state spread out from Sardis. The Lydian kings were not celebrated in myth or song as great warriors, conquerors, builders, or even lovers.

The names of the dynasties and kings are known to us through Hittite tablets and the books of the Greek historian Herodotus, but only one name of ancient Lydia is commonly known today—Croesus. "As rich as Croesus" is a common expression in modern English, Turkish, and other languages around the world.

Croesus ascended to the Lydian throne in 560 B.C. to rule a kingdom that was already rich. His ancestors had made a firm economic basis for the kingdom's wealth by manufacturing some of the best perfumes and cosmetics of the ancient world; yet these goods alone could not have raised Croesus to the level of wealth that myth accords him. For that, he depended on another invention of his ancestors—coins, a new and revolutionary form of money.

Something similar to money and something resembling markets can be found in Mesopotamia, China, Egypt, and many other parts of the world, but they did not actually use coins until the rise of Lydia and the subsequent minting of the first coins, between 640 and 630 B.C.[1] The genius of the Lydian kings can be seen in their recognition of the need for very small and easily transported ingots worth no more than a few days' labor or a small part of a farmer's harvest. By making these small ingots in a standardized size and weight, and by stamping on them an emblem that verified their worth to even the illiterate, the kings of Lydia exponentially expanded the possibilities of commercial enterprise.

The Lydians made the first coins of electrum, a naturally occurring mixture of gold and silver. They made the electrum into oval slugs several times thicker than modern coins, or about the size of the end digit of an adult's thumb. To ensure their authenticity, the king had each one stamped with the emblem of a lion's head. The stamping also flattened the lumps, beginning their transition from an oval nugget to a flat, circular coin.

By making the nuggets the same weight and thus approximately the same size, the king eliminated one of the most time-consuming steps in commerce: the need to weigh the gold each time a transaction was made. Now merchants could assess the value by tale, or by simply counting the number of coins. Such standardization greatly reduced the opportunity for cheating on the amount or quality of gold and silver in an exchange. One did not need to be an expert in handling a scale or in judging the purity of metal in order to buy a basket of wheat, a pair of sandals, or an amphora of olive oil. The use of coins that had been weighed and stamped in the royal workshop made it possible for commerce to proceed much more rapidly and honestly, and it allowed people to participate even if they did not own a scale. The commerce of coins opened up new dimensions for new segments of the population.

The wealth of Croesus and his ancestors arose not from conquest but from trade. During his reign (560–546 B.C.), Croesus created new coins of pure gold and silver rather than electrum. Using their newly invented coins as a standardized medium of exchange, the Lydian merchants traded in the daily necessities of life—grain, oil, beer, wine, leather, pottery, and wood—as well as in luxury goods such as perfumes, cosmetics, jewelry, musical instruments, glazed ceramics, bronze figurines, mohair, purple cloth, marble, and ivory.

The variety and abundance of commercial goods quickly led to another innovation: the retail market. Rather than leaving buyers to seek out the home of someone who might have oil or jewelry to sell, the kings of Sardis set up an innovative new system in which anyone, even a stranger, with something to sell could come to a central market. Numerous small shops lined the market, and each merchant specialized in particular goods. One sold meat, and another offered grain. One sold jewelry, another cloth. One sold musical instruments, another pots. This market system began in the late seventh century B.C., but its descendants can clearly be seen in the later Greek agora, in the medieval market squares of northern Europe, and in suburban shopping malls of the contemporary United States.

Marketing became so important for the Lydians that Herodotus called them a nation of *kapeloi*, meaning "merchants" or "sellers" but with a somewhat negative connotation akin to "hucksters" or "snake-oil salesmen." Herodotus saw that the Lydians had become a nation of shopkeepers. They had changed mere trade and barter into true commerce.

The commercial revolution in the city of Sardis provoked wide-spread changes throughout Lydian society. Herodotus reported with great amazement the Lydian custom of allowing women to choose their own husbands. Through the accumulation of coins, women became free to make their own dowries and thus had greater freedom in selecting a husband.

New services quickly entered the marketplace. Hardly had the first shops been put into operation before some enterprising individual offered a house specializing in sexual services for the many men engaged in commerce. The first known brothels were built in ancient Sardis. In order to accumulate their dowries, many unmarried women of Sardis supposedly worked in the brothels long enough to secure the money necessary to make the kind of marriage they desired.

Gambling soon followed, and the Lydians are credited with inventing not only coins but dice as well. Archaeological excavations clearly indicate that gambling and games of chance such as knuckle-bones thrived in the area around the market.

Commerce created the fabulous riches of Croesus, but he and the elite families of Lydia squandered their wealth. They developed a great appetite for luxury goods, and they became mired in an escalating game of conspicuous consumption. Each family sought, for example, to build a larger tomb than the families around them. They decorated these tombs with ornate ivory and marble, and they held elaborate funerals, burying their deceased relatives with golden headbands, bracelets, and rings. Rather than generating more wealth, they were destroying the wealth that their ancestors had accumulated. The elite of Sardis used their new wealth for consumption instead of investing it in production.

Ultimately, Croesus poured his wealth into the two bottomless wells of conspicuous consumption so common among kings: buildings and soldiers. He conquered and he built. Croesus used his vast wealth to conquer almost all of the Greek cities of Asia Minor, including the grand Ephesus, which he then rebuilt in even grander style. Even though he was a Lydian, not a Greek, Croesus developed a great fondness for the culture of Greece, including its language and religion. Because he was something of a Hellenophile, he ruled the Greek cities with a light hand.

In a famous episode in Greek history, Croesus consulted the Greek oracle of Apollo to ask what chance he might have in war against Persia. The oracle replied that if he attacked mighty Persia, a great empire would fall. Croesus took the prophecy as a propitious one, and he attacked the Persians. In the bloody campaign of 547–546 B.C., the empire that fell was the great mercantile empire of the Lydians. Cyrus easily defeated the mercenary army of Croesus, and he then marched on the Lydian capital of Sardis.

While the Persian army looted and burned the wealthy city of Sardis, Cyrus taunted Croesus by boasting of what his soldiers were doing to the city and to the wealth of great Croesus. Croesus responded to Cyrus: "Not mine any longer. Nothing here belongs to me now. It is your city they are destroying and your treasure they are taking away."

With the conquest of Lydia by Cyrus, the reign of Croesus ended, his Mermnadae dynasty died, and the Lydian kingdom disappeared from the pages of history. Even though the great kingdom of Lydia and its rulers never rose again, the impact of that small and relatively unknown kingdom has remained vastly disproportionate to its geographic size and relatively minor role in ancient history. Many surrounding peoples quickly adopted the Lydian practice of making coins, and a commercial revolution spread throughout the Mediterranean world, particularly to Lydia's closest neighbor, Greece.

THE MARKET REVOLUTION

Even though the great armies of Persia conquered Lydia and many of the Greek states, the highly centralized Persian system could not compete effectively with the revolutionary new mercantile system of markets based on the use of money. In time, these new markets based on money spread throughout the Mediterranean, and they continued to clash with the authority of traditional tributary states.

The great struggle between the market cities of Greece and the empire of Persia represented a clash between the old and the new systems of creating wealth. It represented a clash between the market system based on democratic principles and a tributary system based on autocratic power, and it was a clash that has erupted repeatedly in history right up to the modern day.

Enriched by their newly emerging markets, the Greeks displaced the conservative Phoenicians as the great traders of the eastern Mediterranean. The monetary revolution sparked by the kings of Lydia ended the heroic Greek tradition and set in motion the evolution of the Greeks into a nation based on trade. With the spread of coins and the Ionian alphabet, a new civilization arose in the Greek islands and along the adjacent mainland.

Coinage gave a great impetus to commerce by providing it with a stability it had previously lacked. Coins became, quite literally, a baseline against which other commodities and services could be more easily measured and exchanged. Coins provided the ancient merchants, farmers, and consumers with a permanent medium of exchange that was easily stored and easily transported. That ease of use, standardization of value, and durability as a store of family wealth attracted ever more people to the new commodity.

The classical Athenians enjoyed the advantage of having discovered rich deposits of silver in Laurium, some twenty-six miles south of Athens. The mines produced silver from the sixth to the second century B.C. They averaged 75 to 150 feet in depth, and some reached a depth of nearly 400 feet.

The uniqueness of Greek culture, in contrast to that of Persia and Egypt, did not rest on the heavy-handed authority of the state supported by a massive army. The Greeks could not even unite into a single state; they remained divided into many, each sharing to a varying degree in the economic and cultural flowering of this new land. The power and might of Greece never depended upon the army. Not until after the apogee of classical Greek civilization did the whole area unite under one leader and one army when King Philip of neighboring Macedonia conquered the city-states and when his son, Alexander, made his brief but spectacular path of conquest first around the eastern Mediterranean and then to the Indian subcontinent. The greatness of Greece came as a by-product of the monetary and mercantile revolution from Lydia, the introduction of money, modern markets, and wholesale and retail distribution.

Money made possible the organization of society on a scale much greater and far more complex than either kinship or force could have achieved. Kinship-based communities tend to be quite small: bands of sixty to a hundred people tied through kinship and marriage to similar neighboring bands. The power of tributary systems and the state to organize humans proved far greater than mere kinship. A tributary system could easily include millions of people divided into provinces and classes and administered by a bureaucracy with a well-established system of keeping records. The use of money does not require the face-to-face interaction and the intense relationships of a kinship-based system. Nor does it require such extensive administrative, police, and military systems. Money became the social nexus connecting humans in many more social relationships, no matter how distant or how transitory, than had previously been possible. Money connected humans in a more extensive and more efficient way than any other known medium. It created more social ties, but in making them faster and more transitory, it weakened the traditional ties based on kinship and political power.

Money also became the medium for the expression of more values, making a great leap forward when its use was expanded from the realm of articles and commodities to something as abstract as work.

A man or woman might be paid for cleaning out the stables, for a day's work at the spinning wheel, for help in chopping timber or in feeding the animals, or for a sexual act. Work and human labor itself became a commodity with a value that could be fixed in money according to its importance, the amount of skill or strength it required, and the time it took. As money became the standard value for work, it was also becoming the standard of value for time itself.

People found that money served as a convenient substitute for various services and tributes owed to political or religious authorities. Instead of giving a portion of his crops to the lord, the peasant would simply pay a tax. Instead of giving a portion of their produce to the church or temple, people could make monetary contributions. Even service to God became valued in monetary terms. God no longer wanted the first fruits of the harvest or the firstborn animals in the spring; God, or at least the priests, wanted money.

The value of a work of art or a musical performance could be as easily expressed in terms of money as could the value of a goat or an apple. Even justice itself became a monetarized activity. Instead of paying an eye for an eye, a limb for a limb, or a life for a life, people could pay for their crimes with money. Money spread into marriage and inheritance through dowries, bride purchases, and cash allotments at divorce or death.

With the rapid monetarization of value, virtually everything could be expressed in terms of a common denominator—money. In this way, a system of shared values was established to calculate the value of virtually everything from a loaf of bread to a poem, from an hour's sexual service to taxes, or from a rack of lamb to a month's rent. Everything could be expressed within the terms of one simplified system.

THE GREEK GENIUS

The introduction of coined money had an immediate and tremendous impact on political systems and the distribution of power. The tensions in ancient Greek society appeared starkly in the reforms made in Athenian law by Solon, the great lawgiver, in 594–593 B.C. Debts, for example, had become so out of control in Athenian life that Solon outlawed debt bondage and canceled all outstanding debts in order to begin with a clean financial and commercial slate. Other politicians in the millennia since Solon have attempted to utilize the same strategy, but invariably the cancellation of debts has produced only a short-lived political reprieve and the same financial problems have soon returned.

The most radical of Solon's reforms, however, was the abolition of the traditional practice of limiting eligibility for holding public office to men of noble birth. Money had a liberating effect on the Athenians, and thenceforth eligibility for election to public office would be based on landed wealth. At the time, such a move was radical and much more democratic than the older system. Money was helping to democratize the political process; it was destroying the old aristocracy based on inherited rights, relationships, and offices.

Democracy arose primarily in city-states like Athens, which had a strong market based on solid currency. Of all the Greek cities, Sparta most resisted democracy, coinage, and the rise of a market system. Legend maintains that the rulers of Sparta allowed only iron bars and spear tips to be used as money; this permitted some internal commerce but effectively minimized private commerce outside the city-state. Not until the third century B.C. did Sparta begin to mint its own coins.

The vibrancy of the revolutionary spread of commerce among the Greeks produced new temples, civic buildings, academies, stadia, and theaters, along with a body of glorious art, philosophy, drama, poetry, and science. The center of the classical Greek city was not the palace of a great king, the fortress of the army, or even the temple. Greek public life centered on the agora—the marketplace. Theirs was essentially a commercial civilization.

After thousands of years of empires throughout the world, the marketplace emerged during the Greek era and changed history. Every great civilization prior to Greece had been based on political union and force backed by military might. Greece, which by then was unified, arose from the marketplace and commerce. Greece had created a whole new kind of civilization.

The wealth generated by this commerce expanded the leisure time of the Greek elite, thus allowing the opportunity to create a rich civic life and to pursue social luxuries including politics, philosophy, sports, and the arts as well as good food and festive celebrations. Never before in history had so many people had so much wealth; yet in a world with only a few luxury goods, they spent that wealth on leisure consumption. Scholars still today mine the rich intellectual deposits of words and ideas laid down by these Greeks, and their era marks the beginning of the academic disciplines of history, science, philosophy, and mathematics.

The emergence of the money system and its sibling, the public market, imposed a new kind of mental discipline upon human beings. Long before people needed to become literate, the market had made it necessary for them to be able to count and use numbers. People were forced to equate things that had never before been equated. It is often difficult for us to think back to the pre-monetary era, since we are so accustomed to thinking in terms of groups, sets, and categories of things.

Counting existed long before money, but outside of the city it had only limited utility. A good shepherd did not need to know only how *many* cows or sheep were under his control; he had to recognize each one by its appearance, sound, and hoofprint. It did not help him to know that one cow was missing; he needed to know *which* cow was missing. Knowing that particular cow, its appearance, its history, and its individual habits, the herdsman knew if she was likely to be in the bush giving birth or if she had wandered back to the water hole for one more drink. He knew where to look for the cow and how to spot her if she had joined another herd.

The use of counting and numbers, of calculating and figuring, propelled a tendency toward rationalization in human thought that shows in no traditional culture without the use of money. Money did not make people smarter; it made them think in new ways, in numbers and their equivalencies. It made thinking far less personalized and much more abstract.

Throughout most of human life, religion used stories and rituals to appeal to emotions such as fear of the unseen or to greed to have control over the invisible, to have eternal life, or some other com-

modity otherwise unobtainable on earth. Political institutions also
appealed to emotions, most often to people's fear of outsiders or of
their own rulers. Money and the institutions built on it respond primarily to the intellect rather than to the emotions. Money and the
culture around it force a kind of decidedly logical and rational intellectual process unlike any other human institution. As Georg
Simmel observed in *The Philosophy of Money*, "the idea that life is
essentially based on intellect, and that intellect is accepted in practical life as the most valuable of our mental energies, goes hand in
hand with the growth of a money economy."[2] Through the rise of
their new money-based economy, the Greeks were changing the way
people thought about the world. These new ways of thinking and organizing the world gave rise to new intellectual occupations. Simmel wrote that "those professional classes whose productivity lies
outside the economy proper have emerged only in the money economy—those concerned with specific intellectual activity such as
teachers and literary people, artists, physicians, scholars, and state officials."[3]

THE FIRST ECONOMISTS

The ancient Greeks recognized air, water, fire, and earth as the four
natural elements from which all substances were made. For many of
them, however, money constituted a fifth, albeit cultural rather than
natural, element. This was in keeping with a Greek saying, "*Chre-
mata aner*" (money is the man).[4]

In Greek texts, we see myriad perspectives in the words of individual citizens and even slaves who wrote their own plays, poems, and
philosophical dialogues. The Greeks bubbled over with records of the
most mundane aspects of daily life at home or in the vineyard as well
as with speculations about everything from the origin of life to the
fluctuating price of wheat.

The philosophical trinity of Socrates, Plato, and Aristotle seems
to exemplify the classical age, but just how representative were they
of the spirit and culture surrounding them? After all, the Athenians
themselves condemned Socrates to death. In general, the philoso-
phers constituted a rather aberrant part of the Greek psyche, a psy-

che that offered a much more practical bent than that seen in the great works.

Xenophon probably best exemplifies the character of classical Greek culture. He followed many pursuits over the course of his adult career as a politician, teacher, general, and writer, but he may be described best as a practical philosopher. On a military expedition to Persia, he and his fellow Athenian mercenaries defeated their enemies, but their leader, Cyrus the Younger, died in the battle. This left the Greek mercenaries stranded hundreds of miles from home in an enemy nation. The Greek forces, known in history as the Army of Ten Thousand, put their trust and their lives in the hands of Xenophon, who successfully led them on a three-month journey back through hostile lands to their Greek homeland. Like many famous generals he later wrote a best-selling book about his adventure.

In the *Anabasis*, Xenophon described the long campaign, but unlike Homer, Xenophon did not make himself or his fellow officers into heroes of the type described in Homer's works. As a practical man, he recognized that the focus of the story was the soldiers themselves. Without fancy phrases or high-flown rhetoric, the *Anabasis* probably represents the best Attic prose ever written. In some aspects Xenophon, the practical man, equally as comfortable with workers, soldiers, and farmers as with scholars, seems very much a predecessor to the more modern minds of Michel de Montaigne, Johann von Goethe, and Benjamin Franklin.

In the midst of his civic duties and commercial work, Xenophon wrote another book, *Economics*, in which he described in detail the running of a home. In writing this book he introduced the word *oikonomikos* (economics), which meant "skilled in managing a household or estate." Managing a home—women's work in the Greek world—was certainly nothing that Homer would have shown the least interest in doing. For Homer, women were trophies of war that enhanced a hero's honor, sacrificial offerings in hard times, or mere domestic props who wove and waited eternally for their fathers, husbands, and sons to return from their latest raid or campaign.

Even though Xenophon was not a feminist of the modern sort, he took the practical work of the household very seriously and depicted the woman as the queen bee of a hive. He filled his book with the simplest, most practical information on how to arrange a home, train servants, store wine and foodstuffs, and impose order on every aspect of the domestic economy.

While the wife ran the household, the husband tended the farm and managed his own business as well as the civic business of the polis, or city-state. Like many books of its day, *Economics* is presented in the form of a dialogue, this one between Socrates and Ischomachus, one of the richest businessmen of Athens. In *Economics*, however, Socrates the philosopher does not loom quite so large or appear quite so clever as he does in the better-known Socratic dialogues written by Plato. Instead, Ischomachus, the simple man of business, has much more to say and emerges as the "hero" of the story. Ischomachus did not attain a very important place in literature or philosophy, and even he admitted that with his wealth and simple lifestyle, he was not well liked by many people. On the scale of literary value, Xenophon's works cannot compare with those of Homer; Ischomachus is certainly no Agamemnon or Achilles. Yet practical citizens like Ischomachus pushed and pulled the classical Greek world to the high pinnacle of commercial and artistic success that it attained.

Most Greek scholars lacked Xenophon's wide involvement in war and peace, and they did not share his interest in financial activities. With an attitude that presaged that of many generations of scholars to come, both Plato and Aristotle, his student, had great difficulty with some of the concepts of money and the market.

Plato, ever the dictator in moral issues, wanted to outlaw gold and silver as well as foreign money. According to his work *The Laws*, in place of real money there should have been some valueless coins, a kind of token or government script, to keep records among tradesmen. Anyone returning from a foreign port with money should have been forced to surrender it upon arrival. According to Plato, no honest man could ever be rich, since dishonesty always paid better than honesty; consequently, the richer a man was, the less honest and virtuous he must be. In Plato's view, people should be punished if they attempted to buy or sell their allotted land or home.

Plato's proposals for the regulation of the market seem harsh to us, even in a century of some strictly planned economies. In Book VIII of *The Laws*, for example, he writes that the market should be controlled by wardens who would inflict punishment on anyone violating the rules, of which there were many. Aside from the retail sales made by neighborhood vendors, Plato would permit three product-specific markets to be held each month, one every ten days, and people would have to buy supplies sufficient to last them a month. The first market would sell grain; the second, held ten days later, would sell liquids; and the third would sell livestock, slaves, and other related products such as hides, textiles, and clothes.

Aristotle never shared the totalitarian proclivities of Plato, but he did have some odd ideas about markets. He did not believe that everyone in the marketplace should be charged the same price. To him it seemed only natural that people with more money should pay higher prices than poorer people. He did not see impersonal market principles in operation; he saw individual relationships. The outcome of the interaction, according to Aristotle, should be determined by the status of the participants, not by the value of the merchandise. For him the purpose of the market was not merely to exchange goods but also to satisfy greed. Consequently, the market catered to a basically undesirable human instinct and had to be monitored carefully. Aristotle viewed the operation of the marketplace in personal rather than abstract terms. Even though he was certainly capable of abstract thought, we can see in his works the struggle of a person trying to understand the newly emerging phenomena of money and markets.

Prior to the invention of money in the form of coins, the chapters of history overflow with stories of many civilizations on different continents speaking different languages and worshiping different gods, but we see in virtually all of them a common pattern. Whether we consider the ancient Egyptians or the Aztecs, the Hittites or the Babylonians, the Cretans or the mysterious people of Mohenjo-Daro, we see that they all appear to have risen only to a similar level of civilization. It is almost as though each of them encountered the same invisible wall, which they were unable to penetrate. They developed their own architecture and religion, science and commerce, poetry and music only so far before they stagnated.

The Greeks, however, broke through this barrier. Suddenly, architecture, philosophy, science, literature, and the other arts and sciences soared to a level of attainment unknown to any earlier civilization. Some scholars would have us believe that this breakthrough arose from some superior quality of the Greek mind, psyche, race, or culture, from some more advanced sensibilities about humans and nature; but we see little in history before or after that time to indicate that the Greeks were unique among the many peoples of the world. What was different for the Greeks was that they lived next door to the Lydians, who invented money. Unlike other neighbors, such as the Phoenicians and the Persians who already had sophisticated social systems without money, the Greeks were a largely unformed civilization, and their adoption of money propelled them forward, past all the other peoples of the area. Greece was the first civilization to be transformed by money, but in a relatively short time, all cultures followed the Greeks down the same road and underwent the same metamorphosis.

Humans have found many ways to bring order to the phenomenological flow of existence, and money is one of the most important. Money is strictly a human invention in that it is itself a metaphor; it stands for something else. It allows humans to structure life in incredibly complex ways that were not available to them before the invention of money. This metaphorical quality gives it a focal role in the organization of meaning in life. Money represents an infinitely expandable way of structuring value and social relationships—personal, political, and religious as well as commercial and economic.

Everywhere that money went it created marketplaces. Money created a new urban geography by giving rise to towns and cities centered on the market rather than the palace. The exchange of goods necessitated new commercial routes over land and sea from one urban nodule to the next, thereby linking Greece and neighboring lands in a new web of commerce.

This new social network founded on commerce and money gave rise to a new political system. Philip of Macedonia saw an opportunity to bring all these interconnected points together into a united kingdom under his rule. His son, Alexander, expanded this system to parts of the world that had not yet been fully incorporated into the new commercial culture. As he conquered new lands, Alexander founded new commercial cities, which he often named for himself, that would unite that land to the expanding commercial world of his empire. In Egypt, he founded Alexandria on the Mediterranean so that it could serve as a link between the commercial Greeks and the more isolated riches of the Nile River valley.

Because of Alexander, Greek became the language of commerce. Merchants on the Nile Delta, on the island of Sicily, along the coast of Tunisia, and in the cities of Israel used Greek as the trade language.

The Greek spoken in the markets of Iberia and Palestine was not the classical Greek of Aristotle and certainly not the ancient Greek of Homer. The merchants used a simple, almost pidginized form of shop Greek, but this language proved capable of conveying great ideas far beyond the needs of simple market exchange. The marketplaces of the Mediterranean became focal points for discussing a new kind of religion. The followers of Jesus used the simplified market Greek to spread their ideas from one market center to another. His disciples and followers spoke in the marketplaces of cities such as Ephesus, Jerusalem, Damascus, Alexandria, and Rome. They wrote down their stories in this market Greek—sometimes called "God's poor Greek"—and their writings became the New Testament.

Prior to the rise of the Greek commercial system each country had its own gods. The gods of the Egyptians were different from those of the Greeks, the Persians, and the Hebrews. The common commercial culture, however, provided an opportunity for the rise of a common religion, open to all people. Christianity blazed through the cities of the Mediterranean as a totally new and revolutionary concept in religion. It was a uniquely urban religion that had none of the fertility gods or weather gods of the sun, wind, rain, and moon that were associated with farmers. It was the first religion that sought to leap over the social and cultural divisions among people and unite them in a single world religion. Its followers actively sought to make Christianity a universal religion; they did so in much the same way that money was creating a universal economy.

The coining of the first money in Lydia unleashed a revolution that began in commerce but spread almost simultaneously to urban design, politics, religion, and intellectual pursuits. It created a whole new way of organizing human life. After nearly five hundred years of rapid social change, all of these forces came to focus in the rise of a new type of empire centered in Rome. This unique empire was to be the greatest extension of the classical civilization created by money, but it was also to be the beginning of the end of money as a system based on metal coins. Rome became both the climax of the classical world and its destroyer.

3
The Premature Death of Money

Thy money perish with thee.
—Acts 8:20

THE ANCIENT RUINS OF THE IMPERIAL AGE LIE scattered across the center of modern Rome like whale bones that have washed up on a rocky shore and been picked clean by the birds and rodents that make their nests and burrows amid the debris. The Colosseum stands as the largest of these ruins, a symbolic focus of Roman civilization at its architectural best and its moral worst. Roman engineers turned the floor of that arena into a large pool on which mock sea battles were performed, resulting in real death and blood. An extensive system of underground passageways and cages held the animals and gladiators who fought in the Colosseum, and trapdoors propelled them suddenly into the arena to the delighted roar of the ever-surprised crowds.

Emperors imported lions, tigers, elephants, rhinoceroses, ostriches, crocodiles, bears, and other exotic animals for displays of combat against each other and against humans. Dwarfs fought bears; African Pygmies faced pale Celtic giants. Gladiators chased Christians around the arena, hacking them to death or leaving them to be attacked and devoured by starving animals.

Construction of the Colosseum, which was officially known as the Flavian Amphitheater of Rome, began in A.D. 69, during the reign of Vespasian, and was completed a decade later in the reign of Titus, who opened the Colosseum with a one-hundred-day cycle of religious pageants, gladiatorial games, and spectacles. The common name by which the structure was known even in Roman times was probably derived from *colossus*, in reference to the large statue of the emperor Nero near the arena.

The Colosseum held 45,000 to 50,000 spectators, and to protect them from the fierce summer sun, workers stretched a large canvas canopy over the top. During its half millennium of use, the Colosseum underwent extensive renovation seven times, but with the fall of Rome, it became a quarry for later generations in need of building stone. Today, only about one-third of the original structure remains.

Despite the gory stories associated with the Colosseum and its symbolic importance in Christianity as a place where untold numbers of saints and martyrs met their grisly deaths, the Colosseum was much more a symptom than a cause of the rot of Rome. Behind the gore lies another story, one of an economy seemingly gone berserk, a situation in which the bizarre entertainments of the Colosseum and the persecution of the Christians seemed normal. To understand the economic heartbeat and the story of money in Rome as well as the ultimate cause of the empire's collapse, we need to look beyond the Colosseum toward Capitoline Hill, home of the high god Jupiter Capitolinus, the official deity of the Colosseum games.

Even though it is the smallest of the Seven Hills of Rome, Capitoline Hill always ranked as the most important, for here stood both the great citadel of Rome and the Capitol, the main temple of the empire. The temple served as home to the king of the gods, Jupiter Optimus Maximus, who occupied the center of the temple; and the side chambers honored Minerva, the goddess of wisdom, and Juno, the sister and consort of Jupiter as well as the mother of Mars. Together, Jupiter, Juno, and Minerva constituted the Roman trinity known as the Capitoline Triad, but each one came in several different aspects with a different surname for each aspect.

Money occupied a sacred place in many temples but particularly in the one dedicated to Juno Regina, the highest Roman goddess, who reigned as the queen of heaven and occupied a position much like the goddess Hera, wife of Zeus, in Greek mythology. Juno represented the genius of womanhood and was the patroness of women, marriage, and childbirth. As Juno Pronuba, she watched over marriage negotiations; as Juno Lucina, she protected pregnant women;

and as Juno Sospita, she presided over labor and childbirth.

As an extension of her role as protector of women and guardian of the family, Juno became the patroness of the Roman state. According to Roman historians, in the fourth century B.C., the irritated honking of the sacred geese around Juno's temple on Capitoline Hill warned the people of an impending night attack by the Gauls, who were secretly scaling the walls of the citadel. From this event, the goddess acquired yet another surname—Juno Moneta, from Latin *monere* (to warn).

As patroness of the state, Juno Moneta presided over various activities of the state, including the primary activity of issuing money. In 269 B.C., the Romans introduced a new silver coin, the denarius, which they manufactured in the temple of Juno Moneta. The coin bore the image of the goddess and her surname, Moneta. From her first name, Juno, comes the name of the month of Junonius, or June, the most auspicious month for marriage. Also from Moneta came the modern English words *mint* and *money* and, ultimately, from the Latin word meaning *warning*.

Cognates in other European languages also derive from *moneta*, including the Spanish *moneda*, meaning "coin." From very early classical times, money showed a close relationship to the divine and to the female. We can still see that connection in money-related words in European languages, which are frequently feminine in gender, as in the Spanish *la moneda* and the German *die Mark* and *die Münze* (coin).

The frequent melting and reissuing of coins kept the mints at the Temple of Juno Moneta in nearly continuous operation, whether the supply of gold and silver increased or not. The coins seem to have flowed out of the mint in a constant stream, and it is from the Latin word *currere*, meaning "to run" or "to flow," that the modern word *currency* is derived, along with other, related words such as *current* and *courier*. The devalued coins gushed like a great river from Capitoline Hill throughout the entire empire.

Today, the site of the Temple of Juno Moneta, the source of the great stream of Roman currency, has given way to the ancient but ugly brick church of Santa Maria in Aracoeli. Centuries ago, church architects incorporated the ruins of the ancient temple into the new building; however, with so many more attractive and impressive sites scattered throughout the city, the site of the ancient mint now attracts scant attention.

AN EMPIRE FINANCED BY CONQUEST

Rome developed the most sophisticated economy of any civilization up to that time. Only a few centuries after the minting of the first coins in Lydia, the Greeks had spread the money economy throughout the Mediterranean. The Romans, in turn, carried it across most of southern and western Europe. As no other empire had done, Rome organized an immense area and operated it according to a new system that borrowed heavily from the tradition of ancient empires but combined that tradition with revolutionary new ideas based on markets and money.

Rome built the world's first empire organized around money. Whereas the great Egyptian, Persian, and other traditional empires had largely rejected money in favor of government as the main organizing principle, Rome promoted the use of money and organized all of its affairs around the new commodity.

The Roman Empire reached its economic apogee sometime around the reign of Marcus Aurelius. For the first time, virtually all of the Mediterranean as well as many of the adjacent lands found themselves united under a single political ruler, the Roman emperor. Unification provided protection and therefore encouraged trade. It also promoted the standardization of products and measurements and increased the kinds and the quality of money available in the marketplace.

Most of the commercial growth of Rome occurred during its Republican era, prior to the rise of Julius Caesar and the long line of emperors to follow. Caesar and the early emperors showed a keen awareness of the value of commerce and markets for their imperial power, and using this knowledge, they managed to sustain and even improve upon some of the Republican achievements. Despite the commercial success attained during the early imperial era, later emperors showed little significant or enlightened interest in commerce.

Their fame and glory came from the military and from conquest, and
their riches, too, derived much more from the achievements of the
army than from those of the merchants. As long as the empire continued to expand, the emperor could appropriate the wealth of the
newly conquered lands and use it to finance his army, pay for the government, and support whatever projects he might dream up. Each
conquest brought in a new surge of gold and silver loot as well as
slaves for sale in the markets; it also gave the emperor new soldiers
to train and turn against the next enemy.

Unlike Athens and Sardis, Rome produced very little of anything;
nor did it serve as a major mercantile crossroads of commerce. Rome
was simply an importer of wealth. What came into Rome stayed
there. As H. G. Wells wrote in *The Outline of History*, Rome was "a
political and financial capital . . . a new sort of city. She imported
profits and tribute, and very little went out from her in return."

Rome had discovered money, not just wealth and tribute, which
all civilizations had coveted, but money that could be used for speculation, buying and selling land, and which supported a whole new
equestrian class that rivaled and irritated the traditional patricians.
As Wells wrote, "Money was young in human experience and wild;
nobody had it under control. It fluctuated greatly. It was now abundant and now scarce. Men made sly and crude schemes to corner it,
to hoard it, to send up prices by releasing hoarded metals."[1]

Roman emperors did not operate on a budget; a few of them saved,
but most spent whatever they could get. The acquisition of each new
kingdom or province produced a temporary jump in imperial Roman
income, and subsequently in expenditures. Government spending
doubled from 100 million to 200 million sesterces with the acquisition of the treasury of the kingdom of Pergamum in 130 B.C. (A ses-
terce equaled one-fourth of a denarius.) By 63 B.C. the budget had
grown to 340 million sesterces following the conquest and looting of
Syria, and so it continued with the conquest of Egypt, Judea, Gaul,
Spain, Assyria, Mesopotamia, and all the other nations along the
Mediterranean.[2] During the reign of Augustus, when the empire
reached its zenith, the cost of government surpassed a million sesterces for the first time. After the death of Augustus, the profligate

spending on useless military campaigns, building projects, and personal pleasure by his successors Caligula, Claudius, and Nero became increasingly difficult to calculate.

Conquest and pillage proved capable of financing the empire for only so long. The Roman legions had soon conquered and looted all the wealthy areas around them. By the reign of Trajan, from 98 to 117, the cost of conquest had surpassed the value of riches it brought into the empire. For new conquests, emperors had to probe rather marginal areas such as the British Isles and Mesopotamia, where the cost of the conquest proved hardly worth the expense and where the natural resources and the goods generated by the area did not suffice to pay for the garrisons necessary to occupy and guard it.

Rome produced little, and once it had looted the lands around it, the empire developed a growing imbalance of trade as it continued to import goods from Asia. Unable to offer quality manufactured goods in return for these imported goods, Rome had to pay in gold and silver. This created a drain of bullion, causing the emperor Tiberius to complain that "our wealth is transferred to foreign and even hostile nations." In A.D. 77, Pliny the Elder complained that as much as 550 million sesterces a year went to India to pay for luxuries.[3]

By far the highest expense of the Roman Empire arose from the financing of its huge and widely dispersed army. As the empire's borders expanded, the long and twisted lines of communication and transportation could no longer hold. It became increasingly difficult for the emperors in Rome to retain the loyalty of soldiers who were recruited from many different nations, spoke many different languages, and served far from the city of Rome, which few of them would ever see. Even after the emperors stopped conquering new territories, they had to maintain a massive army and, frequently, utilize it to put down rebellions and fight off the invading tribes who constantly tested the Roman resolve to defend its borders.

Despite its declining ability to produce revenue for the state, the army continued to grow in size. Even during the third and fourth centuries, when the geographical size of the empire declined, the number of soldiers more than doubled from approximately 300,000 to

650,000. Military equipment and weapons became steadily more elaborate and expensive as the army required more horses for transportation over longer inland routes and as military tactics shifted to an increased use of mounted cavalry in place of the traditional Roman reliance on marching infantry. The new equipment and horses further increased the military budget and strained the imperial treasury.

THE GOVERNMENT GLUT

Although considerably smaller in number than the army, the bureaucracy of Rome increased at roughly the same rate even as the empire was shrinking, and it became a paid institution during the time of Augustus, who began to pay officials for the public service that had been performed free during the Roman Republic. Beginning with the reign of Augustus, the number of salaried officials and assistants grew steadily.

Unable to stem the imperial decline with the army, the emperors organized and reorganized their imperial administrations, searching desperately for a formula to help them overcome the mounting problems confronting them. They created more and smaller provinces, split the empire, and divided the job of ruler between an emperor and two or more caesars who acted as assistants or regional emperors. Each change, however, added a new layer of administration to the hierarchy and created new regional and local capitals along with all the supernumeraries, palaces, temples, and other public buildings to which even regional capitals aspired. Despite the constant stream of organizational reforms, officials were rarely cut from the public payroll; instead more were added. According to the best available evidence, during the reign of Diocletian alone, the government bureaucracy may have doubled in size.

Faced with climbing government expenses, emperors searched for new revenue and new ways to make the existing revenue stretch further. Nero began to tamper with the coinage itself. In A.D. 64, in a naive attempt to deceive the populace, Nero decreased the silver content in the coins and made both the silver and gold coins slightly smaller. By collecting the existing coins and reminting them with his portrait bust but using less silver, Nero produced a momentary surplus of silver and gold. The same pound of silver that had formerly produced 84 denarii now produced 96, giving Nero almost a 15 percent "profit." He similarly increased from 40 to 45 the number of golden aurei manufactured from a pound of gold, thus rendering the coins about 11 percent less golden.[4]

When pressed for yet more money, subsequent emperors followed Nero's strategy and continued the debasement of the nation's money supply. By using the available supply of silver and gold to produce more coins, the emperor had more coins to spend without raising taxes. Increasing the number of coins, however, did not actually increase the amount of money.

During his reign, Nero had reduced the silver content of the denarius to 90 percent; by the time of Marcus Aurelius, the denarius had only 75 percent silver, and by the end of the second century, Commodus had reduced the content to only 67 percent. Then when Emperor Lucius Septimius Severus raised the soldiers' pay, he was forced to reduce the silver content of the denarius to less than 50 percent. Caracalla introduced an entirely new coin called the antoninianus, or double denarius, which contained even less silver but had a face value worth two of the old denarii. By the reign of Gallienus, from 260 to 268, the antoninianus contained less than 5 percent silver. Thus over the course of two hundred years, the silver content was cut from nearly 100 percent to virtually nothing. The amount of silver previously used to mint a single denarius eventually produced 150 denarii, and as the silver content decreased, the price of goods increased in direct proportion. Wheat that had sold for one-half a denarius in the second century increased to 100 denarii a century later, a two hundred–fold increase.

So long as the emperors maintained the backing of the army, no other power in Rome seemed capable of challenging them. With such vast political power, the emperors' greed pushed them toward the acquisition of ever greater riches. In addition to seizing the wealth of the foreign peoples conquered by their armies, the emperors coveted the great riches generated by agriculture and commerce within their own empire, and they found new ways to acquire it.

From the reign of Augustus, if not before, the tax income of the empire was derived from two primary sources. The *tributum capitis* was a poll tax paid every year by each adult between the ages of twelve and sixty-five.[5] The *tributum soli* was an annual property tax on all land, from forests to croplands, as well as on ships, slaves, animals, and other movable property. This tax seemed to equal approximately 1 percent of the total property value. The brunt of this tax burden fell much more heavily on agriculture than on commerce, therefore encouraging commercial activity.

Most of these taxes went into the treasury of the central government located in Rome, so cities and provinces levied their own taxes to cover civic projects and salaries. Additionally, they created city and provincial taxes on goods being transferred in and out of their territory.

These two primary taxes sufficed as long as the army brought in great amounts of loot from its conquests, but they began to prove insufficient as government and military costs rose. The emperors had to impose new taxes. They increased taxes on land, with the result that farmers abandoned the less productive fields and agricultural output therefore declined. The emperors turned increasing attention to taxing commerce and inheritance, going so far as to create a sales tax. In the quest for greater tax revenues, Tiberius ordered each man in the empire to take his wife and children with him to the community of his birth in order to make a census from which a head tax would then be made.

According to the Gospels, it was during this time that Joseph of Nazareth returned to his natal city of Bethlehem with his bride, Mary, who then gave birth to Jesus in a stable. Not only did imperial Roman taxation play an odd, indirect role in the birth of Christ, but the New Testament contains repeated references to Roman taxation, to the resentment it caused, to the people's hatred of tax collectors, and even to discussion of whether or not the followers of Christ should pay taxes. Jesus settled this question in the affirmative by showing his followers a coin bearing a portrait of the emperor and then commanding them to "render, therefore, unto Caesar the things which be Caesar's and unto God the things which be God's" (Luke 20:25). Christianity was born just at the beginning of the protracted economic struggles of the Roman Empire, and although few could have suspected it at the time, the new religion would play an important role in that struggle only a few centuries later.

In the third century, the emperor ordered an *indictio*, a special and supposedly temporary levy to requisition oil, wine, wheat, meat, leather, and clothing for the support of the army. These levies soon became a new layer of permanent taxation, very similar to the tributes demanded in the older palace economies.

The small traders and merchants bore an increasingly larger tax burden from the oppressive *chrysargyron* tax on manufactured goods and retail business. Although this tax yielded relatively little for the national coffers, it did great damage to the artisans and small traders throughout the empire. The more people produced, the more taxes they paid. By the time of Diocletian, many Roman subjects were not earning enough money to pay their annual taxes. In order to meet their annual tax assessments, they were forced to sell their animals, tools, or even the land itself. Increasingly, those smaller merchants who lacked land had no alternative but to sell their own children, and sometimes even themselves, into slavery to pay their taxes. Thus more and more families were reduced to poverty.

With fewer external sources to exploit, the government found increasingly grotesque ways to exploit its own citizens. One simple method arose from the ancient practice of confiscating the property of anyone judged to be a traitor to Rome or, more accurately, to the emperor. Soon the emperors used the accusation of treason as a ploy to confiscate the property of anyone rich enough to attract the attention of the emperor but not close enough to him to maintain his favor. Caracalla, for instance, raised the pay of the army by 50 percent in order to ensure its support, then financed much of the increase by confiscating the property of the growing number of people whom he judged disloyal to him.

Late in the fourth century, the Roman soldier and scholar Ammianus Marcellinus wrote one of the first histories of the Roman Empire. He recognized that the empire had already peaked and attributed its decline to taxation and the bureaucracy.[6] Even Emperor Valentinian III recognized the difficulty when he said that "if we claim these expenses from the landowner in addition to what he pays already, such an exaction will crush his last feeble strength; if again we demand them from the merchants, they will inevitably sink under the weight of such a burden."[7] After making this rational and compassionate observation, however, Valentinian imposed a new sales tax.

As taxes increased, the emperor and his favorites were exempt from taxes and enjoyed an ever more luxurious life while the farmers, tradesmen, and craftsmen who created the abundance lived in abject poverty. The entire economy focused on maintaining the government. In the Roman Empire, one did not complete the journey along the path to riches and fortune by hard work, through agriculture or commerce, or even through birth into a noble family. Rather, one completed the journey by becoming a favorite of the erratic emperors, thereby receiving appointment to high office and thus being entitled to claim or steal large sums of money.

Among the elite, the taste for luxuries grew continuously. They eschewed simple linen and woolen garments in favor of silk imported over thousands of miles and at great cost from China. They used large quantities of Arabian perfume and incense. They wore increasing amounts of gold and silver jewelry as well as amber and furs from the Baltic and other precious stones from throughout the empire, and they used more and more cosmetics from Anatolia. Money changed hands many times as these goods traveled laboriously along caravan routes to the most distant parts of the empire, but the money eventually left the Roman Empire in order to pay for the goods at their sources in China, India, Africa, and the Baltic. The desire for these luxury goods consumed ever greater resources, and it created a drain of gold and silver from Europe to Asia that was to continue almost until the nineteenth century.

The Roman desire for Asian luxury goods created the first great trade imbalance on a global scale. Because the Romans produced comparatively little, they had little to offer on the world market other than gold and silver in exchange for the luxury goods of Asia. The continuing desire for Eastern goods enriched the ruling Andhra dynasty of South India and the Han dynasty of China. The extent of the trade between Asia and Rome in ancient times became evident in recent decades when archaeologists and builders discovered some of the largest caches of buried Roman coins as far away as southern India.

THE FIRST WELFARE STATE

The elite associates who surrounded the emperor were not the only people to benefit from Roman successes. Beginning in the days of the republic, before the foundation of the empire, Roman politicians found that they could often increase their power by bribing the masses with bread and circuses. In addition to the exotic free entertainments that were staged in the Colosseum, the politicians exempted free citizens of the city of Rome from taxation and gave them heavily subsidized or even free wheat, paid for by taxes and tribute seized from the hinterlands of the empire. This practice quickly became institutionalized as a public dole.

When Julius Caesar first came to power nearly one-third of the people, approximately 320,000, received free wheat on the public dole, but through skillful maneuvering, he reduced the amount by more than half, to a still substantial 150,000. After Caesar's assassination, the numbers started to climb once again,[8] and the benefits increased. In addition to wheat, Emperor Severus gave the people of Rome olive oil; from time to time, emperors gave cash payments as part of the dole. Emperor Aurelian, who acquired the title Restorer of the Empire, changed the allotment of wheat to a ration of bread so as to spare the masses the expense of baking. He also subsidized the price of wine, salt, and pork for the masses in the city of Rome.

Like people anywhere, once the tax burdens became too high in comparison to the benefits and services offered by the government, the Roman subjects found ways to avoid the taxation. Commerce declined. People produced more of what they needed for themselves and traded less on the open market. While the poor suffered from heavy property taxes, the *latifundia*, the great landed estates, grew greatly, particularly those that had been granted a tax-free status. The high taxes induced more peasants to abandon their land and move to the tax-free estates where they at least had a steady supply of food and the essential goods produced on the estate itself.

As people left the small farms and towns, the large estates grew; and finally, without sufficient commerce to keep them alive and functioning, the great cities began to decline and to fall prey to marauding tribes. Even though no one at the time thought in terms of economic policy, it was the cumulative actions of the government that strangled the economy of Rome and of much of the rest of the Mediterranean and European world as well. The emperors saw the signs of death in the economy and proposed strenuous measures to revive it, but these measures served only to worsen the situation.

Diocletian, who ruled from 284 until 305, was in a sense the first modern ruler to attempt to regulate and fine-tune the economy in recognition of the fact that it was the true engine of empire. In order to preserve the system, in 301, Diocletian issued his Edict of Prices, which ordered a freeze on all prices and wages. In practice, however, rather than freezing prices, the edict prompted merchants and farmers to withdraw their goods from the market. Production declined.

Diocletian then ordered all male citizens to follow the occupation of their fathers. A merchant's son must be a merchant, a farmer's son a farmer, and a bureaucrat's son a bureaucrat. Soldiers' sons had to be soldiers, thus creating a hereditary military class. Even the sons of the workers who produced coins had to become mint workers.

Diocletian's edict forbade the heavily burdened farmers from selling their land, thus permanently tying them to the same plot of land—a practice that foreshadowed the age of feudalism. The empire began to take on the characteristics of a static, caste society, a tendency that grew even stronger in medieval Europe.

In the last centuries of the Roman Empire, the emperors operated without a workable currency; like the ancient empires that had preceded it, Rome turned to conscription and forced labor to meet its needs. The government often would not allow its citizens to pay taxes in the debased money that it still issued; instead, officials demanded payment in goods, crops, or labor.

As tax policies continued to suppress productivity and commerce, the emperors found it increasingly difficult to supply their armies and the bureaucracy with the equipment and goods necessary to rule the far-flung but diminishing empire. The markets had withered; even the emperor could no longer depend on the open market to supply him with the sandals, armor, weapons, saddles, tents, and other goods that an army needed. Out of desperation, Diocletian created government-sponsored workshops to manufacture armaments and supplies. As privately financed shipping and other transport enterprises declined, Diocletian also had to create government transport companies to move the goods that were manufactured in the workshops.

Well before the end of the third century, these changes made the emperor and the government the greatest manufacturers in the empire, in addition to being the largest owner of land, mines, and quarries. Step by step, the imperial government took over the direct administration of the economy and crowded out the small, independent merchants, landowners, manufacturers, and entrepreneurs.

The government workshops and transport systems never functioned as efficiently as the older ones, which had been based on a network of relations among many different merchants. The creation of these workshops further stifled commerce and drove private entrepreneurs either out of business or into total dependence on government contracts. An increasingly greater portion of the economy fell under direct control of the bureaucracy, which consumed ever more of the national output of agricultural and manufactured goods. By its last decades, Rome had become another state-administered economy, an empire without money and markets. It had reverted to a palace system more like that of pharaonic Egypt or imperial China than that of the republican system on which it had been built.

PROFITS FROM PERSECUTION

As the economy of the Roman Empire continued to deteriorate, the desperate emperors searched for even more radical solutions outside the economic realm. To ensure the support of the people while increasing his power over them and the army, Diocletian ordered all citizens to worship him as a god. Then, in 303, he began the horrendous persecution of Christians that was to last for a decade. The persecution of the Christians added money to state coffers and provided plenty of victims for the shows in the Colosseum.

In the short term, Diocletian's measures and those of his succes-
sor, Constantine, helped to contain the increasing cost, but they further stifled the economy. The efforts of Constantine, who ruled from
306 to 337, to revive the empire were even more drastic because he
looked increasingly beyond the economic world to the sphere of religion to find a solution to the empire's problems.

After supposedly receiving a vision of the cross with the words *in
hoc signo vinces* (in this sign, you will conquer) just prior to a major
battle, Constantine reversed the religious policies of Diocletian and
ended the persecution of Christians. He then changed the course of
Roman religious history in 313 by issuing the Edict of Milan, grant-
ing Christians freedom to practice their religion and returning their
confiscated property to them. Even though Constantine himself remained an unbaptized pagan, in 325 he presided over the Council of
Nicaea, which adopted a common theology for all Christians and produced the Creed of Nicaea, a statement of beliefs that faithful Christians of many denominations still recite today.

Constantine recognized that the persecutions had provided very
little benefit to anyone. As it did with all traitors, the state had confiscated much of the Christians' property, but the small sect had relatively little property or wealth. The persecution of a religious group,
however, proved to be a bizarre new tool crafted by the state, and once
it was devised, the state looked for new reasons to use it. If the emperor could not obtain much property from the Christians, then he
needed to target a wealthier group from whom to confiscate property.
Constantine found that wealth in the many well-endowed pagan
temples throughout his empire.

Unable to finance his administration from taxation and unable to
loot new lands, Constantine began confiscating the riches in the temples of his own empire. He conducted a systematic looting of these
temples, and with the gold and silver, he minted gold coins to finance
the construction of his new capital, Constantinople. The building of
the new capital cut off the money supply to Rome and further depressed the economic condition of the Roman lands.

Although it is difficult to determine the precise motive after the passing of so many centuries, it may well be that Constantine's desire to acquire the wealth of the great temples played an important role in his support of the Christians and his eventual conversion to their religion. No matter what his motive, he certainly benefited greatly from the confiscation of temple wealth. Constantine waited until he lay dying before converting to Christianity and allowing himself to be baptized in 337. He left Christianity as virtually the official religion of the empire and, in so doing, further strengthened the position of the emperor in the imperial system.

With the empire firmly established in the East, the western Mediterranean and Europe fell increasingly into chaos even while continuing in name as the Roman Empire for more than another century. Because the peasants lived under such an onerous tax burden from their own government, many of them welcomed conquest by barbarian tribes who offered them far more freedom than was allowed by the Romans. They joined the barbarians, eagerly slaughtering their own rulers and looting the remaining cities of the empire, including the once mighty imperial city of Rome.

In the fourth century, as the western half of the empire decayed, the mint in Rome ceased production of its totally debased currency. The Ostrogoths captured much of Italy and ruled from Ravenna, making the mint there the primary one for their kingdom. When the Byzantine ruler Justinian I conquered Italy, he used the mint in Rome to produce some coins for the Byzantine Empire, but it operated as a mere subsidiary workshop for Constantinople. The making of coins in Rome had come to an end and, with it, the classical economy.

By A.D. 476, the date of the second sacking of Rome and the date usually given for the collapse of the empire, the classical money economy that had survived for barely a thousand years also collapsed. So completely had the Roman economy deteriorated that almost a thousand years would pass before the money economy returned in full force. During the long period known as the Dark Ages and then the Middle Ages, money played only a wispy shadow of the role it had held in classical Greece and Rome at their height. After more than a thousand years of using coins in a culture based on city life, people retreated into a rural and virtually moneyless economy.

THE ROAD TO FEUDALISM

Today, scattered across the face of the former Roman Empire in Europe, from England to Italy, stand many great country estates—manors, châteaux, castles, and monasteries. During the nearly one thousand years from the fall of Rome in 476 until the Renaissance around 1350, these estates served as centers of productivity and power that created one of the greatest rural civilizations ever known.

The medieval era, which might also be called the manorial era because of the importance of manors, represented a major departure from classical Mediterranean culture; whereas classical culture focused on the city, medieval culture focused on the country manor. Whereas classical culture emphasized commerce, medieval culture emphasized self-sufficiency; and whereas classical economy focused on money, medieval economy focused on hereditary services and payment in kind. Medieval culture, then, departed radically from that of the classical era, especially in that the medieval world virtually gave up the use of money. Rather than collect taxes in coins, landowners required payment in crops and service from the peasants. Rather than manufacture trade goods, each manor sought to be as self-sufficient as possible by producing its own food and clothing and even by making its own tools. No longer able to sell their services, people became serfs who were bound to the land. Even slavery virtually ceased during this era with the exception of criminals, pagans, and Muslim captives taken in war.

Because of a decline in education, fewer people could read or figure numbers, which made them all the more suspicious of and reluctant to use coins. Coins continued to be minted during the medieval era, but they varied greatly in quality from region to region and from year to year. They were often made to resemble classical Greek or Roman coins but had frequent misspellings and were easily counterfeited. The general quality of money dropped so low that the average merchant as well as the illiterate peasant needed to be extremely cautious when using coins of any type.

The struggle between the tributary empire and the market system seems to have been won by the empire. Under Roman hegemony, government had defeated and apparently destroyed the market system itself. The Romans seem to have inadvertently managed to do what the Persians had attempted but failed to accomplish in their years of war against the merchant cities of Greece.

Despite the virtual death of coinage systems in western Europe, a reasonably healthy system of coinage continued to operate in the eastern Mediterannean under the aegis of the Byzantine emperors at Constantinople. Money did not grow or develop more complicated institutions, but at least it did survive. After centuries of slumber, the system gradually returned to life during the era of the Crusades, when western Europeans invaded the Mulims lands of the East. Money acquired a newly important role in financing the extensive new trade routes opened between East and West and in financing the large military expeditions that were launched over great distances for long periods of time.

4
Knights of Commerce

In faith there is profit.
—SAIKAKU IHARA

ON TUESDAY, MAY 12, 1310, FRENCH SOLDIERS LOADED fifty-four bound men onto carts and took them into the country outside of Paris, where they stripped off the men's clothes and tied them to stakes surrounded by piles of wood. As the prisoners vociferously screamed their innocence, the guards lit the wood beneath them. The flames crawled higher, singeing their hair and lapping at their flesh. The heat caused huge blisters to erupt and their skin to split open as their fat liquefied and ran down their limbs in delicate rivulets of flame. The roar of the flames gradually drowned out the screams of the burning men.

With this mass execution of the Knights of the Temple in the bucolic fields near the Convent of Saint-Antoine, Europe's first international banking system began to crumble. Even though most of the men burned that day had not been the top leaders of the financial enterprise, the system never recovered from the much publicized execution of its members and the accompanying public humiliation of their enterprise. Within another four years, even the once powerful leaders of these men met the same fiery death on an island in the Seine River, and their entire banking system collapsed with the extinction of their order.

THE VIRGIN BANKERS
The first major banking institution arose not from the merchant community but from an odd and seemingly unlikely order of religious knights known as Templars. Founded in Jerusalem around 1118 by

Crusaders, the Military Order of the Knights of the Temple of Solomon dedicated their lives to serving the church and, specifically, to the task of liberating the Holy Land from the Infidels. The Templars later became businessmen who ran the world's greatest international banking corporation, which they operated for nearly two hundred years. During that time, they laid the foundation for modern banking, but they did so at a huge price to themselves. Their success led not only to the destruction of the order but to the torture and public burning of its leaders as well.

Recruited largely from among the younger sons of nobility, who inherited no titles or riches, the knights pledged themselves to a life of devotion to the church. They lived adjacent to the ruins of the Temple of Solomon in Jerusalem, and from this location they derived their name. They undertook the special obligation of maintaining the safety of the highways for pilgrims coming to the Holy Land.

The Knights Templars did not pursue an easy life, at least not in the early years. Although they fought, strenuously, they ate only two silent meals a day while listening to scriptural readings. They ate meat only three times a week. As a sign of their chastity, they dressed in white mantles emblazoned with a large red cross; they kept their hair short and tonsured like other monks.

Married men could join the order, but they had to live chaste lives apart from their families and, even so, could never don the traditional white mantle reserved for the brothers who lived as perpetual virgins and never married. All knights had to stay away from women and could not kiss any female, even a family member. To forestall any potentially inappropriate interaction, the order did not have a female branch, and, unlike other orders, it did not allow youths to enter. As a final precaution against sin, the Templars slept in shirt and pants with a cord around their waist to remind them of their vow of chastity. They kept a candle burning in their room throughout the night to discourage any immoral acts whether alone or with someone else.

In the twelfth century, according to an eyewitness account, the knights went into battle in silence, but at the moment of attack they burst loudly into song with one of the Psalms of David, "Not unto us, O Lord." They maintained a strict code of warfare that virtually precluded surrender or defeat on the battlefield. Because of their willingness, even eagerness, to die, the Templars were among the most feared warriors in the world. The Templars served as the romantic model for the knights in Richard Wagner's nineteenth-century opera *Parsifal*.

Even the strictest and most well constructed codes, however, contain some cracks that expand and widen with the passage of centuries until the original structure is eventually altered beyond recognition. Though founded in complete poverty, a sequence of papal bulls gave the order the right to keep all spoils that they captured from Muslims during the Crusades. Like virtually all religious orders, they also accepted gifts and bequests from the faithful back home. The most infamous of these gifts came from King Henry II of England, who donated money to the Templars in atonement for the murder of Thomas à Becket, archbishop of Canterbury, by four of Henry's knights in 1170. The king donated enough money to support two hundred knights a year in the Holy Land, and he left in his will an additional 15,000 marks for the Templars and another order, the Knights Hospitalers.

Through the years, the Templars acquired more land and valuables, all designated to support the work of the order in Palestine. The knights regularly transported the proceeds of their European estates to their headquarters in Jerusalem.

Because the Templars owned some of the mightiest castles in the world and because they constituted one of the fiercest fighting forces of the time, their castles served as ideal places in which to deposit money and other valuables. The fierce and respected Templars also offered an ideal means of transporting such valuables over long distances, and even across the Mediterranean, since they exercised responsibility for safety on the highways and in the shipping lanes.

A French knight could deposit money or a take out a mortgage through the Templars in Paris but receive the money in the form of gold coins when needed in Jerusalem. The Templars, of course, charged a fee for the transaction, and since they paid out in different currency from what they received, they could take an additional cut of the money for the exchange.

In addition to serving as a depository for and a transporter of treasure, the Templars administered the funds gathered from religious and secular sources to finance the Crusades. They also made loans to kings, including Louis VII of France, and to those knights who needed funds for themselves and their retainers when going on a Crusade. Knights who were not members of the order customarily stored their valuables in a fortress of the Templars, leaving on file as well their last will and testament, for which the order was to serve as executor if the knight did not return. The order frequently held and supervised mortgages and other financial affairs for kings during their absence, as when Philip II of France left the Templars in charge of revenue from his lands when he marched away in the Crusade of 1190. The Templars' castles soon became full-service banks, offering many financial services to the nobility.

The Templars' headquarters in Paris became one of the greatest treasure-houses in Europe. To ensure scrupulous honesty, the order forbade its knights to own money themselves. This prohibition was so strictly enforced that any knight who died with unauthorized money on his person was considered to have died outside a state of grace. He was denied a Christian burial and thus, according to their religion, condemned to eternal damnation. Such strict rules and beliefs kept pilfering and even petty dishonesty in check throughout the history of the order.

Over the course of the thirteenth century, this order of educated and honest knights served as financial agents for the papacy and handled many accounts for the French kings, including their household accounts. As bankers to the kings and popes, the Templars grew into an institution somewhat akin to a modern treasury department, except that they did not collect taxes. At their maximum strength, they employed approximately 7,000 people and owned 870 castles and houses scattered across Europe and the Mediterranean from England to Jerusalem.

Despite the dedication of the Templars to their mission, they steadily lost ground in Palestine to the Egyptian Mamelukes, an army of fierce military slaves, most of whom had been recruited from Christian families and had converted to Islam. In 1291, the Templars lost the city of Acre, their last stronghold on the mainland, and fled to the island of Cyprus. Despite the military setback, their financial enterprises continued to flourish.

THE DANGERS OF SUCCESS

Despite the poverty of its individual members, the order grew rich and fat, but seemingly beyond the control of any one nation or king. They became an easy target, waiting for a sufficiently strong and greedy monarch to tackle them. That monarch finally appeared in the dashing form of King Philip IV of France, known as Philip the Fair because he was considered the most handsome man in the world. In 1295, Philip took the management of his finances out of the hands of the Templars and established the royal treasury at the Louvre in Paris. He then began a campaign aimed at taking over both the Templars' extensive properties and treasure.

Philip's desperate need for money arose after he tried a trick that Nero had pulled a thousand years earlier: he debased the silver currency of his realm in order to produce more coins by reminting the old ones with less silver. In the short run, he gained from this maneuver, but problems quickly arose when the peasants started paying their taxes with the new coins containing less silver. Like Nero, Philip ended up with more coins but less money, since each coin now had less buying power. Philip then sought to reform the French currency by returning it to its original value, and in 1306, he recalled the coins and reminted them at the value set in 1266 by Louis IX. Philip repeatedly altered the value of the currency in the years that followed, but each alteration hurt him in the end. He needed a constant supply of gold and silver in order to restore the adulterated currency.

In order to meet his constant need for money, Philip turned on the Lombard merchants, whose goods he seized. He attempted to tax the clergy, and then he turned on the Jews, expelling them in July 1306, after seizing their property. Even the wealth of the Jews and Lombards combined with his tax on priests failed to meet the needs of Philip's growing government and his thirst for power. He needed massive amounts of money.

The greatest concentration of wealth in Europe lay just outside Paris in the well-fortified castle that served as the main treasure-house for the Templars' wealth. To obtain that wealth, however, the king would have to destroy the order, and he proved willing and able to do so. In 1307, Philip issued a secret order that began with a bitter denunciation of the order.

"A bitter thing, a lamentable thing, a thing which is horrible to contemplate, terrible to hear, a detestable crime, an execrable evil, an abominable work, a detestable disgrace, a thing almost inhuman, indeed set apart from all humanity."[1] With these words, Philip set the stage for the skillful propaganda campaign he needed to wage in order to topple and loot the greatest financial institution in the world.

Rather than make war on the Templars, the agents of Philip IV coordinated a surprise raid in which they arrested the unsuspecting leaders of the order throughout France. Philip timed his raid so as to arrest Jacques de Molay, the elderly grand master of the order, who had come to France from his headquarters in Cyprus to attend to some business for the Templars and Pope Clement V.

Philip's allies immediately unleashed a public relations war against the Templars, accusing them of the worst sorts of crimes in order to incite public horror and outrage against them. The charges resulted in lengthy court proceedings that culminated in a dramatic series of trials during which French prosecutors accused the order's leaders of heresy, apostasy, devil worship, sexual perversion, and a whole catalog of the worst offenses against the medieval code of morality. Under fierce torture, the elderly officers of the order signed confessions that provided lurid details about their activities as idol worshipers, profaners of sacred objects, conspirators with the devil, and perpetrators of sexual deviance upon one another.

The charges included accusations of Templars having sex with the corpses of noblewomen, worshiping a cat, eating the bodies of dead knights, and making bonds of blood brotherhood with Muslims. Other witnesses alleged that Templars seduced virgins in order to produce infants whose body fat the knights could render to make a sacred oil for their idols. Philip's prosecutors accused the Templars of promoting sodomy within the order, and they cited this sin in particular as the reason why the Templars had lost their Crusades in the Holy Land and control of Jerusalem. The fall of Jerusalem thus paralleled the biblical story of God's wrath and the subsequent destruction of the cities of Sodom and Gomorrah for similar offenses. This charge of sodomy offered even the simplest mind an explanation of why God would have allowed the Muslims to conquer Jerusalem. The charge made understandable a history that otherwise confounded the faithful who had prayed diligently for so many years for liberation of the Holy Land.

Philip's prosecutors even used the very wealth of the order against them. All Christians believed that Satan had appeared to Christ in the wilderness and offered him the wealth of the world if he would but renounce God and follow Satan. Christ had refused and lived in poverty. The Templars, by contrast, had grown to be the richest group on earth and lived in affluence, if not genuine luxury. According to the prosecutors, the Templars, then, must have made a pact with the devil in order to have become so wealthy.

After the initial shock of arrest and torture, most of the Templars recanted their bizarre confessions and defended themselves and their order with the bravery and strength by which the Knights Templars had earned their reputation on the battlefield. Instead of Muslim soldiers, they now faced judges, prosecutors, and torturers who spoke their language and professed to worship their god. In their hour of need, the Templars received no help from the mother church that they had defended with their lives for so many years. For nearly a decade, the French authorities tortured the Templars to extract confessions from them. When put on public display, however, the Templars would rally and recant their confessions, whereupon a new round of torture and confession would commence.

Bowing to pressure from the French monarchy, Pope Clement V abolished the order in a papal bull, *Vox in Excelso*, on March 22, 1312. The pope found it more prudent to sacrifice the knights of his church than to defy the will of the French king. In abolishing the order, the pope hoped to maintain some control over the Templars' property, which he transferred to other religious groups, most importantly to the Hospitalers, another order of religious knights.

Four years after the mass execution of the Templars outside of Paris, Grand Master Jacques de Molay and Geoffroi de Charney were taken from their cells and burned to death on a small island in the Seine River on March 18, 1314. Thus King Philip crushed completely the greatest and most powerful international financial institution of the time. The French government, thwarted in its attempts to obtain the entire treasury of the Templars in Paris, demanded a large portion of it from the Hospitalers as compensation for the money spent on investigations and trials of the Templars. After seeing what had happened to their Templar brothers, the Hospitalers quickly yielded to Philip's menacing threats to purify their order with the same fire that he had used on the Templars.

Pope Clement V and King Philip IV quarreled over the money and property of the order, but not for long. Within the same year, 1314, both the pope and the king lay dead. Many observers, forever seeing the will of God in earthly happenings, concluded that God had called the pope and the king to appear with the burned Templars before the throne of God for final judgment.

On earth, it mattered little who was to blame, since nothing could change what had happened. The total triumph of King Philip over the Knights Templars marked a clear increase in the power of a national government that would not tolerate an international financial rival as powerful as the Templars. Whether Philip and Clement had lived or died, their struggle was settled clearly in favor of the state. For the first time since the fall of Rome, a government in western Europe had successfully reasserted its authority and power to control financial institutions, and it had broken the commercial power of the church. Never again did the church or its institutions exercise so much clout over the financial activities of western Europe.

The destruction of the Templars, however, created a financial and commercial void that the church was too weak and fearful to occupy again and that government was not yet large and strong enough to fill.

THE RISE OF THE ITALIAN BANKING FAMILIES

At this pivotal moment in European economic history, when the financial power of the church had waned and the power of state had not yet grown strong enough to replace it, a new group of men and institutions stepped into the breach. The families of the north Italian city-states of Pisa, Florence, Venice, Verona, and Genoa began to offer the same services that the Templars had offered, albeit on a much more modest scale at first. These families created a new set of banking institutions outside the immediate control of church and state, yet with close ties to both.

A new system of private, family banks arose in northern Italy. These banking families did not operate under a religious mission or within the severe limits regarding money imposed upon the Templars by the church and by Christian doctrine. The Italian banking families dealt as readily and easily with Muslims, Tartars, Jews, and pagans as they did with Orthodox and Catholic Christians. The banking network of the Italian merchant families soon stretched from England to the Caspian Sea, and they financed trading missions throughout the known world from China to the Sudan and from India to Scandinavia. They offered a steady supply of credit at rates lower than those tendered by most other financiers, and they controlled more money and lent it at consistent, if not always low, rates. Unhindered by the religious principles of the Templars, they had only one ambition: to take home a profit.

The Italian families differed in other important ways from the religious knights. They did not operate from well-fortified castles, nor did they travel in heavily armed convoys. Instead, they lived and worked in the marketplace among the people, catering as much to the needs of small landlords, merchants, and vendors as to those of the aristocrats and high officials of the church and state. Whereas the Templars served only the nobility, the new Italian bankers served everyone.

In their financial pursuits, Italian merchants traveled to markets and fairs throughout Europe. Like other itinerant merchants and vendors, they set up tables or large benches from which they not only traded their goods but also exchanged money, made loans, arranged to take money as payment for a debt for someone in the next town, and performed other related financial services.

The modern word *bank* comes from the way in which these early money merchants did business; it is derived from a word meaning "table" or "bench," the prop that literally formed the base of their operations at the fairs. From Italian, the words *bank*, *banco*, and *banque* soon spread into other European languages and eventually throughout the world.

Moneylending in some form or other seems to have been known for as long as there had been money, but the bank became something more than a moneylending institution, because the bankers dealt not so much with gold and silver as with slips of paper representing the gold and silver. Banking, as practiced by the Templars, faced a great limitation in that the church forbade usury, the charging of interest on loans, and getting around that barrier proved to be one of the greatest obstacles that the Italian families had to overcome in order to build their extensive banking enterprises.

The Christian prohibition against usury was based on two passages in the Bible: "Take thou no usury . . . or increase; but fear thy God. . . . Thou shalt not give him thy money upon usury, nor lend him thy victuals for increase" (Leviticus 25:36–37); and "He that . . . hath given forth usury, and hath taken increase: shall he live? he shall not live: he hath done all these abominations; he shall surely die, his blood shall be upon him" (Ezekiel 18:13).

The scriptural prohibition never completely eradicated usury, but it certainly hampered it. Jews often served as moneylenders since, in the eyes of the church, they were already condemned to eternal damnation, but if Christians lent money for interest, the Catholic church excommunicated them, thereby barring them from all services and from Holy Communion. The law stated quite specifically that *quidquid sorti accedit, usura est* (whatever exceeds the principal is usury). The Italian bankers, however, found a way around this prohibition and thus grew rich without endangering their souls.

Usury applied only to loans, so through the fine technical distinction between a loan and a contract, the Italian merchants built a whole edifice of borrowing and lending behind a facade that showed no sign of usury. They scrupulously avoided making *loans*. Instead, they traded *bills of exchange*. A bill of exchange is a written document ordering the payment of a certain amount of money to a certain person at a certain time and place. The Latin name for this document is *cambium per lettras*, which means "exchange through written documents or bills." This transaction was a sale of one kind of money for another kind that would be paid in another currency at a specified future date.

A merchant in need of money went to a banker in Italy. The banker gave him the necessary money in cash, in the florins of Florence or the ducats of Venice, and they both signed the bill of exchange whereby the merchant agreed to pay a slightly higher amount of money in another currency at the next fair in Lyons or Champagne, France. The merchant did not have to go to the fair personally to pay the bill. Both parties knew that if the merchant failed to show up at the fair, the office in Florence would collect the money owed it.

The Italians did not invent the bill of exchange, but they put it to a new and more profitable use. Bankers received a fee for changing the money and therefore were organized into the guild of currency exchange, the Arte del Cambio, which was separate from the lower-class moneylenders and pawnbrokers so despised by everyone. In practice, the bankers became lenders to the rich while the moneylenders and pawnbrokers continued to lend to the poor.

These bills of exchange functioned well in Christian countries, but they did not work in the Muslim world. The Koran prohibited usury even more strictly and clearly than the Bible. It forbade any kind of profit on the exchange of silver or gold. Muhammad said, "Sell not gold for gold except in equal quantity . . . nor silver for silver except in equal quantity." The Koran specifically prohibited bills of exchange by condemning the sale of "anything present for that which is absent."

THE MAGIC OF BANK MONEY

The use of bills of exchange had another beneficial effect on commerce: it helped to overcome a major obstacle of the time, the awkwardness of coins and the difficulty of dealing with them in bulk.

Coins were heavy, difficult to transport, easily stolen, often counterfeited, and subject to dozens of other problems on the poorly guarded highways, in the lands of corrupt nobles, and at the sometimes poorly administered fairs and markets that emerged as the new commercial centers of Europe.

The new Italian bank money boosted commerce by making it transpire much faster. In 1338, a shipment of coins required three weeks to wend its way from Rouen in the north of France to Avignon in the south, a distance of just over four hundred miles, and the shipment faced the hazard of being lost, stolen by robbers, or pilfered by the very people hired to transport it.[2] By contrast, a bill of exchange could be sent in a mere eight days, and if it was stolen, the thief could not redeem it. Bills of exchange, in other words, moved faster and protected everyone involved in the transaction. Despite the extra cost of 8 percent to 12 percent, a bill still proved cheaper than the cost of hiring an armed escort for a shipment of gold and silver coins or bullion. Bills of exchange helped to free money from its spatial limitations.

The bills of exchange also freed money from the confines of any single currency and from the shortages of gold and silver that could occur in the country that minted the coins. The merchant could designate the bill in Venetian ducats, Saxon talers, Florentine florins, Milanese testones, French ecus, or any of dozens of other currencies. The supply of bills that could be written in that currency no longer depended upon the supply of gold and silver that those states had; it merely depended on the merchants' confidence in the currency. If they lost confidence in one currency, they quickly began to write their bills of exchange in another.

The bills of exchange created new money by breaking through the physical limitations imposed by the use of specie, or metallic coins. The bills themselves circulated among merchants as a kind of paper money. Although the activities and services of the banks remained confined to a relatively small number of people and did not involve the average peasant or city dweller, the banks had, in effect, found a way to put more money into circulation.

Under the new system a bag of a hundred florins that might once have sat idle for years in a noble's strongbox could now be deposited for safekeeping in an Italian bank that had access to branches across the continent. The bank then lent the money and circulated the bill of exchange as money. The noble still had his one hundred florins, which were now on deposit in the bank; the bank had one hundred florins on its books. The merchant who borrowed the florins was richer, and the person who held the bill of exchange now had one hundred florins as well. Even though only one hundred gold coins were involved, the miracle of banking deposits and loans had transformed them into many hundreds of florins that could be used by different individuals in different cities at the same time. This new banking money opened vast new commercial avenues for merchants, manufacturers, and investors. Everyone had more money; it was sheer magic.

The Italian merchants conducted banking as a private enterprise rooted in families such as the Peruzzi, Bardi, and Acciaiuoli of Florence, who had relatives serving in branch offices from Cyprus to England. Together, the banking families of Italy financed the English monarchy under Edward I and Edward II in the campaigns to conquer Wales and Scotland. By backing the English monarchy, the Italian banking families made more money than simply what they received in interest on these high-risk loans. With the English king as their debtor, they acquired special access to the English markets, and in particular their special relationship with the monarchy gave them a near monopoly in the marketing of English woolens on the Continent.

According to contracts signed between the pope and the banking houses of Peruzzi and Bardi on June 9, 1317, the money collected from all the Catholic churches in England and destined for the pope would be deposited with the Peruzzi and Bardi representatives in London. They kept the actual money in London but forwarded a bill of exchange to Italy, where the banks paid the pope from their treasury. The Peruzzi and Bardi bankers in London then used the money deposited with them by the church to buy English woolens, which they shipped to the Continent for sale. The bank kept the money from the sale in Italy. The money thus "passed" back and forth between

Italy and England and among the markets on the Continent. It "moved" from the coffers of the state to those of the church; then it went to the bankers and back to the merchants, where it could be paid as taxes before starting its journey anew. Yet all this could be done without the use of a single coin; the movement was of columns in registers and account books. Banking represented a commercial innovation that stimulated commerce in all its phases and benefited everyone—from the peasant to the king and from the local priest to the pope—wherever the banking families opened an office.

Bills of exchange provoked a boom in the European markets by helping to overcome the vastly insufficient supplies of gold and silver coins. By making the system work much faster and more efficiently, they increased the amount of money in circulation. The bills of exchange themselves became money as they circulated to third, fourth, and fifth parties in much the same way that we accept paper currency today. The bills circulated throughout Europe as a specialized type of paper currency accepted by merchants in the main commercial centers across the Continent.

With the spread of Italian banking through Europe, the currencies of Florence and Venice became two of the standards of the Continent. First minted in 1252, the Florentine coin bore the portrait of Saint John the Baptist on one side and a lily on the other; this gold coin became known as the fiorino d'oro, or the florin. The city issued the florin in both silver and gold denominations, the gold having ten times the value of the silver. At a time when every city of any size or with any claim to importance minted its own coins in its own size and with its own name, the florin of Florence, together with the ducat of Venice, helped bring stability to the late medieval markets.

The Venetian doge Giovanni Dandolo introduced the gold ducat in 1284, and it continued in use for six centuries. The Venetian ducat acquired the name *zecchino* after the palace of La Zecca, where the coins were minted. The name *ducat* came from a Latin inscription on the coin. Like the title *doge*, used by the head of the Venetian republic, *ducat* is related to *duke* and *duchy*, from the Latin *ducere* meaning "to lead." The Venetian ducat remained unchanged in size and purity until the fall of the Republic of Venice in 1797.

The new forms of banking money circulating throughout Europe necessitated new ways to keep account of the money's movements across so many jurisdictions and in so many currencies. Innovations in Florence produced double-entry bookkeeping, a simplified form of marine insurance, and one of the most important innovations of all: the check. In the earliest forms of banking, a person could deposit or withdraw money only by appearing in person before the banker, who would give out money only if the depositor himself verbally requested it. Written withdrawals were considered too risky, since such a request might be easily forged unless the person appeared in person before a bank clerk who could later serve as a witness, if needed. Not until the end of the fourteenth century did the first written withdrawals appear in the records of the Medici Bank. These first checks further increased the speed and flexibility of the banking system.

The Italian bankers thrived, but like the Templars before them, they were ultimately undone as a result of their success and their dealings with the government. Several of the major Italian banking families backed Edward III at the start of the Hundred Years' War between England and France, but when Edward III defaulted on his loans in 1343, his bankruptcy caused the bankruptcy of the leading Florentine family banks as well as many of their depositors. The entire system of money based on bills of exchange ultimately rested on the honesty and goodwill of the participants, but when the government became too burdened by debts, it had the power to cancel them, thereby destroying the system. The banking fortunes of the Italians dissolved like sand castles on the beach at high tide. Then, to seal the fate of Florentine banking, the Black Death appeared in northern Italy and ravaged the area until 1348.

Even though the original Italian banking families brought financial disaster upon themselves and the city of Florence, banking itself survived. Their innovative practices spread to other cities, and proved too beneficial for merchants to allow them to die. Genoa and Venice quickly took up the mantle of Florentine banking, and toward the end of the fourteenth century, Florence itself reemerged as an international banking force. Despite great losses in the fourteenth century, banking revived with new vigor in the next century under the leadership of Florence's greatest banking family, the Medici, who entered banking as relative latecomers in the final decades of the fourteenth century.

Even though banking emerged during the Italian Renaissance, it acquired little respect. Their work as money changers and as barely disguised moneylenders placed bankers only marginally above pimps, gamblers, and other criminals. In the aristocratic system of Europe based on land and title, the possession of mere wealth had practical importance but lacked prestige. A Dutch church ordinance passed as late as 1581 prohibited bankers, along with the practitioners of other unsavory professions, from receiving Holy Communion. The law remained in effect until 1658.[3] Many clerics also continued to condemn the collecting of interest as counter to biblical injunctions.

In order to become respectable after becoming wealthy, the bankers needed to acquire the accoutrements of late medieval life. They needed landed estates, urban palaces, aristocratic titles, and high church offices. In their efforts to procure these trappings, the rich banking families of Europe created the Renaissance, and no family succeeded in it like the late arriving Medici.

5

The Renaissance: New Money for Old Art

Bankers are just like anybody else, except richer.
—OGDEN NASH

SOME CITIES CONTINUOUSLY REINVENT THEMSELVES through the centuries by changing their architectural styles, their government, their religion, and sometimes even their names; other cities remain eternally rooted in the history, culture, and ethos of a single, particular era. No city clings as tenaciously to one spot in history as does Florence, located in the Tuscan hills of Italy. Florence remains eternally the city of the Renaissance, the city of Bernini and Michelangelo, the city of the Medici and Savonarola. Even though Florence existed for centuries prior to the Renaissance and has continued for centuries afterward as a large and important city in modern Italy, its heart and facade remain pure Renaissance. Its greatest buildings and monuments arose during that era, a time when its greatest painters, sculptors, poets, and writers flourished.

TOO MUCH HISTORY FOR ONE CITY
The Florentines claim to inhabit the cultural capital of Italy, despite the commercial, political, and religious centers having shifted to other cities. Even though the city developed comparatively late in Mediterranean history as an outpost of Rome, the citizens pride themselves on their city's achievements and will place it second to no other city in the world, much less to another in Italy. They boast of maintaining the highest standard of art, the most magnificent ar-

chitecture, the purest language, and the most glorious history. They even claim that their rather bland cuisine is more sophisticated in flavor and texture than the better-known food of the south, where the cooks apply an excess of spices, oil, and tomatoes. Florence served as the capital of the newly unified Italy for a brief time, from 1865 until 1871, until the government relocated to the ancient imperial and religious center of Rome. Through it all, Florence has produced more history, art, and dreams than one place should be allowed.

Today people make pilgrimages from around the world to experience Florence and to pay homage to the Renaissance. Students study here for a semester or a year, and tourists visit for the day. They all make the same rounds to admire the cathedral, to see the great Uffizi gallery, to visit the Academy of Art, and to marvel at Michelangelo's *David*. They pause for a long lunch in one of the many restaurants or sip coffee at an outdoor caffè; then they head for the many souvenir shops that offer a variety of souvenirs from an iridescent *David* on a thermometer to leather tooled in gold and furniture inlaid with precious stones.

Tucked in among the museums and caffès, around the corner from the restaurants, and across the street from the churches are hundreds of small shops where one can change money. They are not banks, but they proudly offer their service in many languages: Geld Wechsel, Cambio, Money Exchange. They trade cash or traveler's checks in dollars, marks, yen, pounds, and francs for seemingly vast numbers of Italian lire. Because banks have such short daily working hours, the money exchanges can charge high fees for their services during the hours when tourists most need them. In addition to currency exchange, they offer gold coins such as the South African Krugerrand, the Chinese panda, the Canadian maple leaf, and the Mexican peso, as well as commemorative silver coins honoring everything from the Olympic Games and royal coronations to the preservation of wildlife.

The money changers transact their business in small shops or even from vending booths made of reinforced metal, concrete, and thick glass. They do not have the ornate lobbies of the great banks; they do not operate from Renaissance-style buildings with grand staircases, marble floors, and gilded balustrades. Most of them do not wear suit coats and ties or the more stylish dress of the grand banks. Rather the money changers are markedly plebeian in style and manner.

Money changers have been around as long as money has. They can almost always be found near markets where merchants of different lands assemble and, in recent decades, hovering around tourist spots throughout the world. As mundane and undramatic as their daily activities and services are, the greatest banking families of Renaissance Florence came from their ranks, and they had a profound impact on art, architecture, and mathematics as well as world finance.

FIRST AMONG EQUALS

At its height as a banking city in 1422, seventy-two "international banks" operated out of Florence. Of the moneylending families there, none acquired a reputation as grand or as permanently etched in the annals of history as that of the Medici family. Chronicles of the twelfth century mention a family by that name in Florence, but the Medici did not emerge until relatively late in the story of banking.

The merchant Giovanni di Bicci de' Medici (1360–1429) founded the family fortune in banking. From his two sons, known as Cosimo the Elder and Lorenzo the Elder, came two lines of descendants who virtually defined the Renaissance by becoming the most important bankers and merchants, the rulers of Florence, and cardinals and popes of the church. The daughters of the family married into the royal families of Europe, and two of them, Marie and Catherine, became queens of France and mothers of kings.

After coming to great power, the family claimed descent from a Knight Averado, who reputedly came to Italy on a pilgrimage to Rome but stopped in Tuscany long enough to slay a giant who had been terrorizing the peasants. The Holy Roman emperor Charlemagne then supposedly awarded the brave knight a coat of arms bearing three red circles representing the dents made in his shield by the giant. Some sources outside the family, however, claim that the three circles represent the three balls that have traditionally been the sign of the pawnbroker; others say they represent three coins.

The name Medici indicates descent from someone in the medical or pharmaceutical field, professions that were about equal in prestige to pawnbroking or barbering at that time. The three circles on the family's coat of arms may therefore represent pills or the cupping glasses that doctors heated and applied to a patient's flesh in order to draw the "bad blood" up to the skin's surface.

No matter what the source of the family name and coat of arms, the Medici made their money in banking, gained their power in politics, and acquired glory through their patronage of art. They profited from the banking practices and procedures worked out in the previous century, but they were generally more cautious than their predecessors. The Medici dabbled in the bloody politics and unstable finances of the English monarchy. They extended uncharacteristically excessive loans to King Edward IV during the War of Roses, and when he defaulted on those loans, the Medici branch in London collapsed. Their offices in Bruges and Milan also failed due to related causes, but having learned from the experience of earlier Florentine bankers with English kings, the Medici stronghold in Florence withstood the crisis and never repeated those mistakes.

When their bank attained its commercial zenith under Cosimo de' Medici, it flourished as the most important private enterprise operating in Europe. Outside of Florence, the family maintained offices in Ancona, Antwerp, Avignon, Basel, Bologna, Bruges, Geneva, London, Lübeck, Lyons, Milan, Naples, Pisa, Rome, and Venice. Even though the staff in most cities numbered fewer than a dozen employees, the bank provided a great variety of services not usually associated with a bank. The Medici served as merchants as well as bankers, providing their customers throughout Europe with spices from the East, olive oil from the Mediterranean, furs from the Baltic, wool from England, and textiles from Italy. Other wares ranged from the unusual (sacred relics and slaves) to the bizarre (giraffes and castrated choirboys).

Despite the extent of their holdings and the diversity of their commercial services, the Medici never attained a monopoly like that of the Templars, nor did they control as great a proportion of the banking market as had the Florentine bankers of the previous era. By the time of the Medici rise, too many banks were already operating in Venice, Genoa, and in cities outside of Italy for them to exercise quite the same degree of influence, but this lack of a monopoly probably served as their protection. They operated at the center of a network of interrelated merchant and aristocratic families; they served this whole new system as the first among numerous others.

Their bank reached its zenith between 1429 and 1464 under the shrewd control of Cosimo de' Medici who oversaw the branch operations in Rome, Venice, Milan, and Pisa as well as those in more distant offices in Geneva, Bruges, London, and Avignon. In addition to banks and land, the family held financial interests in several textile endeavors, including two wool shops and a silk shop.

The Medici bank operated until Charles VIII of France invaded Florence on November 17, 1494. A few days prior to the arrival of the French army, the Medici family was expelled from the city, and the French confiscated most of their property and left the bank virtually bankrupt. The family returned in 1530 with the collapse of the Florentine Republic, but the heyday of the Medici bank had passed.

The basis of their fortune came from what we might think of today as the private sector, something that hardly existed in any degree of importance in earlier times. The Medici, who had made their fortune and fame in the world of finance, separate from the state and church, now lost their great commercial position as bankers and merchants of importance, but they increased their prominence in a variety of church and secular offices.

The great genius of the Medici family, in comparison to other rich merchant families of Florence, became apparent in their ability to use their wealth and commercial success as a means to acquire political power and aristocratic titles. They were the most upwardly mobile family of their time. Through a series of advantageous marriages, astute political appointments, and well-placed bribes over the course of several generations, the Medici managed to become one of the most powerful families in the civil and religious power structure.

THE MONETARY MYSTERY OF NUMBERS

The Medici, along with the other wealthy families of Florence, financed a great revival in scholarship and later in painting, sculpture, and architecture. Today we remember this era mostly for its great works of art such as the many sculptures of David that can be found in museums and plazas throughout the city. The flourishing of art in Florence, however, derived from an older Florentine emphasis on education that consisted not merely of learning the classics but also of mastering the basic skills needed by merchants and bankers: numbers and mathematics. The Renaissance began not as a movement in arts and letters but as a practical, mathematical revival to help bankers and merchants perform the increasingly difficult tasks of converting money, calculating interest, and determining profit and loss.

In 1202, Leonardo Fibonacci, also called Leonardo Pisano after his hometown of Pisa, published *Liber Abaci*, in which he introduced to Europe what we now refer to as Arabic numerals, even though the Arabs had themselves borrowed the numerals from India. This simplified system offered a great advantage over the clumsy Roman numerals, which were difficult to add and subtract and which virtually defied multiplication and division.

The introduction of Arabic numerals eliminated the need for an abacus, since merchants could calculate the new numbers more easily in their heads or on a slip of paper. The universities, the government, and religious authorities expressed grave suspicions of the new numbers, which came from "infidels" and which merchants and clerks used without the reliable abacus. In stubborn defiance of these shopkeepers' numbers, many European universities continued to use the abacus and to teach mathematics with Roman numerals until as late as the seventeenth century. Most governments also refused to accept the use of Arabic numerals for official purposes, claiming that they could be easily forged, even by a person with little education.[1] Even today, eight centuries after the introduction of Arabic numerals, Roman numerals carry a higher prestige in such acts as inscribing a date on a university or government building.

Merchants, of course, could not afford to wait for the approval of professors and priests. They needed a practical means of calculation, even if it lacked the prestige of the classical Roman numerals, and they immediately began using the new numerical system. When merchants noted an overweight or underweight item, they marked it with a plus sign or a minus sign. These signs soon became the symbols for addition and subtraction and, eventually, for positive and negative numbers.[2]

The new numbers proved to be practical and quick, and their use spread quickly throughout the commercial sector. In the words of mathematics historian J. D. Bernal, the introduction of Arabic numerals "had almost the same effect on arithmetic as the discovery of the alphabet on writing." These numbers brought mathematics "within the reach of any warehouse clerk; they democratized mathematics."[3]

The thirteenth and fourteenth centuries produced a mathematical revolution that moved the calculation of numbers out of the secret realm of magicians and into the streets and shops of Europe, and the expansion of banking made Italy the center of this new mathematical development. The revolution erupted not so much in the discovery of new ideas as in the transmission of the arcane ideas of mathematics to common people, aided in great part by the newly developed printing press.

In 1478, *Treviso Arithmetic*, an anonymous textbook, appeared. It was designed to teach people in the commercial trades more about numbers and calculations. The author taught the reader not merely how to add and subtract, operations that were already fairly well understood at the time, but also how to multiply and divide and how to deal with fractions and arithmetical and geometrical progressions that were important in calculating interest. Only a small number of the best-educated scholars had even a vague understanding of such abstract mathematical operations.

For many students and young shop apprentices, the zero proved difficult to comprehend and utilize when there were several of them in a single number or calculation. It was easier to recognize the Roman numeral M as one thousand than it was to translate 1000 or to distinguish it from 10000 or 100000. In 1484, Nicolas Chuquet, a Paris physician, tackled this problem by writing *Triparty en la science des nombres*, in which he introduced a system to make zeroes more easily understood by grouping them into sets of three with a marker between each set.

He even gave each set of three zeroes its own name. The European languages already had names for the first set (hundreds) and the second set (thousands), but traditionally anyone who wanted a higher number had to express it as "hundreds of thousands" and then as "thousands of thousands." Chuquet introduced *myllions*, *byllions*, *tryllions*, *quadryllions*, and so on up to *nonylion*. Using the system of zeroes grouped by threes, one nonylion would be written, and much more easily read, as 1,000,000,000,000,000,000,000,000,000,000. Although Chuquet used periods where we use commas today, the number represented the largest known at that time.

In 1487, Luca Pacioli, a Franciscan friar, published the six-hundred-page masterpiece *Summa de aritmetica geometria proportioni et proportionalità*, which taught the now-common mathematical operations and moved the student into the greater mysteries of double-entry bookkeeping. With a book such as this, a shopkeeper required no university training to maintain an efficient and profitable business.

Arab mathematicians devised algebra as a means of working with unknown quantities. The word *algebra* comes from *al-jabr*, a word used in the Arabic title of the book *Hisab al-Jabr w-al-Muqabalah* (*The Science of Restoration and Reduction*), by ninth-century mathematician Muhammad ibn-Musa al-Khwarizmi. He borrowed the word *al-jabr* from Arabic medicine, where it referred to the resetting or restoration of bones, a process that he saw as metaphorically similar to his resetting of numbers. Al-Khwarizmi worked in Baghdad and borrowed many of his ideas from the Hindu work of Brahmagupta; al-Khwarizmi's work, in turn, was translated into Latin and spread throughout Europe by Gerard of Cremona.

Al-Khwarizmi also helped to alleviate some of the problems of working with fractions, which were difficult enough for the average merchant to add and subtract, much less multiply and divide. Arab mathematicians also devised a sophisticated system of decimals in place of fractions. This use of decimals, called *algorism*—a corruption of the name al-Khwarizmi—eventually became the modern word *algorithm*, denoting any mechanical or recursive procedure of computation.

Jewish scholars such as Immanuel ben Jacob Bonfils of Tarascon introduced these Arabic ideas to European scholars around 1350; they were episodically used by other scholars such as Regiomontanus in 1463 and Elijiah Misrachi in 1532. Decimal calculation gained little attention until the 1585 publication of *De Thiende* by the Dutch scholar Simon Stevin (1548–1620) of Bruges, who began as a cashier in an Antwerp merchant house. Stevin sought to introduce Italian methods of bookkeeping to the northern Europeans, and he published the first tables of interest so that people could understand the arcane procedure performed by bankers, moneylenders, and other creditors. In 1525, Christoph Rudolff published the first German book on algebra, introducing the sign for square root.

University academics could not help but notice the great strides made in mathematics during the Renaissance, and somewhat after the fact, they searched for the theoretical underpinnings of these new number systems. In so doing, they laid the foundation for a new form of science, an objective discipline based on the apparent magic of numbers. The philosophical groundwork for this mathematical method of science was largely developed by René Descartes, who published his *Discourse on Method* in 1637. Descartes abhorred the study of mathematics for its own sake; instead, he sought to use it as a means of understanding the world in order to achieve practical accomplishments in nature. The use of mathematics to understand nature received a second major boost in 1686 with the publication of *Principia Mathematica* by Sir Isaac Newton.

The rise of the money economy created a new way of thinking. As twentieth-century philosopher Georg Simmel wrote, "money by its very nature becomes the most perfect representative of a cognitive tendency in modern sciences as a whole: the reduction of qualitative determinations to quantitative ones."[4] Money was changing the world's systems of knowledge, thinking, art, and values.

BANKING ON THE RENAISSANCE

The growth of banking that began in the thirteenth century greatly increased the general interest in new forms of knowledge such as mathematics, but the interest spread to other aspects of classical learning as well, leading eventually to a revival of art in the classical style. As banking families such as the Medici grew wealthier, they did what most newly rich families did: they cultivated an interest in the past and connected themselves to the glories of the past through the lavish display of art and literature in their palaces. When they could not find old palaces to buy, they built new ones that looked old. They filled their homes and palaces with the art of ancient Rome and Greece, and they filled their libraries with copies of ancient manuscripts newly translated from Arabic or from Greek and Latin.

These wealthy merchant families could afford to finance their own scholarship and art, freeing it from the restrictive grasp of the church and its monasteries. The new humanism in art led to an emphasis on the human body as seen in the works of Michelangelo and Leonardo da Vinci, who wrote that "The good painter must paint principally two things: man and the ideas in man's mind."[5] The human body became the focal point of this humanistic art.

The Medici and the other rich merchant and banking families of the Renaissance also used classical learning as a means to separate themselves from the religious themes that had characterized so much of European culture during medieval times. The banking families owed their power to the riches earned in their commercial enterprises; they did not owe it to the church. Their art, their home furnishings, and their building styles reached back into the pre-Christian era of Rome and Greece for inspiration. While neither anti-Christian nor anticlerical, this new form of scholarship acquired the name *humanism* because of its emphasis on people rather than gods, saints, and angels.

Like the banking that financed it, the Renaissance was centered in Florence. As the Medici acquired more power in Rome, several even assuming the highest church office of pope, they took their ideas and new standards of art and scholarship into the Vatican and throughout the church. Michelangelo's Sistine Chapel ceiling depicting the creation of man, for example, emphasized man as much as God, a radical departure from older religious art.

In literature the new humanism de-emphasized biblical scholarship and theology in favor of works about humans, such as Boccaccio's *Decameron* (1353); works of secular history, such as Leonardo Bruni's *History of Florence* (1429); and works on the glory of humanity, such as Giovanni Pico della Mirandola's *Oratio de dignitate hominis (Oration on the Dignity of Man)*, published in 1486. The world around these authors excited their interest and inspired their genius far more than could the abstract concept of heaven or of some afterlife in another dimension of reality. Pico della Mirandola's essay echoes the theme that there is "nothing to be seen more wonderful than man," and he compares man to both the animals and the angels. He explains that "[a]t the moment when they are born, beasts bring with them . . . whatever they possess." By contrast, "[w]hatever seeds each man cultivates will grow and bear fruit in him. If these seeds are vegetative, he will become like a plant; if they are sensitive, he will become like the beasts; if they are rational, he will become like a heavenly creature; if intellectual, he will be an angel and a son of God."[6]

The artists, merchants, writers, and aristocrats of the fourteenth and fifteenth centuries did not realize that they were living through a renaissance, since that word did not come into vogue until the nineteenth century. The revival of interest in the past became known as the Renaissance only after the 1855 publication of Jules Michelet's study *La Renaissance*, but this is our name for their time and their culture. During the Renaissance, life and history entered a new golden age that looked forward much more than it looked back.

Even though Florence and the surrounding area of Tuscany achieved a reputation for the rebirth of ancient Roman and Greek learning, it also broke from the past by giving birth to modern Italian as a language distinct from Latin. Dante Alighieri's *Divine Comedy* is acknowledged as the first work written in modern Italian. In the works of Dante, Boccaccio, and Petrarch the Tuscan dialect became the established literary form of modern Italian.

The Renaissance flourished and spread new commercial ideas as well as art styles to France, Germany, the Netherlands, England, and even to Scandinavia. In the writings of the sixteenth-century French essayist Michel de Montaigne, we see evidence of new ways of thinking. Montaigne reflected extensively in his writings on the marketplace and its importance in life. In writing his reflections in *Essais*, which he began around 1571, he is credited with inventing the modern essay. Even the word itself comes from the concept of a test, a trial, or the weighing out of something, and it was closely associated with the testing or assaying of coins and precious metals done in the marketplace. Montaigne described his work as being done in the vernacular, the style and language "of the marketplace."

In his short essay "That One Man's Profit Is Another's Loss," we see the dawn of economic awareness. He makes profit into something natural by placing it within the context of life and decay. He concludes that profit arises from desires that are often not good, much as new life arises from the decay of old matter. Montaigne rarely focused directly on money, but we see in his writing the emergence of the modern system of cost and profit values.

We can detect similar developments in literature and art. Money emerges strongly as a theme in the works of Shakespeare, for example, whose characters struggle not only over honor, power, and love but over money and wealth as well. It would have been unthinkable for a medieval bard or minnesinger to sing about money, but in a play such as *The Merchant of Venice*, money becomes the central focus. Most of Shakespeare's works are based on traditional themes of power and morality, but in the emerging modern world of his era, he recognized money as an important factor and considered it as much of a test of an individual's character as love and war.

Soon after Shakespeare's time, money began to appear in art, particularly in that of the Dutch and other northern European painters. Artists painted bankers counting their money; and in some pictures of domestic tranquillity a box of coins can be seen on the table. People have always depicted in their art items and ideas that they prize, but with the rise of the commercial age, art shifted in focus from religious paintings, mythological scenes, and people with their horses and dogs to portraits of people with their prized possessions: money and the costly things it could buy.

Together with banking and the Renaissance, even the name America must be credited to the vast cultural heritage of Florence. In an odd twist of fate, the name of a Florentine explorer and braggart,

Amerigo Vespucci (1451–1512), inspired the names of the two continents that constitute the New World. Vespucci was one of many Florentine merchants who traveled and explored the world. Soon after Christopher Columbus opened a route across the Atlantic, Vespucci joined an expedition that reportedly visited the coast of what is now Brazil. In his writings, Vespucci made many wild claims about places that he said he had visited but that, in reality, he probably never actually saw. His maps and writings circulated widely, leading a German cartographer to apply *Americus*, the Latin form of Vespucci's first name, to the newly discovered southern continent that was thought to be completely separate from the places seen by Columbus farther north. Soon, cartographers applied the designation to the new northern continent as well, giving us the new names North America and South America. In all the world Amerigo Vespucci is the only person ever to have even one continent, much less to two, named for him, and he too was a Florentine merchant.

With the rise of Italian banking and the Renaissance, a new type of civilization began to emerge. It was marked by novel ways of thinking and new ways of organizing commercial life. By themselves, the bankers and their new monetary system would not have been able to create a whole new civilization, but the changes that they introduced into European life were followed by a unique event in world history. With the expansion of European hegemony to the Americas, the Europeans acquired more wealth than any other people had ever possessed. The new wealth combined with the new financial institutions created a unique hybrid system of banking that dominated the world for the next five hundred years until the First World War.

6

The Golden Curse

Make money, money by fair means if you can,
if not, by any means money.

—HORACE

THE QUECHUA INDIANS, WHO DIG MINES AND EX-
tract the minerals from the Bolivian Andes, toil beneath the
ground in a twilight world of fluttering light ruled by the devil and
his wife. Only the devil holds the power to grant or deny money, success, and wealth to the miners. Aboveground the miners pray to the
Virgin Mary and the saints for help in solving problems of health and
love, but they go to the dark altars inside the mines to ask for favors
from the devil and his consort. The Virgin Mary and the saints control the water above the earth and thus the crops, the animals, and
fertility, but since money is derived from the gold and silver that come
from the devil's domain in the bowels of the earth, only the devil and
his wife can bestow it on humans. In some respects, the devil of the
Bolivian miners resembles the Greek god Pluto who, as ruler of the
underworld, had the power to distribute its metals and was thus also
the god of wealth.

Deep inside the caves, the miners erect altars to the devil, whom
they call El Tío, "the Uncle," and to his wife, China Supay. Statues
depict him with large, twisted horns rising up from his head and with
bulging, bloodshot eyes popping out of their sockets. Mulelike ears
flare out from his head, and two long black tusks rise from his lower
jaw. His other teeth are usually sharp daggers made from strips of mirrors that reflect what little light there is in the dark cave, giving the
devil a smile that sparkles with menacing ferocity. He wears a large

crown topped with a snake or a rampant lizard, whose mouth is open and twisted in what seems to be a scream of rage. The statue of the devil usually stands next to the rather plain figure of his wife, who has a broad moon face and a deep red complexion, and who looks somewhat like the Bolivian women one sees scurrying along the streets aboveground.

The miners make regular supplications before the images of El Tío and China Supay. They offer candles to the lords of the underworld, and each miner brings a daily offering of a cigarette, a libation of alcohol, or some coca leaves for the devil and a lump of sugar for his wife. In special rituals of appeasement during times of earthquakes or tragic cave-ins, large sacrifices such as sheep or llamas must be made. In such sacrifices, blood is scattered around the altar, and the shaman pulls out the pulsating heart of the sacrificial animal to spray blood in the four sacred directions of Inca cosmology. This act forms a contract, or *k'araku*, between the worshiper and the deities. In return for the offering, the devil will grant the miner life. Such sacrifices usually occur in August, the devil's sacred month, when the miners traditionally buy their equipment and supplies for the coming year. Sacrifices to the devil also abound during the pre-Lenten carnival season, when normal restraints are loosened.

According to local lore, some greedy petitioners want more than just life, more than just the sustenance to get through another day's work. They want true wealth. To get such riches, the petitioner must bring a very special offering of a fellow human being who is sacrificed in the same way as a llama. Whenever the body of a person, almost always a previously healthy young man, shows up on the mountains near the mines, and especially if he has any unusual marks, the Indians say that he was sacrificed to the devil and China Supay. Such a *k'araku*, a golden contract, with the devil would be made only for money.

For nearly five centuries, the Indians of Bolivia have mined the greatest silver deposits in the world, and for five centuries they have remained among the poorest people on earth. It is little wonder that, for them, a magical curse must be associated with the mining of silver, the minting of coins, and the making of money. All around them, the Indians see ample evidence of the success of the curse and pacts with the devil. They point to historical evidence such as the killing of the last Inca emperor, Atahualpa, by Pizarro, who then inherited all the wealth of the Inca Empire. They point to countrymen who have made millions of dollars in the cocaine trade and who could have done so only with the help of the devil and his wife. How else could these uneducated men have defied all the efforts of the Bolivian army and the sophisticated technology of the U.S. government to capture them? Even in their own lives, the miners know that they risk sacrificing themselves to an early death by accident or from the ravages of poverty, while others, who live far away and never work in the mines, live the luxurious lives of millionaires. They insist that such inequities in wealth can be explained only by magic and special sacrifices to the devil.

TREASURES OF THE AMERICAS

After Columbus arrived in America in 1492, it took the Spaniards approximately fifty years to locate all the major treasures accumulated by the Indians. The Spaniards looted the great Aztec capital Tenochtitlán in 1521. Soon thereafter they raided Central America and conquered the Chibcha people of Colombia, the original El Dorado, before moving on to battle the Incas in the 1530s. The Spaniards melted most of the gold and silver immediately so that it could be made into ingots for efficient shipment back to Europe. They saved some of the more unusual pieces, such as a giant sun made of gold and some of the gold and silver plants from the Inca emperor's garden, and shipped these back to Spain to give the king some idea of what kind of country they had captured for him.

One description of these Indian gold and silver treasures survives. The German artist Albrecht Dürer visited an exhibition of the captured American treasure on display in Brussels and wrote, "I saw the things which have been brought to the king from the new land of gold, a sun all of gold a whole fathom broad, and a moon all of silver of the same size. . . . All the days of my life I have seen nothing that rejoiced my heart so much as these things, for I saw amongst them wonderful works of art, and I marveled at the subtle *ingenia* of men in foreign lands."[1] Soon after the exhibit, royal officials ordered that the gold and silver be melted in order to mint coins.

After half a century of constant looting, the Spaniards ran out of rich Indian nations to conquer. In need of new sources of riches, they turned their attention to the source of the silver and gold—the mines. In Mexico and Peru they found more deposits of silver than the meager mines of Bohemia and other European sites had ever produced. The Spaniards immediately expanded the mining of these deposits, and the silver mines of Mexico and the Andes made Spain the richest nation on earth, but these riches came at what ultimately proved to be a very high price for Spanish society and culture.

The two primary centers for mining in America arose in Zacatecas, New Spain (Mexico), and in Potosí, Upper Peru (now Bolivia). Through the centuries, the two colonies jockeyed for the lead in silver production, their position depending on the discovery of new mines and the introduction of new technology. Despite variations in production, America remained the greatest source of silver in the entire world throughout the Spanish colonial era.

As early as 1536, only fifteen years after Cortez's conquest, the Spanish government established a mint in Mexico to make coins from the vast deposits of silver. Colonial officials applied for royal permission to begin issuing coins in other parts of the Americas, and the king granted permission to establish mints in Lima (1568) and then in Potosí (1574).

At that time, Spain owned the Americas, except for the easternmost territory of South America, which became Portuguese Brazil. The monarchs owned the land by virtue of a papal bull backed by the Treaty of Tordesillas signed on June 7, 1494, by Castile and Portugal. As God's spokesman, the pope could assign such lands as he saw fit, but in addition to the backing of God, the two powers held the land by right of discovery and conquest. This gave them several theoretical layers with which to enforce their claim. With the backing of God and the pope, the Spaniards and the Portuguese did not need to enact the charade of signing treaties with the native peoples themselves, as the English and other European powers later felt compelled to do in order to make their rule legitimate.

Under the laws of Castile laid down by Alfonso X and Alfonso XI, the monarch could grant ownership of land to individuals, who could then buy and sell such lands. No matter who owned the surface rights to the land, however, the Crown continued to own all mineral resources in perpetuity. Additionally, the Crown demanded payment of 50 percent of any buried treasure discovered in Indian tombs, pyramids, and temples.

The monarch owned many of the mines outright, but for a high enough fee, the Crown's agents would lease, grant, or even sell to individuals and groups the right to mine the resources. Even after such a sale, however, the Crown continued to collect a fee called the *quinto real* (the royal fifth), or 20 percent of all silver and other minerals; the percentage decreased in later decades. Even though the *quinto real* supposedly allowed 80 percent of the silver to remain in the hands of the mine owners, the government enacted restrictive laws that took away much of that as well. The miners had to buy from the royal government all of the mercury and other substances needed for the mining process. The royal government also exercised a monopoly on the trade of salt, tobacco, gunpowder, and most minerals.

The Spanish Crown acquired further profits from mining through the supplies shipped from Spain. These came from a government monopoly that charged the colonists exceptionally high prices, and of course the goods had to be shipped in government-controlled ships in government-organized convoys, adding even more to the cost of the goods. On every transaction in Spain, there was a sales or gift tax called the *alcabala* that gradually increased over time from 2 percent to 6 percent. This tax had to be paid on any transfer of goods whether by barter, sale, or gift; the king exempted only the clergy from it. In 1572, the government extended the *alcabala* to include all the Spanish territories in America. In addition to paying the same taxes as people in Spain, the Americans had to pay the *almojarifazgo*, a 7.5 percent import tax, on all goods shipped from Europe.

The Spanish government also collected the *diezmo*, or tithe, for the church, with the officials keeping a portion of it as a collector's fee. This *diezmo* did not apply directly to the output of the mines, but it did apply to all agricultural products, including those used to supply and feed the miners. Indians, whether they worked in the mines or not, were forced to pay special tribute taxes in the form of silver coins.

A minimum of 20 percent and perhaps as much as 40 percent of all the silver shipped to Spain from the Americas went directly into the government treasury.[2] The remainder went into the pockets of assorted government officials and various aristocratic families who owned rights in the American mines.

To keep the silver flowing, Spanish officials completely reorganized the social life of the native peoples. Upon arrival in Mexico and Peru, the Spaniards found a number of Indian societies of peasants growing crops and paying taxes and tribute to local chieftains and a central ruler. They quickly changed these independent nations into colonies organized around one single activity: the mining of gold and silver. Agriculture was important to the colonial authorities in that it produced food for the miners, who could not stop mining to grow their own crops. Ranching was important in that it produced horses, mules, and oxen for transport to and from the mines and cows for dairy products and meat. Roads were important because they allowed for easy transport of materials and men to the mines and silver to the coasts for shipment across the sea.

Prior to the arrival of the Europeans, the production system of Indian America had centered around the family, but under Spanish administration, the hacienda became the primary focus of the production of food, men, and animals for the mines. The very name *hacienda* was derived from the Spanish *hacer*, meaning "to make," referring to all the things produced on these estates. The peasants attached to the haciendas grew the crops and raised the animals that would feed the miners; they produced the mules, donkeys, burros, and oxen need for transportation to and from the mines. They tanned the leather to make saddles, aprons, tethers, ropes, lashes, whips, and the other accoutrements for work in the mines. They chopped down the trees for mining supports and gathered the firewood and made the tallow for the torches used in the mines. They made the sacks used to haul the silver down to the coast, and they supplied the ships with the food and material needed for the return voyage to Spain carrying their heavy cargo of silver bars.

THE BRIDGE OF SILVER

The wars and struggles among the European powers from the sixteenth through the eighteenth century focused on controlling the wealth of the Americas and the trade with Asia. First Spain struggled against Portugal, and then they both struggled against England, France, and the Netherlands.

From 1500 until 1800, the mines of the Americas provided 70 percent of the world's output of gold and 85 percent of its silver.[3] The amount of gold and silver extracted from the American mines increased in each century as new deposits were discovered from Canada to Chile. Even as late as the beginning of the nineteenth century, when the Spanish colonies were poised for independence, Mexico alone produced half the world's annual output of silver.

The Indians who worked the mines had no way to measure the amount of silver that they produced for shipment abroad, but oral tradition maintains that they mined enough silver to build a bridge from America to Spain. The precious metals poured forth out of the mines and away the Americas at a rate unprecedented in the history of the world. Spanish galleons transported the gold and silver from the Caribbean to Spain, and from there, merchants of many nations distributed it throughout Europe and the Mediterranean. From Acapulco each year, the Manila galleon sailed with its cargo of silver for the Spanish colony in the Philippines, and from Manila, other merchants traded the silver up and down the Asian coast from Siam to Siberia.

Outsiders have attempted to estimate how much wealth the Spaniards and Portuguese took out of the Americas. The colonial powers, of course, went to great effort to keep the amounts secret, causing much scholastic effort to have been spent gathering and evaluating records from around the world. Researchers have measured the amount of ore mined and the amount of metal extracted. They have compared it with the food provisions for the miners and with the amount of mercury used in the treatment of ore. They have compared shipping records with the arrival records in Europe and, most importantly, with the records of the Casa de la Contratación, the bureau in charge of Spanish shipping. Scholars have dug through records, some of which were falsified, and have tried to determine how much gold and silver was pilfered or shipped illegally.

Based on all of these methods, a range of estimates has emerged. Historians calculate that from the European discovery until 1800, between 145,000 and 165,000 tons of silver were shipped out in addition to 2,739 to 2,846 tons of gold. At the price of $400 per ounce, the total gold production would have a value of approximately $36 billion.[4] Even these numbers, however, cannot convey the significance of such an amount of gold and silver. In an age without paper money, the introduction of this much specie into the monetary system had an effect that would be difficult for us to imagine.

The Portuguese colony in Brazil lacked the silver of Mexico and Peru. Portuguese officials never derived as steady a flow of wealth from their colony as the Spanish did from theirs, and the Portuguese monarchs and aristocrats largely ignored Brazil in the early years in favor of their more lucrative spice trade with India and the Spice Islands. For the Portuguese government, Brazil remained a secondary colony that produced cheap sugar and bought many slaves but supplied few of the exotic goods provided by the colonies in Africa and India.

Portugal's indifference toward its American colony ended dramatically in 1695 with the first of a series of Brazilian gold booms. Prospectors found that some sections of the flat, alluvial soil of Brazil harbored rich deposits of gold flecks and nuggets, the extraction of which required much work but relatively simple technology. The district of Minas Gerais (General Mines), north of Rio de Janeiro, became the center of world gold production. Unlike the Spaniards, who relied mostly on Indian labor to work their mines in Mexico and Peru, the Portuguese imported African slaves to work theirs. The Brazilian emphasis on gold mining became so obsessive and so important in the colonial economy that the Portuguese authorities made it illegal to engage in any enterprise in Minas Gerais that did not relate to or promote gold mining.

Gold production in colonial Brazil climbed to its zenith in the two decades between 1741 and 1760 when it averaged more than 16 tons a year (14,600 kg).[5] The mining and transport of gold required the work of some 150,000 slaves, approximately half of the total population of Minas Gerais.

Prospectors discovered other gold deposits and even precious gems farther west in the provinces of Goiás and Mato Grosso. To the flow of gold, the Brazilians added approximately three million carats of diamonds for the treasury of the Portuguese kings.[6] In the search for gold and gems, the Brazilians pushed ever deeper into the continent and eagerly passed far beyond the line established in the Treaty of Tordesillas to separate Portuguese from Spanish colonies.

THE PRICE REVOLUTION: FROM RICHES TO RAGS

While the Spanish kings squandered their wealth on foreign adventures and wars, the Portuguese kings squandered theirs on palaces, pomp, and pageantry. The rulers wasted money on sumptuous excesses and poured money and gifts into the hands of their relatives, lovers, and other court favorites.

The wealth proved to be a mixed blessing for the governments and peoples of Spain and Portugal. It caused tremendous inflation—the more silver people had, the more goods they wanted to buy, and the more people who wanted these goods, the higher the prices charged for them. The quantity of goods produced could not keep up with the volume of silver shipped from America; consequently, inflation increased, thus eating away at the value of the silver and gold. Writing in 1776, Adam Smith noted that "the discovery of the abundant mines of America reduced, in the sixteenth century, the value of gold and silver in Europe to about a third of what it had been before."[7] It is estimated that between 1500 and 1600, the first century of Spanish colonization of the Americas, prices in Spain rose by 400 percent, and for this reason these great changes are known as the price revolution.

Although this phenomenon of inflation amazed and annoyed people, they seemed to understand it quite clearly. As early as 1556, Martín de Azpilcueta, a professor at the University of Salamanca, compiled a list of reasons why the value of money changed. The most important reason was that "in times when money was scarcer, salable goods and labor were given for very much less than after the discovery of the Indies, which flooded the country with gold and silver."[8] This was later amplified and explained in more detail by the French political economist Jean Bodin. A special commission, the Junta del Almirantazgo, issued a report in 1628 blaming the poverty of Spain on the riches from the Americas. The report stated that the "Indies have been the cause whereby these kingdoms find themselves with few inhabitants, no silver, and a burden of commitments and expenses, serving as a bridgehead for the transfer of silver to other kingdoms, all of which would have stayed in these if what went to the Indies were of our harvesting or manufacture."[9]

Spanish farmers, ranchers, craftsmen, and manufacturers produced few goods; so they had to be imported from other countries, adding even more to their cost and hastening the flow of silver out of the country to the point that it left nearly as fast as it arrived. Italy sold them glassware, Hungary sold copper, England offered woolens, and the Netherlands offered weapons. So much silver was being exported by Spain that even its shipment became difficult to arrange; foreign shippers soon had to step in because most of Spain's ships were occupied in the transportation of silver from America to Spain.

The Spanish monarchs had exacerbated their financial situation by expelling the Jews and Muslims in 1492, the same year that Isabella and Ferdinand united the country and Columbus made his first voyage to America. Most Christian Spaniards at that time worked as peasants tilling the soil, growing wheat and olives, and raising cows and goats, or else they served as soldiers. Whether soldiers or peasants, they had little education; they could not read and write, nor could they work with numbers. The Jews and the Arabs had constituted the educated class of administrators and merchants; without them, the Spaniards proved highly ineffective in managing their financial and commercial affairs. People of many nations rushed in to help the Spaniards. Italian merchants, German moneylenders, and Dutch manufacturers quickly moved to fill the mercantile void left by the Jews and Arabs, but they took their profits back to their home countries. Without a native merchant class, the Spaniards watched their silver flow through their hands and into the coffers of the other Christian nations of Europe.

In describing the impact of American silver on Europe, Voltaire wrote that the wealth "entered the pockets of the French, English, and Dutch who traded with Cadiz under Spanish names; and who sent to America the productions of their manufactories." He added that "a great part of this money goes to the East Indies to pay for spices, saltpeter, sugar, candy, tea, cloths, diamonds, and monkeys."[10]

Silver shipments from America arrived once a year, but the kings usually spent their portion before it arrived. To do this, they had to borrow money in advance of the ships' arrival and without knowing how much silver might be lost at sea or to pirates. At first the kings borrowed from their loyal subjects, but since they felt no obligation to pay it back, the already overtaxed subjects hid their money and quit lending it.

The kings then turned to foreign creditors. Although the Spanish monarchs ruled over one of the largest and richest empires in the world, they were constantly at the mercy of their bankers and creditors in Italy, Germany, and the Netherlands at rates of interest up to 18 percent per annum. In 1575, Philip II refused to pay his creditors, and they stopped funds flowing to his army in the Spanish Netherlands. The army revolted the following year and sacked the city of Antwerp to make up for their loss of salary. This disrupted trade and taxes, causing further harm to Philip and costing him considerably more than if he had continued to pay the Genoese bankers in the first place.

King Philip II borrowed money constantly to finance his adventures. He launched his expensive and disastrous Spanish Armada against England in 1588, and Spain pursued campaigns against the Protestants in the Netherlands in 1568 and 1618, fought revolts in Germany in the 1540s and 1550s, and launched wars against the Ottoman Turks in the 1530s and the 1570s.

By the 1640s, many of the Spanish provinces themselves had risen up in rebellion against the harsh taxation and repressive government of the Hapsburg monarchs. In some years, the Crown's expenditures surpassed three times its income. Aristocrats and commoners also borrowed lesser amounts, making Spain one of the world's greatest debtor nations and eventually resulting in national bankruptcy. The first bankruptcy came in 1557 during the reign of Philip II; another followed in 1597, the year before Philip's death.

The noble families of Spain were steeped in too much aristocratic pride to bother themselves with mundane business and cheap commerce. They continued to picture themselves and their class as conquerors of the world, whose lives centered on swords, horses, tribute, and booty. They did not see themselves as mere merchants who transported cloth or grain by mule train and old barges to be sold to wholesalers on rat-infested wharves or to barter and truck with common people in the muddy markets of the city. They too borrowed heavily in order to keep up their lavish forms of conspicuous consumption. Large-scale public and private debt exacerbated the inflation.

Gold had much the same effect on Portugal that silver had on Spain. It created an appetite for new goods, but Portugal produced little other than wine, cork, and cattle. To meet their needs, the Portuguese turned to the English for manufactured goods. They formalized this relationship by treaty in 1703, and even more Portuguese gold and wine began to flow to England.

The trading partners of Portugal and Spain benefited from the influx of gold and silver from America, but they experienced much the same kind of inflation that had beset the Iberian countries. John Kenneth Galbraith noted that by the end of the seventeenth century, prices in England had risen to three times what they had been before the first trading voyages to America. During the same period, wages had only doubled.[11]

The mining and trade of America's gold and silver continued very much under the control of the Spanish and Portuguese governments and that of their agents. In keeping with the economic thinking of the time, silver and gold were regarded as the keys to wealth; for most people, they were wealth itself. The man with the most silver or gold was the wealthiest, as was the country with the most gold and silver. The rich officials and court favorites of Spain and Portugal used their wealth to buy what they wanted—soldiers and equipment to fight their wars and luxurious silks, porcelains, and spices for themselves and their palaces. They used the precious metals to decorate their homes and cathedrals and to adorn themselves, their furniture, and their coaches.

BAROQUE GOLD

Like many people when offered the opportunity, the Spaniards indulged themselves in the ostentatious display of gold. The Spanish baroque and rococo eras have probably never been matched for the lavish use of gold in decoration. They covered their walls with gilded molding of fruits, cherubs, urns, and flowing garlands. They applied gold to window frames, mirrors, and wall hangings. They used gold leaf on doors and balustrades. They covered their coaches with gold, and they applied it to the wooden frames of chairs, sofas, beds, chests, and cabinets. They dripped it on their hunting guns and knives. They put it on their belts and shoe buckles. They made dishes and snuffboxes from it. They covered their books with gold filigree and added golden hinges for their bindings. They embroidered golden threads into their clothing and the upholstery for their chairs as well as into their tablecloths, draperies, and tapestries. They lavished yet more gold and silver on the elaborate clothing of their footmen, coachmen, and dining room servants.

It is said that some of the altar objects in the cathedral of Toledo were made of gold that Columbus himself brought back from America and gave to Queen Isabella. In Rome, tradition maintains that the ceiling of the basilica of Santa Maria Maggiore was covered with the first of the American gold donated to Pope Alexander VI. The new wealth of the Americas revitalized the languishing Catholic church and financed its forays against the rising tide of northern Protestantism. As the Protestants denounced ostentation and turned toward starkly simpler forms of architecture and decoration, the newly enriched Catholic church encouraged an exaggerated level of decoration as a way to keep and inspire its followers.

In imitation of their monarchs and the pope, the wealthy aristocrats lavished even more gold and elaborate decoration on their churches and cathedrals than on their palaces. They hid the ceilings and walls of old churches behind flocks of golden angels holding golden banners and attached to one another by long garlands of golden flowers, leaves, and baskets of golden fruit. From every corner and from behind every pediment peeked the cute faces of mischievous golden cherubs armed with golden bows and arrows.

The faithful parishioners covered the statues of their favorite saints with gold leaf and then clothed them in silk garments embroidered with gold and silver threads. To accentuate the glittering gold inside the churches, architects cut new windows out of the walls, opened skylights in the roof, and installed gilded mirrors in the niches. This allowed reflected light to strike the gold and make it sparkle and glitter dramatically in the newly brightened and sunny church interior. Artisans made the excess gold and silver into baubles for the table, decorations for the body, and objects for devotion. They did everything they could with it except eat or invest it.

This era, known as the Siglo de Oro (Century of Gold), marked the apogee of Spanish civilization. Its most treasured and abiding accomplishment, however, proved to be not its gilded architecture but its gilded literature. In literary terms, the Golden Age opened in 1522 when Garcilaso de la Vega began to write, and it closed in 1681 with the death of playwright Pedro Calderón de la Barca.

THE MONEY CULTURE

Even though Spain and Portugal encountered many difficulties managing the gold and silver that they extracted from the Americas after 1500, many other parts of the world profited handsomely. The spread of American gold and silver across the Atlantic and Pacific oceans opened the modern commercial era. During the sixteenth and seventeenth centuries, silver coins and even gold coins became more readily accessible than at any prior time in history. No longer would the use of precious metal coins be limited to wealthy individuals. Now the baker could use coins to buy flour from the miller, who used them to buy wheat from the farmer, who used coins to buy bread from the baker. The butcher, the weaver, the wheelwright, the seamstress, the dyer, the coachman, and the cooper began to buy their materials and sell their products more often for money and less often in barter for other goods and services. Increasingly, taxes and tithes were paid in money rather than in produce.

Just as the banking revolution had increased the amount of money in circulation and brought merchants from all over western Europe into a single commercial and financial system, the increase of silver coins brought the lower classes into the system. The discovery of the great wealth of the Americas produced a far more immediate impact on the lives of common people than did the banking revolution. Professions that had traditionally depended upon money such as soldiers, artists, musicians, and tutors, now became even more focused on payment rather than on exchange of services such as room and board or rations paid in bread, alcohol, and salt. Even prostitutes and innkeepers became less willing to accept produce and goods in payment; they too wanted gold coins or at least silver ones.

Particularly in the seventeenth century, the new allocation of wealth gave rise to a middle class of merchants. They in turn spawned entirely new professions centered on money. As banking expanded, brokers appeared who specialized in the buying and selling of anything from real estate to shares in a trading voyage to China. Insurance men specialized in spreading out the risk of one voyage over many.

All of these new professions created new sources of wealth that, until now, had been small and unimportant, or entirely unknown, in aristocratic society. In feudal society, wealth had been derived from titles, privileges, and land bestowed by the monarch or taken by force during war. Now men without title, grant, or land had more money to spend than had the old aristocrats. In an era when warfare was increasingly the responsibility of a professional army rather than of the aristocratic class, the rising merchants found themselves able to buy large amounts of land that did not need to be seized in warfare. In the new social system, title and privilege increasingly followed the accumulation of family money and the careful arrangement of profitable marriages.

The greater supply of coins also facilitated international commerce and financial ties that gradually began to knit together the regional economies of the world. Merchants outside Europe would not accept the bankers' bills of exchange, but they eagerly accepted the new silver coins minted in Peru and Mexico. The greatest initial impact occurred in Africa, where the new wealth stimulated the traditional slave market to grow larger than ever. Very quickly after the tapping of American wealth, Africa became a part of the triangular trade with Europe and America. African slaves went to Caribbean plantations. American silver and Caribbean sugar went to Europe. Much of the silver and European manufactured goods then went to Africa to buy more slaves to ship to America.

During the eighteenth century, the commercial ties stretched from the northern and mid-Atlantic to include the Pacific and Indian oceans and, eventually, even the Arctic. The network expanded from the slave trade to include the spice trade with south Asia, the silk and porcelain trade with China, the opium trade with India, and the fur trade with Siberia, Canada, and Alaska.

In conquering America, Spain opened a pipeline that pumped a torrent of silver into the world's economy, but Spain was helpless to control that flow. Neither Chinese emperor nor Ottoman sultan, neither Persian shah nor Russian czar proved any more adept at channeling and controlling it than the Spanish kings. Spain had unleashed a power that raced around the globe and operated with a force of its own, independent of both church and state. The wealth of America had run amok, and the world would never again be the same.

Phase II

PAPER MONEY

Geld regiert die Welt
(Gold rules the world.)
—GERMAN PROVERB

7
The Birth of the Dollar

Money, not morality, is the principle of commercial nations.
—THOMAS JEFFERSON

ONLY THE MUSE OF HISTORY, TOTALLY UNAPPRE-
ciative of coincidence, irony, and symbolism, could have
written a scenario in which both the dollar and the atomic bomb originated in the same little European hamlet. The history of the Czech
village of Jáchymov reads like a cheap Hollywood script that no
reader would find credible and no producer would be willing to film;
yet it was from this tiny town that the dollar developed and grew to
become the preferred currency of the world.

The movie opens when Count Stephan Schlick, a Bohemian no-
bleman, discovers a rich vein of silver near his ancestral home, the
Castle of Joy, and from that silver he secretly mints his own coins,
which become the world's first dollars. The action then fast-forwards
to the end of the nineteenth century when a young girl named Marie,
eager to overcome the double handicap of being both female and Pol-
ish, uses uranium from the same mines to discover radium and rise
to the top of the science world. After winning a Nobel Prize with the
man she loves, he is killed in a traffic accident, and Marie Curie, in
her sorrow, devotes the rest of her life to working in the laboratory
on radium, which she is convinced is a miracle medicine but which
is slowly poisoning her to death.

Almost as soon as our heroine dies, German troopers storm into
the Czech village, bringing with them inmates from nearby concentration camps to mine the uranium for the atomic bomb their scientists are striving to perfect. Before the Germans can complete their

bombs, however, the Russians arrive, fill the camps with their own prisoners, and successfully use the uranium to make their first atomic bomb.

Jáchymov, a Bohemian village of 2,700 inhabitants, perches at the head of a steep valley in the Krušnéhory, the Ore Mountains in the western part of what is now the Czech Republic. Its broad main street ascends the mountain at a sharp angle, creating an ideal passageway for that peculiarly fresh, cool, and moist air that seems to be found only in mountains. A conglomeration of buildings spanning the last five centuries lines the street, but the old yellow and white paint and stucco have been chipped and broken from their facades. Shutters have rotted away, and tiles have fallen off the houses only to be replaced by tin roofs painted in bright shades of red, blue, green, and gray. No matter how shabby the old buildings may be, they still look better than the six-story apartment buildings of corroded cement and rusted metal erected on the edge of town during the Communist regime. The ugliness of the buildings is relieved only by the deep green of the trees and the carefully cultivated lilac bushes that bloom along the main street in June.

Because the village lies only a few kilometers from the German state of Saxony, many of the signs along the main street are written in German and advertise ice cream, champagne, and other goods that sell for less on the Czech side of the border. An occasional car can be found beside the road covered with deer antlers, animal skins, or other hunting trophies that the owner is trying to sell to visiting Germans. On summer weekends, the Natashas, Russian girls in short skirts and skimpy blouses, hang out along the street selling their services to foreign truck drivers en route to Prague.

At the entrance to the town, some of the shops have a platoon of garden gnomes standing in front of them. The Vietnamese women who run the shops stand in the doorway and wave cartons of cigarettes at passing motorists, most of whom are Germans in search of cheap meals, cheap sex, or cheap merchandise. The Vietnamese women came to Czechoslovakia in an era of friendship between the two Communist nations. Too poor to pay for the manufactured goods that it received from Czechoslovakia, Vietnam paid in the only currency it had—its own people, whom the Vietnamese government shipped to Czechoslovakia and the other socialist states as workers. After the fall of the Communist Party in Czechoslovakia and the division of the country into the Czech and the Slovak republics, the Vietnamese found themselves suddenly free and far from home. They then sought out small niches in the newly emerging economy where they could thrive but not succeed so much that they would pose a threat and therefore be deported. Many of them ended up in places like Jáchymov selling garden gnomes and cheap cigarettes.

In the center of the village looms the Renaissance-style city hall, which was built as the home of Count Hieronymus Schlick between 1540 and 1544. Behind it sits the squat half-timbered building constructed by order of King Ferdinand I between 1534 and 1536 to be the imperial mint. It was made into a museum in 1976, but closed after only a decade due to structural damage and deterioration. The building has a bay window on the corner and a coat of arms depicting two crossed miner's hammers topped by a crown. It bears the date 1536.

At the opening of the sixteenth century, Jáchymov came under German administration when Bohemia became part of the Holy Roman Empire. Count Schlick and his family ruled the remote and largely unsettled area from Hrad Freudenstein. It would have been quite an unlikely location in which to imagine a future event that would have a radical impact on the monetary history of the world. Miners discovered silver deposits in approximately 1516, but silver mining was not new to Bohemia. Farther east, in the center of the country, major silver mines had been in operation in Kutná Hora for centuries.

Rather than merely mining the silver and selling it to others, Count Schlick surreptitiously began minting silver coins called *groschen*. According to local tradition, he made the very first coins in 1519 in his castle, even though he did not receive official permission for such minting until January 9, 1520.

From the German name of the valley, Joachimsthal, the coins were called *Joachimstalergulden*, or *Joachimsthalergroschen*, names that were far too long for daily use even by German speakers. The coins became more widely known as talergroschen and eventually as talers, or thalers. Because of the ample supply of silver in the mines of western Bohemia, the heavy and substantial talers steadily increased in number, and because of the economic and political connections throughout the Holy Roman Empire, the talers spread to all parts of it, including Spain.

Saxon mineralogist and general scholar Georg Bauer, whose Latin name was Georgius Agricola, began a systematic study of the minerals in the Jáchymov area and the ways in which they were mined. He published in 1530 a book on the mines, and he wrote some of the first scientific treatises on mines and minerals. He later became known as the Father of Mineralogy.

With the opening of Jáchymov to mining, the community quickly grew to 18,000 inhabitants, who stripped the surrounding mountains of trees, which were used as timbers in the mines and to make charcoal with which to smelt the silver ore. Mining nearly ended when a plague erupted in 1568 and killed nearly one thousand community residents. By the next century, the miners had become strict adherents of the new Protestantism sweeping the German states, including neighboring Saxony, but the Bohemian monarchy began a fierce campaign of forced conversion to Catholicism. Many villagers fled or were killed until the population had dropped to only 529 inhabitants by 1613. In 1627, the government closed the Protestant church for one year and then reopened it as a Catholic one; they also shut down the village school, calling it a nest of Protestantism. The village and its mines never recovered, and the government finally moved the official mint to Prague in 1651.

In the century between 1519 and 1617, however, when talers were minted in Jáchymov, production began with about 250,000 talers in the first year. At maximum production, from 1529 to 1545, the mines supplied enough silver to mint 5 million talers. It is estimated that by the end of the century, Jáchymov had put nearly 12 million talers into circulation in addition to the many smaller coins produced by its mint.

THE SPREAD OF THE DOLLAR

The coins of Jáchymov spread around the world, influencing the names of many different European coins. Initially, for example, the taler was a large silver coin worth three German marks, but it eventually gave its name to any large silver coin. The word passed into Italian as *tallero*, into Dutch as *daalder*, into Danish and Swedish as *daler*, into Hawaiian as *dala*, into Samoan as *tala*, into Ethiopian as *talari*, and into English as *dollar*. It also became part of the name of the Swedish *riksdaler* and the Danish *rigsdaler*.

"Taler" became a common name for currency because so many German states and municipalities picked it up. During the sixteenth century, approximately 1,500 different types of talers were issued in the German-speaking countries, and numismatic scholars have estimated that between the minting of the first talers in Jáchymov and the year 1900, about 10,000 different talers were issued for daily use and to commemorate special occasions.

The most famous and widely circulated of all talers became known as the Maria Theresa taler, struck in honor of the Austrian empress at the Günzburg Mint in 1773. In a century of powerful women, she stands out; she reigned as empress, and her father, husband, and son were all emperors. Born in 1717, the daughter of Emperor Charles VI, Maria Theresa became archduchess of Austria and queen of Hungary and Bohemia. She married the duke of Lorraine, who became Holy Roman Emperor Francis I. She participated in seemingly every war, treaty, and other major event in Europe during her lifetime, from the War of Austrian Succession (1740–1748) to the partition of Poland (1772).

The coin bearing the portrait of Maria Theresa became so popular, particularly in North Africa and the Middle East that, even after she died, the government continued to mint it with the date 1780, the year of her death. The coin not only survived its namesake but outlived the empire that had created it. In 1805, when Napoleon abolished the Holy Roman Empire, the mint at Günzburg closed, but the mint in Vienna continued to produce the coins exactly as they had been with the same date, 1780, and even with the mintmark of the closed mint. The Austro-Hungarian government continued to mint the taler throughout the nineteenth century until that empire collapsed at the end of the World War I. The new Austrian Republic continued to make the Maria Theresa taler until Hitler seized the country in 1937.

When Mussolini conquered Abyssinia (Ethiopia), he found that the economy depended heavily upon the Maria Theresa taler. In fact, the natives proved so unwilling to accept any substitute for it that Rome had to mint its own talers between 1935 and 1937. Later, Brussels, Prague, Leningrad, London, Rome, and Bombay started making them, and after the Second World War, the new Republic of Austria resumed minting the coins from 1956 until 1975. Numismatic historians estimate that a total of 800 million silver Maria Theresa talers were struck between 1780 and 1975, all bearing the date 1780.

Other countries began copying the design of the Maria Theresa taler shortly after it went into circulation. They minted coins of a similar size and put on them the bust of a middle-aged woman who resembled Maria Theresa. If they did not have a queen of their own who fit the description, they used an allegorical female such as the bust of Liberty that appeared on many U.S. coins of the nineteenth century.

The name *dollar* penetrated the English language via Scotland. Between 1567 and 1571, King James VI issued a thirty-shilling piece that the Scots called the sword dollar because of the design on the back of it. A two-merk coin followed in 1578 and was called the thistle dollar. The Scots used the name *dollar* to distinguish their currency, and thereby their country and themselves, more clearly from their domineering English neighbors to the south. Thus, from very early usage, the word *dollar* carried with it a certain anti-English or antiauthoritarian bias that many Scottish settlers took with them to their new homes in the Americas and other British colonies. The emigration of Scots accounts for much of the subsequent popularity of the word *dollar* in British colonies around the world.

Despite the widespread use of the dollar, or taler, from the sixteenth century onward, no major country adopted it as its official currency until the formation of the United States. It might seem that, as the offspring of Britain, the thirteen American colonies would be accustomed to using the British currency of pounds, crowns, shillings, and pence, but the British colonies in North America suffered from a constant shortage of all coins. The mercantile policies then in vogue in London sought to increase the amount of gold and silver money in Britain and to do whatever was practical in order to prohibit its export, even to its own colonies. Beginning in 1695, Britain forbade the exportation of specie to anywhere in the world, including to its own colonies. As a result, the American colonies were forced to use foreign silver coins rather than British pounds, shillings, and pence, and they found the greatest supply of coins in the neighboring Spanish colony of Mexico, which operated one of the world's largest mints.

The Spanish coin bore a face value of eight reales in the Spanish system, *real* being the Spanish word for "royal." Eight of these royals equaled a peso, a coin originally established by Queen Isabella and King Ferdinand in their currency reform for the united Spain in 1497. The Americans rejected both *real* and *peso* as a name for the money, but the number eight stuck to the coin so that it was often referred to as eight bits or pieces of eight. Today the phrase "two bits" still refers to a quarter.

Because of the great wealth produced in Mexico and Peru, Spanish coins became the most commonly accepted currency in the world. The Spanish word *real* also gave rise to *rial*, which is used in Oman and Yemen while an alternate spelling, *riyal*, is used in Saudi Arabia and Qatar. The English-speaking peoples, however, preferred the already familiar word *dollar*.

The most common Spanish coin in use in the British colonies in 1776 was the pillar dollar, so named because the obverse side showed the Eastern and Western hemispheres with a large column on either side. In Spanish imperial iconography, the columns represented the Pillars of Hercules, or the narrow strait separating Spain from Morocco and connecting the Mediterranean with the Atlantic. A banner hanging from the column bore the words *plus ultra*, meaning "more beyond." The Spanish authorities began issuing this coin almost as soon as they opened the mint in Mexico with the intent of publicizing the discovery of America, which was the *plus ultra*, the land out beyond the Pillars of Hercules.

Some people say that the modern dollar sign is derived from this pillar dollar. According to this explanation, the two parallel lines represent the columns and the S stands for the shape of the banner hanging from them. Whether the sign was inspired by this coin or not, the pillar dollar can certainly be called the first American silver dollar.

In 1782, Thomas Jefferson wrote in his *Notes on a Money Unit for U.S.* that "The unit or dollar is a known coin and the most familiar of all to the mind of the people. It is already adopted from south to north."

The American colonists became so accustomed to using the dollar as their primary monetary unit that, after independence, they adopted it as their official currency. On July 6, 1785, the Congress declared that "the money unit of the United States of America be one dollar." Not until April 2, 1792, however, did Congress pass a law to create an American mint, and only in 1794 did the United States begin minting its first silver dollars. The mint building, which was started soon after passage of the law and well before the Capitol or White House, became the first public building constructed by the new government of the United States.

In using the word *dollar*, the Congress may have yielded to popular usage, but neither Thomas Jefferson nor Alexander Hamilton showed much fondness for the term. Yet they never suggested an alternative. They wrote the laws to refer to the currency as the dollar, or unit, apparently with the idea that they would think of a better name later. *Unit* was never much used outside of the law, and the people continued with *dollar*.[1] In accepting the dollar as the national currency of the United States, the Congress made official what had already become common practice in most parts of the colonies. With virtually no access to gold or silver, the U.S. government lacked the ability to mint coins other than by melting the silver coins of other nations and reminting them as American; rather than go to such effort, U.S. authorities allowed the Spanish dollar to continue as the de facto currency of the new nation. After Mexico gained its independence from Spain in 1821, the new Mexican government issued its own pesos with a slightly higher silver content than the old Spanish reales. The new Mexican peso—or Mexican dollar, as it was usually called—immediately became legal tender in the United States and remained so throughout most of the nineteenth century.

In order to determine the initial value of the U.S. dollar, the newly formed American government set up a study to weigh the Spanish dollars circulating in the United States, and found that they averaged 371¼ grains of silver, rather than the 377 grains claimed by Spain. In accordance with this finding, the U.S. Congress set the value of the American silver dollar at the rather odd standard of 371¼ grains, and it remained at that assigned weight for as long as the United States minted silver dollars.

In 1787 the United States issued its first coins. The copper coins worth one cent bore the motto "Mind your business." The sun appeared above a sundial with the inscription "Fugio," meaning "I fly." Because of this inscription, the coins became known as fugio cents.

The other side of the coin bore the image of a chain of thirteen linked circles, each inscribed with the name of one of the thirteen newly united states. The chain encircled the inscription "We Are One," and for the first time in coin history, it bore the name "United States." The image of the chain came from the Iroquois, who depicted the unity of their five tribes in a wampum belt composed of interlocking links and known as "the great chain of friendship."

By using emblems such as the chain in addition to the eagle, stars, or the bust of Liberty, the colonists had made an important decision to distinguish their American dollar from European coins. Because European coins bore the likeness of a monarch—George III on British coins, for instance, and Carlos III on Spanish ones—some Americans thought that U.S. coins should bear the likeness of President George Washington. The majority, however, rejected that idea. Most newly independent Americans felt that the use of a president's image, even that of George Washington, smacked too much of elitism and royalty. They claimed that the money of a free, democratic people should bear inscriptions and allegorical figures, not portraits of politicians. This steadfast refusal to put the picture of a person on the coin persisted in the United States for almost a century.

THE PACIFIC DOLLAR

The use of Spanish, Mexican, and American dollars spread north into Canada where they became the de facto currency of the land. In 1858, authorities in the Dominion of Canada, which then included only Ontario and Quebec, acceded to popular usage and created the Canadian dollar as its official currency. They pegged the value of the Canadian dollar at a one-to-one equivalent with the U.S. dollar. The provincial government issued small denominations in copper but relied on American and Mexican silver dollar coins even after the formation of the Dominion of Canada. Canada did not issue its own silver dollars until 1935.

Throughout the Caribbean, the Mexican dollar played a primary role just as it did in the United States. Virtually all of the former British colonies in this area adopted it as their currency. The dollar also became the name of the currency of Anguilla, Saint Kitts and Nevis, Antigua and Barbuda, Montserrat, Dominica, Saint Lucia, Saint Vincent, Guyana, the Bahamas, Belize, Barbados, the Cayman Islands, the British Virgin Islands, Trinidad and Tobago, the Turks and Caicos Islands, and Jamaica.

Even though the word *dollar* originated in Europe and spread to every continent, it has rarely been used as an official name for a European currency, that is until 1991, when Slovenia gained its independence from the old Yugoslavian Federation and chose *tolar*, a variation of *dollar*, for its new national currency. The new name clearly set Slovenia monetarily apart from its Yugoslavian, Turkish, Italian, and Austrian neighbors and former rulers.

The Spanish and Mexican dollars became so closely associated with commerce in the Pacific Basin that in the nineteenth century, other countries also began to mint their own coins, which were known as "trade dollars." By a congressional act of February 12, 1873, the United States issued special trade dollars for American commerce with China, but they served more generally for trade with any Asian nation. Britain began issuing such trade dollars in 1895 and marked them in English, Chinese, and Malay-Arabic script.

The Chinese called these many different silver dollars *yuan*, meaning "round things," and that became the name of the standard currency in China and modern Taiwan. The association between *yuan* and *dollar* in Taiwan has been so close that the two words are used interchangeably. The Japanese adopted the Chinese name but reduced it in from *yuan* to *yen* in 1871. The Japanese issued gold and silver coins, and, staying true to its original meaning of dollar in the late nineteenth century, the yen and the U.S. dollar shared an approximately equal value.

The use of trade dollars in the Pacific Basin solidified the use of the word *dollar* throughout the area. The Kingdom of Hawaii and the later republic used the dollar as its primary currency in a system based on that of the United States. Their silver dollars bore the bust of the monarch on the front and the national coat of arms on the back.

In the Pacific area of today, the U.S. territories and affiliated commonwealths of Guam and the Federated States of Micronesia continue to use the U.S. dollar as their currency. In addition, the name *dollar* was adopted for the currency of the Pacific nations of Australia, New Zealand, Fiji, the Cook Islands, Kiribati, Brunei, Singapore, Hong Kong, the Solomon Islands, Pitcairn, Tokelau, Tuvalu, the Marshall Islands, and Western Samoa. By contrast, the franc became the second most common denomination in the South Pacific, but it was used only in the French colonies such as New Caledonia, French Polynesia, and the Wallis and Futuna Islands. In the eastern Pacific, most of the Latin American countries from Chile to Mexico use the peso, which descends directly from the same Spanish reales as did the dollar, making both the dollar and the peso offspring of the same mother despite their different names.

As of 1994, some thirty-seven countries and autonomous territories around the world had adopted the name *dollar* for their national currency. Although countries such as Belize pegged the value of their own dollar to that of the U.S. dollar, and other countries such as the Cook Islands pegged their dollar to the New Zealand dollar, most countries operated independently of one another with their own values set in the world currency exchanges.

The Last Silver Dollar

After reaching its maximum usage around the beginning of the twentieth century, the American silver dollar coin began to die. In 1935, during the Great Depression, the U.S. Treasury ended the minting of silver dollars; then, with the passage of the Coinage Act of 1965, they ceased using silver in American coins, replacing it with copper covered in cupronickel.

In Africa, only Liberia, one of the oldest independent countries on the continent, and Zimbabwe, one of the most recently independent countries, have named their national currencies *dollars*. In Liberia, founded in 1822 by emancipated American slaves, the first currency consisted of American coins that the settlers brought with them to their new homeland. Although supplemented by various tokens and by the coins of other African colonial powers such as Britain, the use of the dollar continued in Liberia until 1943 when the government banned the use of all foreign currency except the U.S. dollar. Beginning in 1960, Liberia had its own silver dollars minted at the Royal Mint in London, but it continued to use American paper dollars for all denominations higher than one dollar. Liberia became one of the last countries to mint and use silver dollars, thereby bringing to a close a long chapter that had begun over four centuries earlier in the distant mines of Jáchymov.

Beginning in 1987, the government of Liberia began withdrawing the silver dollars from circulation and issuing in their place a cupronickel dollar that looked like the old silver dollar and bore the date 1968 but contained no silver. They continued minting and using these fake silver dollars stamped with the year 1968 until the 1990s. To profit more from foreign sales, the corrupt Liberian government issued its own Kennedy dollar in 1989, but they misspelled *memoriam* as *memorium*, thereby increasing the novelty value of the coin among collectors but doing little for the respectability of the Liberian currency.

8

The Devil's Mint

*The trouble with paper money is that it rewards the
minority that can manipulate money and makes fools of the
generation that has worked and saved.*
— ADAM SMITH [GEORGE GOODMAN]

A T ONE END OF FOURTEENTH STREET IN WASHING-
ton, D.C., prostitutes and drug dealers brazenly ply their trade
night and day. At the other end, near the White House and the bridge
into Virginia, the federal government prints money night and day in
the workrooms of the Bureau of Engraving and Printing, a part of the
Treasury Department that advertises itself to tourists as "the money
factory."

On weekday mornings tourists begin lining up well before the
opening hour of 9:00 A.M. to see how America prints its paper money.
The visitors enter the building through a sequence of security checks
leading into a dilapidated wooden corridor. Large color portraits of
the president, vice president, and secretary of the treasury beam
down from the walls. Visitors pass a sequence of photographs
and paintings detailing the history of paper money in the United
States and culminating with a life-size re-creation of President Lincoln signing the legislation authorizing the federal government to
print money.

At the end of the long corridor, visitors watch a short video on
the history of paper money, after which guides divide them into small
groups before they enter the work area. These small groups wend their
way through the carefully marked visitors' corridors past glass-
enclosed galleries from which they can watch the sheets of dollars

being printed, examined, cut, and stacked as the guides dispense a constant flow of facts about America's money:

- The dollar is printed on textile paper made by the Crane Company using a mixture of 75 percent cotton and 25 percent linen with a polyester security thread.
- The printing machines are made by Germans and Italians.
- Nearly half of the bills printed in a day are one-dollar notes, and 95 percent of the bills are used to replace worn-out bills.
- The average life span of a bill varies from eighteen months for the one-dollar note to an ancient nine years for a one-hundred-dollar note. A bill can be folded four thousand times before it tears.
- Approximately three thousand people work for the Bureau of Engraving.
- It takes 490 notes to make a pound, and it would require 14.5 million notes to make a stack one mile high.
- Coin and paper account for only about 8 percent of all the dollars in the world. The rest are merely numbers in a ledger or tiny electronic blips on a computer chip.

At the end of the process, the workers bundle the bills into packages of 100, which they then stack into bricks of 4,000. These bricks are loaded onto a pallet for transport to the basement from where they will be sent to the various Federal Reserve offices around the nation for distribution to banks and the public. Along the way, the curious visitors pepper the guides with questions:

Q. Why are so many employees listening to music on headphones?
A. To block the loud sound of the printing, cutting, and stacking machines.
Q. Why are some of them eating?
A. They are on break.
Q. Why are all of the checkers so fat?
A. Because they sit all day and watch money go by with little chance for exercise.

Following the tour, the guides usher the visitors into a cavernous hall where interactive displays invite them to press buttons to learn about the different parts of the dollar or to hear about its history. Children press the buttons, but the lights do not go on, and so none of the questions are answered. They rush to the next interactive display only to find that it too no longer interacts. The large room also offers souvenirs for sale, such as a souvenir pen filled with shredded money. In a corner, Japanese tourists buy sheets of uncut American currency from women behind security windows of thick glass. They take the money home with them to use as novelty wrapping paper for gifts and flowers.

The twentieth century became the era of paper money. Never before had so much of it been manufactured in so many countries and in so many denominations. Behind the perpetually operating machines of the U.S. Treasury lay a long process whereby paper money won the confidence of ordinary people.

MULBERRY MONEY

The Chinese economy has always operated by its own monetary rules, which were usually created and enforced by a powerful state with a large bureaucracy and a strong army. Whether China was under the rule of a dictatorial emperor, rival warlords, or the Communist Party, its commerce has almost always been controlled by state forces rather than market forces. In such a system, gold and silver coins rarely had any role. For much of Chinese history, the emperor's government issued simple tokens, usually known as cash and made of brass or copper. These tokens had a square hole in the middle so that they could be strung together in sums of up to one hundred.

Since the cash itself was bulky and merely a token anyway, it was a small step to simply drawing a picture of the cash on a piece of paper. The drawing could then stand for one thousand or even ten thousand coins. The invention and dissemination of paper money in China marked a major step forward in government control of the money supply, a development that could have occurred only in a great empire with a ruler powerful enough to impose the will of the state on the economy—even to the point of executing those citizens who dared to oppose its monetary policy.

The invention of paper money, of course, had to await the invention of paper and printing. Unlike metal technology, which came early in human history, the discovery of paper and the dissemination of paper-making technology came relatively late and spread slowly. The ancient people of the Mediterranean used parchment made from sheepskin for recording information. For a while during the Hellenistic era and the time of the Roman Empire, papyrus was exported from Egypt for use as a simple writing material, but it was not durable enough to be used as paper money.

It is no accident that printing, papermaking, and paper money all originated in China. In the first or second century A.D., Ts'ai Lun supposedly made the first paper from the bark of the mulberry tree, whose leaves fed the caterpillars of the lucrative Chinese silk industry, but actually papermaking may be centuries older than that. The technology for making paper seems to have been confined to China for at least a millennium. The use of paper money in China was mentioned as early as the T'ang dynasty and some illustrations of it have survived, but no examples from that era have been found.

Of all the strange customs Marco Polo encountered during his travels to Asia in the thirteenth century, none seemed to astound him more than the power of the state to produce paper money and to compel its use throughout the empire. Chinese bureaucrats made paper bills from the mulberry bark paper. Once stamped with the vermilion seal of the emperor, these bills carried the full value of gold or silver. Chinese notes were as large as napkins. A note representing one thousand coins measured nine by thirteen inches. Despite its awkward size, the bill weighed very little and thus represented a great improvement over the coins, a thousand of which weighed about eight pounds.

The use of paper money in China reached its peak under the rule of the Mongol emperors. They needed to administer the largest empire in world history, and like any ruler of a great bureaucracy, they found paper an invaluable asset. The paper bills made collecting taxes and administering the empire much easier while greatly reducing the need to transport large quantities of heavy coins.

In 1273, Kublai Khan issued a new series of state-sponsored and -controlled bills. To enforce their use he utilized essentially the same methods that any government must use to back up its currency: he gave payment only in the form of paper money and compelled everyone to accept it in payment under penalty of great punishment. To ensure its use in circles wider than merely the government, the Chinese government confiscated all gold and silver from private citizens and issued them paper money in its place. Even merchants arriving from abroad had to surrender their gold, silver, gems, and pearls to the government at prices set by a council of merchant bureaucrats. The traders then received government-issued notes in exchange. Marco Polo saw clearly that this system of paper money could work only where a strong central government could enforce its will on everyone within its territory.

Much the same observation of governmental power over paper money was made by the Moroccan traveler Muhammad ibn-Batuta, who visited China in 1345. He reported that it was impossible to pay with gold or silver coins in Chinese markets. Such coins had to be converted to strips of paper about the size of the palm of the hand and bearing the seal of the sultan. He also reported that every foreign merchant was required to deposit all of his money with an official who then paid all of his expenses, including the cost of a concubine or slave girl, if the merchant so desired. At the end of the merchant's stay, the official returned what money he was due as he departed from China.

Ibn-Batuta described China as the safest country in the world for merchants. No matter how far they traveled or how much paper money or other goods they carried with them, they were almost never robbed. To create this level of safety the government operated a police state in a surprisingly modern sense. Bureaucrats sketched detailed portraits of all entering foreigners so that their pictures could be quickly circulated if they committed a crime. At each stop, the merchant had to register with the police, and his name was forwarded to authorities at the next stop before he could leave. At each stop an army official inspected foreign merchants each morning and night and locked them up in a hostelry for the night.

Ibn-Batuta, however, observed a possibly unintended consequence of the outlawed use of coins: since merchants were forbidden to own silver or gold coins, they melted the contraband coins into ingots, which they stored in the rafters above their doorway. Ibn-Batuta may have been witness to a form of resistance that had escaped Marco Polo's notice; or, more likely, the power of the emperor and the central state was in decline during the fourteenth century, more than half a century after Marco Polo's visits to the court of the powerful new Mongol rulers.

Today no known copies of the Mongol money survive, but museums exhibit the few remaining Kwan notes issued by the Mongols' successors, the Ming emperors, between 1368 and 1399. The Chinese then abandoned their paper money system, and it did not reappear until the dawn of the twentieth century and the economic colonization of China by the various European empires.

By using paper money and brass or copper tokens instead of gold or silver coins, the Chinese authorities never had to worry about the purity of their coins. Herein, however, lay a crucial distinction between the money system of China and that which developed in the Mediterranean. The purpose of paper money in China was to allow the government a monopoly over silver and gold. Paper flowed from the capital to the provinces while gold and silver flowed from the provinces to the capital.[1] Paper functioned as part of the tribute system and stifled the development of healthy commerce. By contrast, the paper systems that developed in the West, at least initially, were designed to increase the flow of goods. Only later did they fall into the Chinese trap of becoming a way for government to confiscate gold and silver.

In the West, paper found its most important use as a means of keeping ledgers in banks. Long before it was used as a means of printing more money, it was used by bankers to increase the money supply. Only later did it gradually emerge as a replacement for coins in daily commerce. The initial development and circulation of monetary bills made of paper came about as a side effect of banking.

Paper money helped to solve a major problem in handling gold.

Because even minute amounts of gold had great value, people had always found ways to adulterate gold coins. One of the simplest was to "sweat" the coins by vigorously shaking them in a pouch so that they hit and scraped against one another, a process that invariably left a little gold dust behind. One of the earliest solutions to this problem by merchants in the Mediterranean was to seal gold coins in a small purse with the exact value and type of coin written on the outside. Thus merchants became accustomed to accepting in payment a coin that they could never touch or see. The merchants had to have faith in the stamp of the person who first sealed the coin—usually another merchant, a government official, or a banker. It was only one more step from this process to keep the gold coins in a safe place and circulate only the label.

THE DUKE OF ARKANSAS

Despite the importance of paper money in Chinese history, the modern world system of paper money did not develop in China, or even in the Mediterranean homeland of Marco Polo or ibn-Batuta. It evolved in the trading nations around the North Atlantic. Repeatedly in European records we find mention of money made from leather during times of warfare and siege. Reports indicate that European monarchs occasionally used paper money during periods of crisis, usually war, and they do maintain that in Catalonia and Aragon, James I issued paper money in 1250, but no known examples have survived. Then, when the Spanish laid siege to the city of Leyden in the Lowlands in 1574, Burgomeister Pieter Andriaanszoon collected all metal, including coins, for use in the manufacture of arms. To replace the coins, he issued small scraps of paper.

During the time of Gutenberg, the technology for both printing and superior papermaking spread through Europe. Some scholars maintain that the boom in paper production came as an indirect result of the bubonic plague, which killed a third of the European population. The old clothing left behind by the millions of plague victims became a cheap raw material for papermakers and thus encouraged new uses for the paper. Regardless of the importance of the plague in stimulating the paper business, the invention of movable type for printing certainly created a new and greatly expanded market for printed materials and made possible the expanded use of paper money.

In July 1661, Sweden's Stockholm Bank issued the first bank note in Europe to compensate for a shortage of silver coins. Although Sweden lacked silver, it possessed bountiful copper resources, and the government of Queen Christina (1634–1654) issued large copper sheets called *platmynt* (plate money), which weighed approximately 4 pounds each. In 1644 the government offered the largest coins ever issued: ten-daler copper plates, each of which weighed 43 pounds, 7¼ ounces. To avoid having to carry such heavy coins, merchants willingly accepted the paper bills in denominations of one hundred dalers. One such bill could be substituted for 500 pounds of copper plates.

It was unclear at first whether paper money should be created by the government or by private institutions such as banks. Generally, local banks lacked the ability to create a truly national currency. The first national experiment for such paper money was undertaken in France.

By royal decree on May 5, 1716, the French chose a Scotsman, John Law, to head up a bank named Law and Company, but quickly renamed Banque Générale. John Law—a handsome, wealthy, and popular ladies' man—had written several pamphlets on trade, money, and banking, including *Money and Trade Considered with a Proposal for Supplying the Nation with Money*, published in Edinburgh in 1705, in which he proposed that paper money could create wealth. Law was a self-taught banker who was also a heavy gambler and a convicted murderer in England. He allegedly claimed that he had found the true philosopher's stone to make gold from paper by printing money.[2]

The creation of the bank proceeded in clear imitation of the already successful Bank of England. Under special license from the French monarch, it was to be a private bank that would help raise and manage money for the public debt. In keeping with his theories on the benefits of paper money, Law immediately began issuing paper notes representing the supposedly guaranteed holdings of the bank in gold coins.

Initially, the bank operated quite successfully, but it remained independent for a mere two years before the duc d'Orléans, who ruled as regent for the Louis XV, a minor, took control of the bank by decree on December 14, 1718, and changed it to the Banque Royale, the official bank of the French government. The bank continued under the administration of John Law, who had by now become the duc d'Arkansas and who issued ever more paper with the confidence of the government behind him.

Law was also instrumental in establishing the Compagnie d'Occident of 1717, generally known as the Mississippi Company and formed to bring home the great wealth of France's holdings in Louisiana. Investors received their profits from subsequent investors in a giant pyramid scheme. To maintain the illusion of great profits lying just over the horizon, the company directors hired unemployed men to dress as miners and march through the streets of Paris with shovels and axes on their shoulders as though they were off to rake in great wealth from Louisiana. The Banque Royale printed paper money, which investors could borrow in order to buy stock in the Mississippi Company; the company then used the new notes to pay out its bogus profits. Together the Mississippi Company and the Banque Royale were producing paper profits on each other's accounts. The bank had soon issued twice as much paper money as there was specie in the whole country; obviously it could no longer guarantee that each paper note would be redeemed in gold. The Mississippi Company collapsed when it became obvious that the wealth would never materialize, and the bank fell with it. By the end of 1720, the Banque Royale lay devastated with a trail of worthless paper notes behind it.

In "The Great Mississippi Bubble," American writer Washington Irving vividly described the scene in Paris: "The doors of the bank and the neighboring street were immediately thronged with a famishing multitude, seeking cash for bank-notes of ten livres. So great was the press and struggle, that several persons were stifled and crushed to death. The mob carried three of the bodies to the courtyard of the Palais Royal. Some cried for the Regent to come forth and behold the effect of his system; others demanded the death of Law, the impostor, who had brought this misery and ruin upon the nation."[3]

The disgraced and hated John Law, the mastermind behind the

whole paper affair, fled to England and then to Venice, where he died in 1729. His title, the duc d'Arkansas, died with him.

Half a century later, during the French Revolution, the new Republican leaders sought to finance the government and their revolution with a new form of paper money, the *assignat*. In all, the various governments of the French Revolution issued some 40 billion assignats before 1796. The government finally bowed to public anger at the paper assignat in a great public spectacle at the Place Vendôme on February 18, 1796. Before a great crowd, government officials solemnly destroyed all the machines, plates, and paper used in printing the assignat in an effort to show that the assignat itself, rather than the government's manipulation of paper money, bore the guilt for the monetary collapse. The government began the unfortunate cycle anew by issuing yet more paper money but calling it by yet another name: the *mandat*.

THE FATHER OF PAPER MONEY

The idea and the technology for paper money had become firmly established in Europe, but its first successful application occurred across the ocean. Neither China nor Europe became the cradle of paper money; rather, it was to be North America, the continent that was perpetually short of coins. John Kenneth Galbraith observed that "if the history of commercial banking belongs to the Italians and of central banking to the British, that of paper money issued by a government belongs indubitably to the Americans."[4]

As early as 1690, the Massachusetts Bay Colony printed the first paper money in North America. Colonists later printed various types of money geared for local use over short periods of time, but one man was largely responsible for creating paper money in much greater amounts for use in three of the colonies on a nearly permanent basis. Benjamin Franklin holds the honor of being the father of paper money. In honor of his role in this creation, the hundred-dollar bill— the highest denomination currently issued by the United States for general circulation—bears an engraved portrait of Benjamin Franklin.

Born in 1706, the tenth and last child of a Boston chandler, a candle and soap maker, Franklin grew up in a family lacking the money and the social connections to educate him. Instead, they apprenticed him into the chandling business at the age of ten after he had completed only two years of school. At twelve, he quit his apprenticeship to become an apprentice to his half brother James, a Boston printer who published the *New England Courant*, which he had founded in 1721. James's questioning of colonial officials in his newspaper sometimes landed him in jail and in other types of trouble with the British authorities.

As a printer's apprentice, Franklin gained his education through his work. He became a skilled reader who developed a great interest in the ideas behind the documents he printed as well as in the technology of printing. Because of a stormy relationship with his brother, Franklin left Boston for Philadelphia where he found work as a printer's assistant. Then, after working in London for a brief time, he returned to Philadelphia where he and a partner acquired their own press; soon Franklin was not only publishing books but writing them as well.

Despite his lack of a formal education, Franklin became the quintessential scholar of the Enlightenment—and perhaps the most beloved of all the Founding Fathers. Through his printing, Franklin developed an early interest in the manufacture of money. In fact, he wrote one of the first pamphlets on paper money at the young age of twenty-three. At a time when paper money existed only as an emergency substitute for "real" money, he printed some of the first paper money used in America, and he continued to print money periodically throughout his life.

In 1729, Benjamin Franklin published *A Modest Enquiry into the Nature and Necessity of a Paper Currency*. The colonies attempted to follow Franklin's plan by issuing paper money, and Franklin himself was contracted to print the money issued by Pennsylvania—a service that sometimes caused his newspaper, the *Pennsylvania Gazette*, to be late in delivery. Colonial authorities in London, however, saw the issuing of paper money as an impudent usurpation of power by the colonists. In 1751 the British Parliament outlawed the use of paper money in New England and, in 1764, extended the ban to the other American colonies. In response to this parliamentary ban, Franklin himself went to London in 1766 to petition Parliament to allow more money to be printed.

Despite his later reputation as a diplomat and scientist, Franklin supported himself throughout his life as a craftsman, using his entrepreneurial talent to run a modest printing business. At the dawn of the information age, he was an information specialist, printing and distributing the ideas of his time to an increasingly literate public. His message focused sharply on a creed of thrift, honesty, and commerce.

Franklin's commitment to his ideology is demonstrated clearly in a letter dated July 11, 1765, which he wrote regarding the Stamp Act more than a decade before the Declaration of Independence. "Idleness and pride tax with a heavier hand than kings and parliaments," he wrote. "If we can get rid of the former, we may easily bear the latter." His dicta have become a part of the American language and public psyche:

- Remember that time is money.
- Early to bed and early to rise, makes a man healthy, wealthy, and wise.
- There are three faithful friends—an old wife, an old dog, and ready money.
- No nation was ever ruined by trade.
- In this world nothing is certain but death and taxes.

Franklin's creed was not one of greed or miserliness. It was one of conscientious work. He advocated this creed not merely as a means of making individuals prosperous but as a way to improve the whole society. He believed that the world would be a far better place if everyone produced more and consumed less.

For Franklin, money always had to be made within the confines of a strict social and personal morality. Because of this, he could not sanction the enslavement of one person for the financial gain of another. Later in life, after the United States had won its independence from Britain, he turned his attention to the issue of slavery, calling for its abolition throughout the new nation.

Benjamin Franklin was a man of deep morality; yet he eschewed and even mocked the hypocrisy of established religion. He rejected religious dogma and the hierarchy of officials who dominated the church, but not the morality of religion. He had a dictum for this philosophy as well: "God helps them that help themselves."

He served the community and country well with his creed. He organized not only the first public library in Philadelphia but also a hospital, a fire department, a police department, and the Academy of Philadelphia, which became the University of Pennsylvania. He also founded a discussion group that developed into the American Philosophical Society. He helped found the U.S. Post Office and, as a convention delegate, made the census a part of the U.S. Constitution. He invented the lightning rod, bifocal eyeglasses, and the Franklin stove, which generated safe, efficient indoor heat yet released a minimal amount of smoke into the house.

In his devotion to the public good, Franklin declined to apply for a patent on his inventions; he wanted them to be manufactured by anyone who wished to do so. Such decisions kept Franklin from becoming a wealthy man, despite being quite successful throughout most of his life. He died on April 17, 1790, as a famous and much admired man but a man of only modest financial means.

A CONTINENTAL EXPERIMENT

The foundation of the United States of America offered the chance to put many of Franklin's ideas about paper money into practice. The newly forming nation provided the first modern experiment with paper money on a national scale, and the American Revolution has the distinction of being the first war to be financed with paper money, albeit a rapidly depreciating paper money.

The Second Continental Congress created paper money before it had declared independence from Britain. To enforce its claim of independence the new country needed to raise an army to fight a war, but Congress lacked the money to finance it. They issued paper bills of credit supposedly backed by gold and silver and with a stiff penalty for any traitor who refused to accept them as currency. In 1777, Congress issued $13 million worth of paper bills called Treasury notes but dubbed "continentals" by most people because of the label *Continental Currency* printed on them.

The continentals began with a nominal value of one Spanish milled dollar of silver, but they quickly traded at two continentals for one silver dollar. As Congress issued more continentals to pay for its prolonged war, their value declined proportionally. By the beginning of 1780, Congress had issued some $241 million in continentals, and they were trading at a rate of forty to one silver dollar. A year later the value of the bills had dropped to seventy-five continentals to one silver dollar.[5]

In 1791, James Madison wrote for the *National Gazette* that "[t]he situation of the United States resembled that of an individual engaged in an expensive undertaking, carried on, for want of cash, with bonds secured on an estate to which his title was disputed; and who had besides, a combination of enemies employing every artifice to disparage that security."[6]

The American Congress stopped issuing the virtually worthless paper money in 1780, but most of the states continued to issue their own paper money. By 1781 the continental had lost so much value that it gave rise to a new cliché: "not worth a continental." Fortunately for the United States, however, Britain was giving up its struggle to hold on to the reluctant colonies and directing its commercial attention elsewhere in its search for profits.

After much debate over what to do with the continentals following the Revolution, the newly forming U.S. government agreed to redeem the continentals in government bonds paid at the rate of one cent for each continental.

The whole experiment with paper money so disgusted most Americans and provoked such a deep mistrust of paper currency that the United States printed almost no paper money for nearly a century. Even the delegates to the Constitutional Convention could not decide what to do about paper money. In Article I, Section 10, of the Constitution, they forbade the states to mandate any substance other than gold or silver as legal tender: "No State shall . . . make anything but gold and silver coin a tender in payment of debts." Even though Article I, Section 8, of the Constitution gave the federal government the power to regulate the value of money, the delegates could not agree on giving it the power to issue paper money. Because of grave and tumultuously voiced differences of opinion among the delegates regarding the value and usefulness of paper money, the Constitution remained silent on the federal government's ability to issue it.[7]

For many Americans, the experiment with paper currency during the American Revolution was a great failure because they lost so much money, but to the rest of the world, the experiment appeared to be a great success because the Americans had won their war using the novel technique of issuing paper money.

THE MINT OF MAMMON

In the years following the early experiments with paper money in Europe and North America, one of the most interesting treatments of the subject was penned by Johann Wolfgang von Goethe in his poetic tragedy *Faust*. In some ways, *Faust* should be treated as two works since Goethe published Part I in 1808 but did not complete Part II until 1831, shortly before his death. The two parts represent the contrasting vision, interest, and style of a young versus an old man, and in some ways they represent the contrast between the medieval world of romance, belief, and magic and the modern world of finance, rationalism, and skepticism.

The story of Dr. Faust, as related by Goethe in Part I, was already an old one when Goethe tackled it. It deals with a medieval alchemy professor who seeks to make gold from base metals and, more importantly, to acquire ultimate knowledge about the universe and human pleasure. Toward these ends, he makes a wager with the devil, promising his soul if the devil can grant him a moment of ecstasy that Faust will want to last forever. Faust sets out on a quest that includes seducing a beautiful young maiden and abandoning the pregnant girl after killing her brother. The story told in Part I of Goethe's *Faust* is a highly emotional tragedy written by a young genius at the start of his great career. Some scholars call it the quintessential literary work of the Romantic era.

In the second part of the play, written at the end of Goethe's life, Faust and Mephistopheles visit the court of the emperor during the pre-Lenten carnival season of masquerades and tricks. The emperor is besieged by his treasurer and stewards reporting the lack of funds and the need to pay the wages of the soldiers and servants. His moneylenders demand payment on debts, and even the wine bill has come due.

Mephistopheles offers the emperor a way out of his financial mess. He has found the key to making gold, the secret that all alchemists had sought for centuries. He obtains from the emperor permission to print paper money—"the heaven-sent leaf."

Faust comes to the emperor's carnival ball dressed appropriately as Plutus, the god of wealth, and through magic, he and Mephistopheles show the emperor the riches he can have by printing money. They convince the emperor to sign a note bearing the inscription "To whom it may concern, be by these presents known, this note is legal tender for one thousand crowns and is secured by the immense reserves of wealth safely stored underground in our Imperial States."[8] He has based the value of his money on the *future* mining of gold, the untapped treasures still buried in the earth. By the next morning, the emperor has forgotten that he signed the note, but during the night Mephistopheles has had thousands of copies of it made in various denominations. The new money has been unleashed to the great joy of creditors, debtors, soldiers, and other citizens. Already people are ordering new clothes, and business booms for the butcher and baker. Wine is flowing freely in the taverns, and even the dice roll more easily. Priests and prostitutes scurry about their business with greater enthusiasm because of the new money, and even the moneylenders are enjoying a brisk new business.

"And people value this the same as honest gold?" asks the incredulous emperor. "The court and army take it as full pay? Much as I find it strange, I see I must accept it."[9]

Like John Law and Benjamin Franklin, whose experiments with money made a lasting impression on Goethe, Faust found the key to the modern economic world in money. It was a system for borrowing against future earnings and using those earnings today. With this supply of seemingly endless paper money, Faust literally remakes the land by draining marshes, building factories and new farms, and digging canals.

Goethe had shown that the modern money economy based on its strange new money was a "continuation of alchemy by other means."[10] Writing in the first decades of the nineteenth century, Goethe seemed to forecast many of the industrial achievements of that age. In other writings, he predicted the building of the Suez Canal, and nearly a century before the opening of the Panama Canal and long before the United States had made an important appearance on the stage of world history, Goethe predicted that the young nation would build a canal to connect the Atlantic and Pacific oceans. As a scientist and statesman as well as a poet and playwright, he foresaw the great accomplishments and the shortcomings of the emerging industrial world that would be financed on the newly emerging monetary system of paper money.

At first, the spread of Faust's new money brings happiness and improvement, but soon the hidden costs begin bubbling to the surface. Peasants are killed while developing their land. A new class of government functionaries arises with names such as *Quick-loot* and *Get-quick*, describing their attitudes toward life. Soon social unrest in the newly enriched nation leads to rebellion, and a new anti-emperor rises to challenge the old one.

The many versions of Faust's bargain with the devil all end the same way when the devil finally claims his due and descends with Faust into hell. Of all the writers and composers who tackled the story of the Faustian bargain with the devil, only Goethe, after a lifetime of studying human passion and behavior, gave the story a different ending. In the poem's final verses, a host of heavenly angels take the body of Faust away from Mephistopheles and sing that "for him whose striving never ceases, we can provide redemption."[11]

The seventeenth century marked the inauspicious debut of paper money onto the modern world scene, but as demonstrated by both the French and American cases, paper money carried great potential dangers. As long as it was supported by gold or silver, all seemed well and paper seemed just as reliable, and far more convenient, than precious metals. Invariably, however, the government or bank in charge of printing the money issued more paper than it had metal to back it. No matter how important the reason or how pressing the cause, once begun, the devaluation process spiraled, with more and more bills being issued at less and less value.

The dangers and temptations as well as the great mystery surrounding paper money weighed heavily on the thinkers and poets of the nineteenth century. In the play *Oedipus Tyrannus*, written in 1820 by Percy Bysshe Shelley, greed incites people to abuse paper money. This perspective on paper money becomes clear when Mammon appears and asks another character: "What's the matter, my dear fellow, now? . . . Does money fail? Come to my mint, coin paper, till gold be at a discount, and ashamed to show his bilious face."

Money began as a specific, tangible commodity, as cowrie shells and stone disks, cacao beans and metal nuggets. In its second stage, it came in the form of paper which retained its tangibility but lost its value as a commodity. Paper money could not be eaten, as could salt blocks or cacao beans, nor could it be melted and formed into metal tools or ornaments, like copper, tin, gold, and silver coins. Paper money lacked usefulness except as money. The use of coins and other commodities involved tremendous abstraction, but the use of paper made money even more abstract.

Whether seen as a solution to practical problems, as portrayed by Benjamin Franklin, or as a Faustian bargain with the devil, as portrayed by Goethe, paper money was to play a crucial role in the nineteenth and twentieth centuries, bringing great profit to some at a great cost to others.

9
Metric Money

Money, like number and law, is a category of thought.
—OSWALD SPENGLER

PAPER, BACKED BY GOLD, MADE POSSIBLE THE WIDE-
spread use of money. Paper expanded the role of money to new
markets, new applications, and new clients. In addition to the new
technology of paper, however, people also needed new ways of thinking about money. Paper could simplify the use of money, but for it to
have widespread use, the intellectual system of monies had to be simplified as well. Money came in many units that were difficult to relate to one another, much less to the units of other countries. The
simplification came through the gradual decimalization of money, a
process that began in Russia but reached its fullest expression in the
fledgling currency of the United States and later in revolutionary
France.

As early as 1535 the Russians used a system of one hundred denga
to one Novgorod ruble. Peter the Great upgraded the system and
changed the denga to the kopek, creating a system that survived into
the twentieth century.

On March 15, 1719, Peter the Great issued a royal order making
one of the barracks in his new capital into the city's first mint. The
equipment in the Moscow mint was then moved to Saint Petersburg
in order to make the czar's new coins, the first of which were merely
silver coins from other countries, which the Russian mint restruck
in Peter's honor.

America Goes Decimal

No matter how rational the new Russian system might have appeared to be, no other monarch wanted to copy Russia, which they regarded as a backward country. All of them rejected the decimal currency, preferring their traditional and confusing, but more easily manipulated, systems. The Russian system found its first imitators not in the palaces of other European monarchs but in the revolutionary meeting halls of the British colonies in North America. Eager to break with all things royal, including the royal money bearing portraits of the British monarch George III, the American colonists searched for a new system. Even the names of British coins, such as *crown* and *sovereign*, evoked too much of the royal mystique for the radical Americans, who sought a truly republican yet scientific monetary system.

In 1782 the U.S. superintendent of finance sent a report to President Washington and the Congress recommending that the United States adopt a decimal system of currency. The proposed decimal system would divide the dollar, or "unit," into one hundred equal parts. Thomas Jefferson recommended that the smallest part, one-hundredth of a dollar, be called a *cent*, from the Latin word meaning "hundred," and that a tenth of a dollar would be a dime, from the Latin meaning "tenth." The proposed monetary system of the new country received further elaboration in the *Report on the Establishment of a Mint* by Alexander Hamilton, probably the most financially sophisticated American of the time. Congress adopted the basics of this system in 1785 and 1786 and finalized it in Alexander Hamilton's Coinage Act of April 2, 1792.

Since the Russians had decimalized only the ruble, using it in conjunction with other coins, theirs had not been a wholly decimal system. The United States coinage system became the first wholly decimal monetary system in the world.

This country's adoption of the decimal system so soon after the Revolution strongly influenced the attitudes of European monarchs, who associated the decimal system with political revolt and subversion of the established order. This association strengthened the monarchs' dislike of the decimal system and reinforced their commitment to their own system, no matter how antiquated and awkward it may have been.

Most countries at this time divided their money into arbitrary units. The Spanish dollar, for example, consisted of eight *reales*. Through the centuries, the English used a confusing mélange of shillings, farthings, crowns, sovereigns, pennies, guineas, and pounds made of various metals with constantly changing values relative to one another. A shilling contained 12 pence, and a pound contained 20 shillings; thus it took 240 pence to make a pound. The guinea, a larger gold coin, was worth 1 pound plus 1 shilling, or 260 pence, and each pence contained 4 farthings. To add to the confusion, each coin had its own abbreviation—£, s., or p.—but they could not be expressed in decimals. In 1971, the United Kingdom finally abandoned this arcane system and became one of the last countries in the world to adopt a decimal currency. The pound now consists of an even one hundred pence, and prices can be expressed in terms of the pound alone, as in £1.47.

Under the Bourbon dynasty, France's coinage system centered around the louis d'or, which consisted of 10 livres; each livre consisted of 20 sols; and each sol consisted of 12 deniers. In addition to the gold coins, 60 sous constituted 1 silver ecu. On October 7, 1793, France, in the throes of its own revolution, followed the example of the United States and Russia and adopted the decimal monetary system, *calcul décimal*, but this was a largely symbolic move, since the government could not stop to alter the coinage in the midst of a raging revolution and the subsequent Reign of Terror. In 1795 the French replaced the name *livre* with *franc*, which consisted of one hundred centimes. Not until 1803 did France actually mint new coins using the decimal system, but that system has survived to the present.

Revolutionary France took its decimal system to all the areas its army conquered. For the French revolutionaries, the decimal and metric systems symbolized the rationality of the revolution. In the belief that their revolution represented far more than mere political change, the French imposed their decimal system as part of the broad benefit package conferred on the people whom the struggle had lib-

erated from the tyranny of monarchy. In 1798 the French conquered
Switzerland, transformed it into the Helvetian Republic, and imposed
upon it a unified coinage system of ten rappen to the batzen and ten
batzen to the Swiss franc. Most of the Italian states accepted similar
decimal systems during the Napoleonic years, and gradually throughout the nineteenth century other countries followed suit, often as a
result of revolution or major political change.

THE METRIC FETISH

Through a series of decrees in 1793, the Convention, as the national
legislature of France then called itself, imposed the decimal system
in weights and measures as well as coinage, carrying the decimal and
metric ideas far beyond their original purpose. The radicals of the
French Revolution sought to associate revolutionary democracy with
decimalization. They then turned their attention to the measurement
of space. The Convention abolished the 90° right angle and substituted in its place the 100° right angle. They further divided each degree into one hundred minutes, giving the circle a full 400° rather
than an awkward 360°.

In an enthusiasm for decimalization that overshadowed that of
Thomas Jefferson and the other ardent Americans, the Convention
decided also to base timekeeping on the decimal system rather than
on the odd Babylonian system of sixty units for seconds and minutes
and twelve for hours. On November 24, 1793, the Convention specified that one hundred seconds would constitute a minute, and one
hundred minutes would constitute an hour. A few new clocks were
made, but with the need to operate at the rate of 10,000 seconds
an hour, they proved difficult to construct, to operate, and to comprehend.

Under the new system, ten hours would equal a day, and ten days
would make a week, which was to be renamed a *decad*. Three decads
would compose a month. According to their new calendar, the
French would celebrate New Year's Day on September 22, the au-
tumnal equinox, and all years would be numbered from the establishment of the French Republic on that date in 1792. The new
calendar left the number of months at twelve, but they were given

new names to identify them with the weather in France during that month. The months were organized into four seasons, each with its distinctive set of suffixes. The three months of the first season, autumn, ended in *aire*. What had been September 22 on the Georgian calendar became the first day of Vendémiaire.[1]

Virtually no one liked the new French day of 100,000 parts, and the French government abandoned it on 18 Germinal an III (April 7, 1795), but the months stayed in effect in France until January 1, 1806, when Napoleon abandoned Republican time completely and returned to the Gregorian calendar.

Despite the failure of the revolutionary decimal clock and calendar, the decimal system for coinage, weights, and measures gained respectability due to their usefulness, and Napoleon helped spread them throughout Europe as his army fought from Spain to Russia. A platinum meter was constructed and deposited in the Archives of the State of France to serve as the official meter of record.

In France, decimal thinking developed nearly into a national fetish of the revolutionary class and their academic allies. The adoption of the decimal system for coinage helped to prepare lawmakers and the public for a decimal system in other areas such as weights and measures. The first systematic proposal for a decimal system of weights and measures had originated far back in history with Gabriel Mouton, vicar of Saint Paul's Church in Lyons, France, in 1670. This odd idea attracted little attention at the time, but scholars tinkered with Mouton's proposal until it gradually evolved into what we now know as the metric system. Scientists set the length of the meter at one ten-millionth of the terrestrial meridian that ran through Paris. Using the meter as the determining measure of distance, scientists multiplied it by 1,000 to create the kilometer and then divided it into 100 centimeters and 1,000 millimeters. They also established the liter as a wet and dry measure equivalent to a cube measuring one-tenth of a meter on each side.

Throughout the world, the scientific community came to appreciate very early the value of standardized units. Each country, however, regarded its own system as the best one, the one that the whole world should adopt. No one, especially not the British, wanted to accept a set of weights and measures based on the terrestrial meridian that ran through Paris.

One of the first important proponents of a scientific decimal system in Britain was the Scottish engineer and inventor James Watt, who invented, among other mechanical devices, the modern condensing steam engine. In 1783 he created a set of measures that he called the philosophical pound. It was composed of ten philosophical ounces, each of which contained ten philosophical *drachms* (drams). Although no country, including England, ever adopted Watt's complete system, his name was applied to the unit of power that is still called the watt. He also coined the term *horsepower*, for a unit of power equal to 747.5 watts.

Watt's system of weights and measures differed in specifics from the French metric system, but the underlying rationale was much the same. Watt's plan had a great and largely unintended impact on the committee overseeing the construction of the French system.

Even though government edicts established the new weights and measures, commerce made them universal. The Netherlands, which included Belgium, adopted the metric system in 1816. The many small nations of Europe needed such a system to simplify the growing trade across national boundaries. Instead of making the metric system compulsory, the French government at first allowed it to operate side by side with other, older systems until 1837, when it decreed that, by 1850, only the metric system would be acceptable for business in France.

One of the great factors propelling the switch to metric measurements came with the creation of international trade shows, which later became known as world's fairs and which started with the London Exposition of 1851. Britain itself did not switch to the new metric system of weights and measures because of the system's close association with the strange political ideas and practices of France, but the exposition created a heightened awareness of the system, which won the allegiance of all scientific groups. It also won greater support from the commercial community, which saw its importance in building international markets for their products.

At the urging of industrialists and other supporters of the metric system for coins, weights, and measures, scientists gathered for an international statistical meeting during the next world's fair, held in Paris in 1855. The International Jury of the Paris Exposition recommended that all nations switch to metric and decimal systems as a way of expanding science and commerce. With a burst of optimism, the jury also concluded that use of the metric system would promote world peace. As scientists have been prone to do when waxing philosophical, they confused simple scientific practicality with world utopia. Despite such lofty ideals, World War I proved in the next century that governments could be just as adept at waging war with weapons measured by the metric system as by any other set of measurements.

The Vienna Coin Treaty of January 24, 1857, helped move forward the adoption of the decimal system for coinage, and it encouraged the adoption of metric weights and measures. Following the unification of Italy in 1861 and of Germany in 1871, the new governments adopted the metric system as a way of standardizing the many different systems of their constituent nations. Austria followed in 1873, and one by one, the other European nations adopted the change, followed by Mexico (1862), Siam (1889), Japan (1891), Egypt (1892), Tunis (1895), and Russia (1900). To force compliance with the new laws, some countries took drastic measures. The sultan of the Ottoman Empire, for instance, ordered the switch to metrics in 1886 and, in 1891, had all other weights confiscated to make sure that only metric ones could be used.

Although the United States was the first nation to adopt an exclusively decimal system for its coinage, it will probably be the last to adopt it for weights and measures. As early as 1866, the U.S. Congress approved the metric system as an optional system for use by American businesses, but the idea has never caught on with the American public.

Americans, however, did apply the decimal system in an unexpected way through the work of an otherwise little known New York librarian and Columbia University professor, Melvil Dewey. He divided library books into ten classifications, which he further divided and redivided into what became known as the Dewey decimal system. In 1876 at the age of twenty-five, he published details of the system in *Decimal Classification and Relativ Index*, which he updated constantly almost until 1931, the year of his death.

THE SCIENTIFIC REVOLUTION

As the use of money spread to ever lower strata of society and the use of markets spread around the world, even the poorest peasants needed to know some basic math and market principles. This transition to a new way of thinking can be seen in the folktales and children's stories of this period. The myths and sagas of earlier eras had emphasized heroes and monsters, weapons and conflict, honor and pride, and superhuman struggles against supernatural forces.

But if we look at stories from the feudal period, we encounter characters like the protagonist of "Jack and the Beanstalk," who nearly devastates his widowed mother by trading her prize cow for a handful of beans. The story turns on a silly barter made by a youth who did not understand the market. Fortunately, the beans turn out to be magic, and Jack enriches his family by stealing from a giant. Similar stories deal with a goose that lays golden eggs, or with the search for gold at the end of the rainbow. As we move into the later feudal period and on into early modern times, more and more of the peasant stories deal with markets, money, and how to manage it—or at least how to avoid being made a fool of by someone with supernatural powers.

Money forces humans to reduce qualitative differences to quantitative ones. It forces a numbering of things, and this quantification allows things that are very unalike to be compared. This numbering pushed ahead the development of mathematics, and when applied to other fields, it made science possible. This tendency toward numbering has become the basis of modern thought from the rise of mathematics and science through the increased objectification of law, medicine, teaching, and virtually all other professions.

The decimal system and its twin, metric measurement, not only changed the way people handled money and numbers but also transformed the way people thought. A new empiricism in thought, coupled with money's strict discipline in the use of numbers and categories, had a great impact on the intellectual development of the Enlightenment, which emerged in the eighteenth century. The new class of intellectuals no longer sought to discover knowledge only through studying the works of ancient scholars and religious writers. They themselves could create knowledge through observation and the recording of events around them. Knowledge could thus be induced from evidence rather than merely deduced from sacred Scripture or established dogma. In their daily lives, people had always learned by induction and empiricism via the lessons of experience, but such a path to knowledge had little legitimacy in the universities.

With the new ways of measuring and the increasing importance of numbers in scientific research, scientists invented new equipment for measuring. In addition to improving the older weight scales and the clock, innovators developed the thermometer for measuring temperature, the barometer for measuring air pressure, and the hydrometer for measuring humidity.

The men who led the scientific revolution were not scholars in the traditional or classical sense. They generally lacked university training and did not occupy university chairs or hold professorships. Instead, they carried out their work in the practical realm of men who worked with their hands for a living. This group of innovators included such men of the world as Benjamin Franklin. It also included men like Joseph Priestley, the son of a Yorkshire dressmaker. Young Priestley studied to be a Congregationalist minister, but he devoted himself to science until his sympathy with the French Revolution caused him to be burned out of his home. He then emigrated to Pennsylvania because it was the home of his hero, Benjamin Franklin, and there he discovered oxygen and spent most of his life experimenting in science.

Another such man was Louis Pasteur, who worked to improve the brewing of beer and the manufacture of wine. His initial work in health came in searching for a cure for silkworm diseases so as to save the silk-manufacturing industry.

Following the Enlightenment came a succession of new sciences: chemistry, physics, biology, and geology. Without the changes in thought and measurement made by the spread of market systems and money and by the accompanying spread of the metric and decimal systems, it is difficult to imagine that scholars could ever have devised something like the periodic table that identified and cracked the code of the basic elements and arranged them by atomic weight. It is no coincidence that chemist Dmitri Ivanovich Mendeleev (1834–1907), who devised the periodic table of elements, was the director of the Russian Bureau of Weights and Measures in Saint Petersburg.

The scientific revolution and the industrial revolution arose in sequence, although it is difficult to separate them clearly. As science historian J. D. Bernal wrote, "It is no accident that the intellectual formulations of science, the technical changes of industry, and the economic and political domination of capitalism would grow and flourish together at the same times and in the same places."[2]

German Socialist Friedrich Engels first coined the term *industrial revolution* in 1844 to refer to the rapid technological and scientific changes that had occurred in manufacturing throughout the preceding century. This revolution grew directly out of the earlier commercial era. A world trade system allowed textiles manufactured in England to be effectively and cheaply sold in Africa, India, and the Americas. Most important was the establishment of European contact with the American Indians who supplied a vast array of new crops and products such as dyes, tobacco, superior cotton, and rubber. The new products, together with a vastly expanding commercial market, created a revolution first in the manufacture of textiles and then in all types of production.

Mining gave rise to major industrial achievements such as the improvement of the pump, which led to development of the steam engine. The use of explosives in mines expanded chemistry and the understanding of gunpowder. The need to transport ore easily in wheeled vehicles led to the development of carts on tracks, and when this innovation was combined with the steam engine, it produced the first locomotives and trains.

The telecommunications and electricity industries arose from the need for better business communication. Electricity had no apparent practical use beyond entertaining people at parties until it was discovered that it could be used to send messages through a system known as Morse code. The group that most urgently required quick communication was made up of businessmen for whom news was money, since it affected the rise and fall of stocks and agricultural prices.

As had happened so often in the past, the university communities were painfully slow to admit these new areas of research and knowledge into their system of studies. Not until the middle of the nineteenth century, under great pressure from manufacturers and governments, did the major universities of Europe reluctantly begin to open their doors to these new scientific disciplines. Germany took the lead, followed by England and France, both of which were inspired in great part by the success of the early world's fairs, which emphasized the unity of science and manufacturing. The great exhibition in London in 1851 resulted in the creation of the Royal College of Science, modeled in part on the French École Normal Supérieure and the École Polytechnique.

The disciplines of science found great difficulty integrating into the established university curriculum. They were often shunted into special polytechnic schools. The large universities reluctantly made room for science, often because a group of industrialists had paid for the new program. Administratively and spatially, the sciences were separated from the humanities and established their own sections of the university.

Over the course of the nineteenth century, scholars began applying the principles of science to areas outside of mathematics and the realm of natural phenomena. They adapted scientific methodology to the study of society, politics, and economics. This new rigor shows clearly in the writings of Karl Marx, who sought to bring a scientific study to human history and to its political and economic systems. He translated his scholarship into action through his support of communism, a movement that found little support during his lifetime.

The new disciplines of economics, sociology, and anthropology followed the methods introduced in the natural sciences, albeit with less precise and effective results. Economics, which Scottish historian

Thomas Carlyle later labeled *that dismal science*, emerged as one of the offspring of the Enlightenment and as a new discipline of study and analysis created by the expanded emphasis on numbers, measurements, and money. Through the works of scholars such as Sir James Denham Steuart, who in 1767 published *Inquiry into the Principles of Political Economy*, and the more famous Adam Smith, economics slowly emerged as a distinct discipline and approach to human social life and organization. Beginning with Smith in particular, economics showed how life is organized through exchange.

10

The Gold Bug

Time will run back and fetch the Age of Gold.
—John Milton

L IKE MOST GREAT CITIES, LONDON HAS MULTIPLE
faces, but it is best known for the aristocratic visage that it presents to the world on public occasions marked by elaborate royal rituals. That face is the imperial countenance of ceremony, pomp, and
circumstance of a government that now operates behind the facade
of its tradition-steeped monarchy. This official image and drama can
usually be seen in London, in the district known as Westminster in
the triangular area bounded by Westminster Abbey, Buckingham
Palace, and Trafalgar Square. Large open parks and the uniform buildings of the royal guards and the government offices flank its straight
streets. In this area, most of the major ceremonies of the British
monarchy unfold, from coronations and the opening of Parliament
to funerals and celebrations of the queen's birthday. The Westminster area was designed and landscaped specifically for imperial
pageants with grand coaches, prancing horses, waving plumes, and a
variety of military and official uniforms unmatched by those of any
royal court since the fall of the Ottoman Empire.

Less recognized by outsiders and casual visitors, London's other important face appears in the one-square-mile area known officially as
the City of London, but referred to locally simply as "the City." It oc-
cupies the oldest part of London where the original Roman settlement grew up and the medieval city operated. The City includes
the area along the north bank of the river Thames roughly between
the Tower Bridge on the east and Saint Paul's Cathedral to the west.

The City was destroyed by the Great Fire of London in 1666 and again by German bombs during World War II, but it has risen again and again on the same awkward medieval pattern of streets, although the restored and rebuilt buildings are now jumbled amid completely modern ones. The layout of the City, however, is roughly the same today as it was in the ancient Roman settlement of Londinium.

The ruins of the Roman walls still mark the limits of the City, but modern police squads now patrol the area, protecting the financial heart of the nation from terrorist attack. They stand on all streets leading into the City; unlike the colorful Beefeaters, Warders, and other ceremonial guards scattered around London, these men are dressed strictly for protection from violence. Wearing bulky bullet-proof vests and sturdy helmets, and carrying submachine guns loaded and ready to fire, the special guards stop all vehicles, from bicycles to trucks, entering the City. Despite their vigilance, an occasional bomb blasts another hole in the street or rips out the front of a pub or an office building in the densely packed area.

The City has been a financial center ever since the Romans chose it as the site on which to build a bridge spanning the river Thames. For approximately a thousand years, that bridge was the only one across the Thames, and thus the area became a major trading point. Most of the older markets now survive only in the names of the streets, which long ago acquired new functions. The medieval grain market, for example, occupied the area still known as Cornhill. The main markets stood on Cheapside, with smaller ones along Wood Street, Poultry Street, Ironmonger Street, Milk Street, Bread Street, and even Love Lane. While these markets have disappeared through the centuries, they have been replaced by larger and far more important ones for the world economy.

All streets in the City seem to lead to a seven-way intersection that forms the heart of the City. Here stand the imposing edifices of the Bank of England; the Royal Exchange, which houses the London International Financial Futures Exchange and Mansion House, where the lord mayor presides; and the gray concrete fortress of the modern stock exchange. Nearby rises the headquarters of the world's great collection of insurers, known as Lloyd's of London. Since 1986,

Lloyd's has been housed in a steel-and-glass edifice that looks like an overgrown but dilapidated oil refinery and which probably qualifies as the ugliest urban building constructed during the twentieth century.

The relationship between the City and the Crown—as the British government still calls itself—has never been an entirely cordial one. In 1066, the City secured itself behind its thick walls and, at first, refused to surrender to William the Conqueror even after the Battle of Hastings by which he won the rest of England. Only gradually did the City reach an accommodation with the new monarch whereby it acknowledged him but continued to manage its own affairs through its corporate guild. After accepting this compromise, the still mistrustful William built his most imposing castle at the edge of the City so that he could watch it, and for eight centuries most political executions were carried out between William's castle and the City. The castle, which eventually became known as the Tower of London, still looms over the Thames just beside the City.

The City ends just outside the walls of the Tower of London, where the crown jewels and other treasures of the British monarchy are kept under guard. This treasure trove, which probably ranks as the most valuable collection of jewels ever assembled, includes the world's largest diamond. Until well into the nineteenth century, the Tower of London also served as the national mint, producing most of the English coins prior to the Victorian era.

To the present day even the monarchs of Great Britain, who otherwise have the right to go anywhere in the United Kingdom including all the other boroughs of London, must stop and request the permission of the lord mayor of the City of London in order to enter his one square mile of the city. The medieval ceremony of the sovereign seeking permission to enter the City preserves the memory, if not the fact, of the ancient separation of the City and the Crown. As though to further emphasize that distinction, the road that runs parallel to the Thames and connects Buckingham Palace and Whitehall with the City is occupied by the Royal Courts of Justice, which often had to mediate between the government and financial institutions. The part of that boulevard known as Fleet Street was also the traditional home of most of London's newspapers, which reported the activities of both the financial and government centers of power as well as the many scandals seeping out of the royal palaces.

The separation of the City from the rest of the kingdom gave the merchants of London a limited autonomy and the guarantee of certain rights that have seldom been allowed by strong monarchs. While this separation of commerce from the Crown did not allow for true independence, it did offer enough protection for the British economy to grow stronger and more vibrant than that of France, Russia, Spain, or most of the other European countries. The affluence created by the London financial institutions is mentioned in the 1797 play *The Heir at Law* by George Colman the Younger:

> *Oh, London is a fine town,*
> *A very famous city,*
> *Where all the streets are paved with gold*
> *And all the maidens pretty.*

Here in the City of London in the nineteenth century, bankers created a monetary system of paper money based on gold. This system spread around the world and became the first completely global money system in the world. This system brought banking and the circulation of paper money to a new public. In this global system, paper money—in the form of the British pound and its descendant, the American dollar—together with the invisible money of accounts created by banks brought the banking system to its historical zenith.

The City continues as one of the world's great financial forces even though it no longer dominates the world's economy quite the way it did in the nineteenth and early twentieth centuries. There is no greater accumulation of financial institutions in any square mile anywhere on earth. Something comparable to the City could be imagined if the U.S. Department of Treasury, Fort Knox, the Federal Reserve headquarters, and Wall Street were all located within one square mile, along with the headquarters of all major American banks, insurance companies, and the nation's top five hundred corporations.

If Buckingham Palace, Westminster Abbey, and the Houses of Parliament constitute the official, public, and imperial face of British government, the City is certainly its heart. From the offices, conference halls, and trading rooms of the City flowed the money that kept Nelson's ships supplied at Trafalgar, financed the conquest of India, underwrote the mines of South America and the railroads of the world, supervised the banks of the largest and most far-flung empire in the world, and insured the legs of Hollywood movie stars.

THE OLD LADY OF THREADNEEDLE STREET

The commercial district of London rose around the Bank of England, which still stands as the most important financial institution in the City. The bank emerged from the momentous changes in British history known as the Glorious Revolution of 1688, when both the Whigs and the Tories in Parliament agreed to remove King James II, who was a convert to Roman Catholicism, and to invite his daughter, the Protestant Mary, and her Dutch husband, William of Orange, to reign jointly as the British monarchs William III and Mary II. The monarchs took over a virtually bankrupt government and an antiquated monetary system handled by goldsmiths. The new monarchs needed money desperately because they had to put down the rebellion of supporters of James II while waging war with France.

In his search for funds, William agreed to charter a national bank that would raise money from private sources and lend it to the government. On an engraved marble plaque in the bank today, Sir William Petty is quoted as saying in support of the bank in 1682, "And we have in England Materials for a Bank which shall furnish Stock enough to drive the Trade of the whole Commercial World."

Even though it started as the banker to the government, the Bank of England was strictly a private holding company. The Scottish financier William Paterson and his associates organized it and immediately lent the King £1.2 million at 8 percent annual interest. The investors received stock in the bank in proportion to their investments. Chartered as Governor and Company of the Bank of England, the bank raised money to finance the conquest of the world's largest empire over the coming centuries.

Depositors brought their coins to the Bank of England and received a receipt for deposit. According to some reports these paper receipts gradually began to circulate as money, but little evidence of such paper money survives. We do know, however, that in time the bank began to issue receipts in standard denominations to its depositors. These receipts circulated as money and were thus the first bank notes designated in British pounds.

Throughout most of the eighteenth century, the Bank of England issued bank notes in ten- and twenty-pound denominations. At that time, a twenty-pound note had the purchasing power of roughly one thousand modern dollars, and because of their great value, the notes were used exclusively in large business transactions, particularly those among the financiers and rich merchants within the City of London. For most people, coins of much smaller value usually sufficed for daily transactions.

During the financial crisis provoked by the Napoleonic wars at the beginning of the nineteenth century, the bank began issuing one- and two-pound notes to compensate for the shortage of coins and to expand the supply of money needed to purchase materials and pay the soldiers. Even a one-pound note, however, represented a relatively large amount of money, equivalent to about fifty modern dollars, and it would not have been used by an average person in the course of a normal day's transactions.

Other banks could also issue receipts for deposits, but none of these banks carried the prestige of the Bank of England since it was the bank of the royal government. In 1844, Parliament passed the Bank Charter Act, which gave the Bank of England a virtual monopoly on the right to issue bank notes in the United Kingdom. As a nod to local Scottish pride and national sentiment, some banks in Scotland retained their right to issue monetary notes, but even they were required to back their currency offerings with notes issued by the Bank of England. The Bank of England, in turn, had to guarantee the convertibility of all of its paper notes into gold on demand, thus making a paper pound just as valuable as a gold one.

Unlike the paper money issued by the United States and France during their revolutions, the paper money of England was not issued directly by the government. It originated instead from a private bank operating under a government charter but still distinct from the government. The Crown continued to issue its coins, including the golden one-pound coin with a picture of the monarch impressed on it. The Bank of England, as a private venture, issued no coins at all but could issue paper money so long as it did not bear the monarch's image. Somewhat insulated from politics, or at least from the daily ebb and flow of political sentiment and temporary expediency, the Bank of England operated under close government scrutiny but functioned first and foremost as a bank—that is, as a fiscally responsible institution that needed to generate a profit for its stockholders.

During the nineteenth century, the Bank of England became the focal and stabilizing institution of the world monetary and banking system. As John Kenneth Galbraith wrote of the Bank of England, "Of all institutions concerned with economics none has for so long enjoyed such prestige. It is, in all respects, to money as Saint Peter's is to the Faith. And the reputation is deserved, for most of the art as well as much of the mystery associated with the management of money originated there."[1]

Most of the world operated on a gold standard, but a few countries, including Mexico and China, continued on a silver standard. Despite variations in the prices of the two metals and some difficulties in synchronizing the two, they essentially functioned as part of a single world money system in which all currencies had the backing of either gold or silver.

After the defeat of Napoleon, Britain dominated as the greatest empire in the world with the support of the world's most powerful navy. The Bank of England became the prototype of the centralized national bank, emulated by national banks around the world. The era from the beginning of Queen Victoria's reign until the outbreak of World War I was one of the most stable periods in monetary history, and it produced the greatest general prosperity known in history to that time. Under the leadership of the Bank of England, the world operated on a single monetary system based on common adherence to the gold principle. In effect, gold was the world currency.

Often the interests of the Bank of England took precedence over those of the government. The bank had to play a very active role in maintaining the value of gold, and sometimes its intervention came at a cost to British citizens, who still had a stable currency but with a reduced purchasing power. Britain was providing a service to the world, but British citizens paid the price for it.

For roughly seventy years, from 1844 until 1913, the English pound sterling reigned as the most steadfast and important currency in the world. During this same period, the world's financial center focused on the small City of London. Britain maintained a unique balance of power, with the currency and financial institutions in the hands of private interests in the City of London and with the military and the empire administered by the government from the cluster of buildings around Parliament, Whitehall, 10 Downing Street, and Buckingham Palace. As long as the imperial government and the private financial interests operated separately yet in concert, Britain ruled the largest and most far-reaching empire in world history.

A TALE OF TWO CITIES

Throughout the nineteenth and early twentieth centuries, the directors of the Bank of England resisted governmental interference in their business. When the government established a royal commission to inquire into the activities and reserves of the bank, the bankers would only respond that the reserves were "very, very considerable." When asked to be a bit more specific, they said that they would be "very, very reluctant" to add to what they had already said.[2]

Under the Bank of England, Britain prospered. With a solid pound sterling, industrialization and trade grew steadily and prices for most commodities dropped just as steadily throughout the century of peace. In economic terms, it was the best of times for Europe. Gold provided the underpinning of that peace and prosperity, not because of any special quality of gold but simply because the gold standard acted as a huge restraint on governments so long as the country could not print paper money greater than the supply of gold backing it. When asked "Why gold?" one monetary expert reportedly answered, "because you can't trust governments, least of all democratic governments."[3]

As nineteenth-century economist David Ricardo noted, "neither a State nor a bank ever has had the unrestricted power of issuing paper money, without abusing that power; in all States, therefore, the issue of paper money ought to be under some check and control; and none seems so proper as that of subjecting the issuers of paper money to the obligation of paying their notes, either in gold coin or in bullion."[4] Throughout the Victorian era, the gold standard imposed the needed discipline on politicians.

The economic boom of the nineteenth century gave the world new systems of railroads, steamships, telegraph and telephone lines, and electricity as well as architectural wonders from the Brooklyn Bridge and the Eiffel Tower to the Suez Canal. During the nineteenth century, more goods were produced for more people than ever before, and the era culminated in the Gilded Age, an era of great excess marked by conspicuous consumption.

By the end of the nineteenth century in democratic countries such as the United States and Great Britain, the newly emerging wealthy class of bankers and industrialists lived a life of privilege and luxury that probably no monarch in history had ever enjoyed. This greatly resented class lived largely above the law and manipulated politicians like puppets. The general public and, in particular, the politicians developed an extreme hatred for the capitalist class. Attacking and, if possible, destroying the capitalist class was seen as a simple solution by many radical ideologues as well as democratic politicians throughout Europe and North America.

Perhaps in an effort to counter the hostility directed toward them, the richest of the plutocrats began performing massive and highly publicized works of charity. Service became an important part of acquiring great wealth, particularly in the United States. The wives and daughters of the wealthy sponsored balls and other functions as benefits to aid the poor, and they formed charitable organizations and public service groups. Steel industrialist Andrew Carnegie built libraries and other educational buildings throughout the United States and established a large public endowment in his own name. Swedish manufacturer Alfred Nobel made a fortune in oil and explosives with which he endowed the international peace prize that bears his name. Henry Ford, John D. Rockefeller, and W. K. Kellogg also established large endowments. Other industrialists and financiers created small colleges and universities under their family name: retail and export magnet William Marsh Rice created Rice University in Houston, Texas; the families and heirs of tobacco brothers Benjamin N. and James B. Duke created Duke University in Durham, North Carolina, to honor the two men; and railroad magnate Leland Stanford founded Stanford University in honor of his deceased son.

GOLD DISCIPLINE

Throughout the nineteenth century, the European governments found themselves severely limited by the gold system around them. Unable to give away lands and make grants as earlier monarchs had done and unable to print endless amounts of money, the governments needed to find new ways to enrich themselves. If gold was the ultimate valuable behind the currency, then to make more money, they needed more gold. This need for gold set off the greatest international scramble since the conquest of America in the sixteenth century. The European governments sent out armies around the world in search of gold. They found it in South Africa, Australia, Siberia, and the Yukon. Even the United States became a major producer of gold in the California territory, which had recently been taken from Mexico.

The British navy ruled the oceans and transported the British army to every continent. The British Empire stretched from England and Ireland to Canada, British Honduras, Guiana, and most of the Caribbean islands. Britain controlled the western entrance to the Mediterranean Sea from its base at Gibraltar and controlled the central area of the sea from Malta. The British base in Egypt gave them control over the eastern entrance to the sea via the Suez Canal, along with control of the surrounding countries. South of Egypt, Britain's empire included Sudan and Nigeria—respectively, the largest and the most populous countries of Africa—as well as South Africa, the richest country on the continent. In addition, the empire included the connecting points of Kenya, Uganda, Ghana, Gold Coast, Rhodesia, and Zambia. In Asia, Britain held all of India (including Pakistan), Malaysia, Ceylon, Burma, and the important ports of Aden, Singapore, and Hong Kong. The British virtually turned the

Pacific into their private pond through control of Australia, New Zealand, Tonga, Fiji, the Cook Islands, and New Hebrides.

The European governments built imperial bureaucracies and armies with which they conquered new lands and brought new subjects into their empires. The British fought wars from the Khyber Pass in Afghanistan to Khartoum in the Sudan and from Hong Kong in China to Zululand in South Africa. The French army fought its wars of colonial conquest from Timbuktu to Tahiti, and even the Germans, Dutch, Belgians, and Italians sent out their soldiers on campaigns of conquest in distant parts of the globe. The Austro-Hungarian Empire pushed farther into eastern Europe and the Balkans, taking over the territory of the declining Ottoman Empire. Russia began its push deeper into the Caucasus and Central Asia. Japan began its imperial expansion into the islands and adjacent mainland as it absorbed Korea, Taiwan, and the islands off the Siberian coast.

Only the Americas managed to shake off the colonial yoke during the nineteenth century as one colony after another followed the example of the United States and declared its independence from Spain, France, and Portugal. In a cultural paroxysm that shook the Americas from the Arctic to Tierra del Fuego, the governments of the newly independent republics launched the worst wars against their own native Indians to be seen in America in two hundred years, since the *entrada* of the Spanish conquistadores in the early sixteenth century. Argentina exterminated the tribes of Patagonia, and in the south, Chile went to war against the Mapuches. Brazil began to clear the Indians out of the jungle as they made room for the rubber industry. Mexico declared war against the Yaqui Indians in the north and their Mayan citizens in the Yucatán. The United States declared a policy of "removal" of Indians from east of the Mississippi River; they then opened a war of extermination on the peoples of the Plains.

For native peoples around the world, the nineteenth century was the worst of times. And these campaigns cost money. Throughout the nineteenth century, spending on armaments and armies increased constantly. As government budgets for the military and the growing bureaucracies expanded, their expenditures made greater claims on the economy and began to put pressures on the gold reserves of these nations.

In the process of conquering the inhabited continents and making them into colonies, the European powers created massive standing armies, navies, and the industrial and organizational structures needed to support them. With these enormous military resources available and virtually no new lands to conquer, they fell upon one another in the First World War, the greatest bloodbath known up to that time. With the outbreak of war, the governments of Europe had an excuse to take over management of their own economies, to expand the internal power of the government over all sectors of public life, to impose taxes such as income tax in the United States. If they lacked the gold to finance their new undertakings, then—in the name of patriotism and war emergency—they simply printed the money anyway and took the country off the gold standard. As long as a country stayed on the gold standard, it limited the amount of money in circulation and thereby limited the amount of money that the government could borrow. If the people lacked the money to buy government bonds, then the government had only its tax revenues to spend.

The autonomy of the Bank of England, already chiseled away by repeated government assaults, ended with the First World War. The need of the British government to finance its army once again took precedence over the discipline of the gold standard, and the bank printed far more money than it could convert into gold. Once the government had seen how easy it was to get money without the discipline of the gold standard, it was reluctant to return to the restraints of that yoke. After the war there was a brief attempt to return to the gold standard, but in 1931, Britain permanently dropped any pretense of tying the value of its currency to its deposits of gold. The era of gold and the heyday of the Bank of England had ended.

The gold standard, which formed the heart of the international currency system administered from the Bank of England in the City of London, represented the first completely global system uniting the world. Gold had done what no conqueror or religion had managed to do: it had brought virtually all people on earth into one social system. With the collapse of that system following World War I, the governments of Europe and North America searched for new systems to replace it, because they did not want to return to the gold standard and thereby surrender the power that had been so newly won by the politicians. Instead, they tried to create international political systems, beginning with the League of Nations and later the United Nations and dozens of other political entities such as the International Monetary Fund and the World Bank, some of which have had a small practical impact in certain areas but which, for the most part, have been ineffective.

The First World War marked the end of the great era of the world currency system based on gold. H. G. Wells said that "the war arrested and ultimately broke up this unpremeditated monetary cosmopolitanism. . . . At the close of the war the practical monetary solidarity of the world had disappeared, and the overprinting of paper money continued."[5] In a certain sense World War I ended the nineteenth century and started the twentieth century, which was to be a much different era. The war crushed the delicate balance that had existed between the separate and relatively independent spheres of government and economy in Britain. Power flowed increasingly into the hands of the politicians and government administrators.

With the old monetary and economic order in ruins at the conclusion of the war, many politicians and political theorists came forward with new systems, all of which increased government power. The Communists came to power in Russia with their extreme plan for ending capitalism, destroying all markets, and having a unified economic and political system administered solely by the government in a form of international socialism. Opposed to *international* socialism, the followers of Hitler imposed a system of *national* socialism, a name that they abbreviated to *Nazism*, which imposed an equally harsh governmental control over the economy, even to the point of allowing a revival of slave labor so long as it met the political ends of the state.

Everyone seemed to be looking for a scapegoat to take the blame for the calamitous monetary and economic fallout of the era. In each country, politicians attacked the wealthy class or some particular segment of it—the aristocrats and landed peasants in Russia and the Armenians in Turkey, for example, or the Jews in Germany.

The liberal democracies of western Europe and North America settled for less extreme ideologies and measures, but they greatly increased the power of their governments over the economy. In each country, political and bureaucratic coalitions formed with certain parts of the economy. One such coalition formed around military production and deployment in what President Dwight Eisenhower called the "military-industrial complex." Later in the century another part of government formed a new set of alliances to create massive social service networks in a welfare-industrial complex. Both needed substantial amounts of government money, which had to be derived from the part of the economy that was neither welfare nor military.

THE QUEEN'S PORTRAIT

After more than two hundred years as a private institution, the Bank of England proved unable to survive the twentieth century movement toward national control over financial institutions. In a rising tide of Socialist sentiment, the Labour government nationalized the Bank of England in 1946. Because the bank was already regulated by the government and working so closely with it, the nationalization was more of a formal recognition of what had already occurred. Control over the bank's activities passed to the politically appointed chancellor of the exchequer.

Soon after the nationalization of the bank, the government decided to put the picture of the sovereign on the bills, as it has been on the coins minted by the government. Queen Elizabeth II became the first monarch whose portrait appeared on British paper currency. The monarch's portrait on the currency clearly signified that the government now held supreme control over the currency and all institutions associated with it. The nationalization of the Bank of England marked the end of a long process by which the government steadily increased its power over the financial sphere of British life and over British currency. It was the first of a long series of steps toward nationalizing the British financial system and economy.

By the end of the twentieth century, the Bank of England—the

Old Lady of Threadneedle Street—had become just one more of the world's national banks. And in comparison with the Bundesbank, which regulated the powerful deutsche mark, the venerable Bank of England could not even claim to be the most important bank in Europe, much less in the world. Not only had the U.S. dollar surpassed the British pound in importance in international markets, but so had the Japanese yen, the German mark, and the Swiss franc.

No longer independent and no longer presiding over an independent money supply based on gold, the Bank of England became one more administrative office of the government. Rather than creating monetary policy and issuing money in accordance with its gold reserves, it carried out government policy and issued the amount ordered by the politicians on the other side of London. The subordination and eventual nationalization of the Bank of England represented a major victory of politics over banking and of government over money.

For many commentators and activists on both the Right and the Left, the new power of government over money—the nationalization of money—came as a welcome relief following the nineteenth century's emphasis on wealth.

Oswald Spengler, a historian and philosopher who lived through the transition from the Victorian to the modern era, wrote that in the twentieth century, the rise of strong governments, which he labeled *Caesarism*, finally "breaks the dictature of money." He regarded the revitalized power of the state as a needed antidote to the power of the wealthy and the interests of the market: "After a long triumph of world-city economy and its interests over political creative force, the political side of life manifests itself after all as the stronger of the two." He predicted the end of the age of money: "The sword is victorious over money."[6]

11

The Yellow Brick Road

All you have to do is to knock the heels together three times and
command the shoes to carry you wherever you wish to go.

—L. FRANK BAUM

FORTUNATELY, THE ISLAND OF MANHATTAN RESTS on a solid bed of schist. A less stable material might not have been capable of holding the massive number of skyscrapers while being honeycombed with tunnels for subways, water pipes, sewage, and electrical cables. Although some of its street names—Broad Street and Broadway, for example—suggest spacious thoroughfares, in the automobile age, the streets now seem like narrow trails. They cut through the warren of granite, marble, and sandstone cliffs erected by the greatest financial institutions of the world—the Bank of Tokyo, the Federal Reserve Bank, the Chase Manhattan Bank, Citibank, the Morgan Guaranty Trust Company, the American Stock Exchange, the Equitable Building, the World Trade Center, Manufacturers Hanover Trust—and the major exchanges: the Cotton Exchange; the Coffee, Sugar and Cocoa Exchange; the Mercantile Exchange; and the Commodity Exchange. In the center of the Financial District pulses the heart of capitalism itself, the New York Stock Exchange.

On Broad Street in even the worst weather, workers from the New York Stock Exchange line the sidewalk where they smoke cigarettes and eat during lulls on the trading floor. They form a gauntlet for the lines of tourists from around the world who must undergo repetitive security checks before being admitted into the gallery.

During the latter years of the nineteenth century, New York began to replace London as the world financial center. The center had slowly worked its way from ancient Lydia across Greece and Rome, through Renaissance Florence, and then on to London during the early industrial era. Gradually, in the decades after the American Civil War, the financial center shifted from the Old World to the New.

FROM WILDCATS TO GREENBACKS

From the beginning of its history, the United States has been a nation built around money and commerce more than around its army, government, or ruling class. Founded without the European feudal system and its culture of church and chivalry, American society rested, as had perhaps no prior society in history, on a solid basis of monetary relationships. As the aristocratic French observer Alexis de Tocqueville wrote of America in the early nineteenth century, "I know of no country, indeed, where the love of money has taken stronger hold on the affections of men."[1] That hold soon created the most dynamic economy in world history.

A century after de Tocqueville, this sentiment must have been shared by President Calvin Coolidge who, on January 17, 1925, told the American Society of Newspaper Editors that "the chief business of the American people is business."

The current system of paper money in the United States is very much a product of the Civil War. Following America's first disastrous foray into printed money—the issuance of continentals during the American Revolution—the United States printed no more money for nearly a century, with the one exception of a brief period during the War of 1812.

During the first half of the nineteenth century, the United States underwent a long struggle over the control of money. It chartered and unchartered its national bank twice. The Supreme Court ruled that the individual and sovereign states could authorize state banks to issue their own notes, and consequently almost all of the paper money in circulation came in the form of state and private bank notes. Almost always desperately short of coins and without any national paper money, Americans had to find substitute forms of currency, so the banks offered the only practical substitute in the form of their own bank notes. Unfortunately, as with any newly developing system, Americans occasionally felt the sting of unscrupulous and unregulated bankers bilking them out of millions of dollars in deposits and worthless paper money. While the profession of banking in continental Europe was rising in prestige, respect, and responsibility to previously unknown heights of public trust and support, bankers in the United States became ever more despised and mistrusted for managing a disreputable, though necessary, business.

In the United States during the first half of the nineteenth century, the federal government issued all coins of silver, gold, or copper but no paper money. Since there were no federal banking laws or charters, all paper money was issued by banks operating under state law but backed by gold. From the beginning of the Republic, however, a strong political faction favored management of money and banking by the federal government. They worked hard to discredit the local banks with stories about "wildcat bankers" who printed money and then went bankrupt or of unscrupulous bankers whose chests of gold coins turned out to be filled mostly with nails or lead ingots. Such anecdotal evidence gave them a basis on which to push for the federal chartering of banks, and thereby to increase federal power over the paper notes that the banks issued.

Computer technology has allowed researchers to perform detailed empirical analyses of the records of nineteenth-century banks. They have found that despite the anecdotes about rogue banks on the frontier, most of the free banks managed the flow of paper money quite responsibly.[2] The final stripping of local banks of their power to control money came not because of financial failures but as a result of political movements to centralize power in Washington. The proponents of increased federal power found their opportunity to move against the banks during the Civil War.

The era of free banking—or wildcat banking, as its detractors called it—ended in the United States when Congress passed the National Bank Act in 1863 and thereby placed a tax on the notes issued by state banks beginning in 1866. This act established a truly national currency controlled by the federal government and federally chartered banks; but in the next few years, the federal government abused that monopoly grievously by overissuing greenbacks.

Under the administration of President Abraham Lincoln and Secretary of the Treasury Salmon Portland Chase, the federal government needed to pay for an army, but it lacked the resources. Like many governments before and since, the United States turned to the printing presses as the solution and issued paper money that was not redeemable in gold or silver. By the first Legal Tender Act, signed by President Lincoln on February 25, 1862, the government printed $150 million worth of notes in denominations of five dollars and higher. This created a multitiered currency system in which the United States demanded import taxes paid in silver or gold coins and agreed to pay interest on all government bonds in coins, but it would pay its soldiers and creditors in the second-class greenbacks streaming out of the U.S. Treasury and backed by nothing but promises.

Although issued as currency, the greenbacks might more accurately be thought of as low-denomination, non-interest-bearing government bonds. The government promised to pay the value of the notes at some unspecified time after the war. The greenbacks, then, were loans that the banks and the citizens were forced to make to the federal government in order to finance the Civil War. The government might lose the war, however, and whether it won or lost, it might decide at some future date not to pay the full price, or anything at all, for the notes. The value of the greenbacks reflected the people's confidence that the Union would actually win the war and that the government would quickly redeem its notes in gold.

A second Legal Tender Act followed on July 11, 1862, authorizing an additional $150 million to be printed. It also allowed the government, for the first time, to issue bills as small as one dollar and even to use postage stamps as change when coins could not be found. A third Legal Tender Act was passed March 3, 1863, authorizing yet another $150 million in greenbacks. As the government issued more greenbacks, their value declined until June 1864, when one hundred greenbacks had the value of only 35.09 gold dollars, slightly more than a third of their face value. But by this time it appeared that the United States would win its war, and hope that the greenbacks might day be redeemed at something near their face value gradually increased. That day did not come for another fifteen years: on January 2, 1879, citizens finally could exchange their greenbacks for an equivalent value in gold coins.[3] By then, however, the United States had recuperated from the war and had built up gold reserves worth $114 million. With the government standing behind the currency, few people felt the need to turn the greenbacks in for gold coins.

In the meantime, in the case of *Hepburn versus Griswold*, the U.S. Supreme Court in 1870 declared the issuance of greenbacks by the federal government to be illegal and unconstitutional.[4] The Court ruled that the federal government could not force a person to accept paper greenbacks in settlement of a debt made in gold-backed currency before the war. The judge behind the decision was Salmon P. Chase, whom Lincoln had appointed chief justice in 1864. In declaring the greenbacks unconstitutional, Chase ruled against himself since, in his earlier capacity of secretary of the treasury, he had been the one who first issued the greenbacks. The following year, a new Court overturned the ruling.

While the federal government faced serious monetary problems financing the war, the government of the Confederate States of America faced difficulties far more severe. According to one etymology, the name *Dixie* derived from the ten-dollar notes first issued in the 1830s by the Bank of Louisiana in New Orleans and printed in English and French. Since *dix* in French means "ten," people called the ten-dollar notes dixes. A song written by Dan Emmett for a minstrel show in 1860 included the sentence "I wish I wuz in de land of de Dixes." Thus the Confederacy came to be called Dixie. Whether this is a valid etymology or not, it would be fitting if the nickname of the South derived from paper money because money played such an important role in the short history and devastating destruction of the Confederate States of America.

Whereas the United States eventually issued a total of $450 million in paper during the Civil War, the Confederacy issued more than twice as many notes totaling approximately $1 billion. Prices rose at a rate of about 10 percent a month until March 1861, and throughout the remainder of the war they increased another ninety-fold. Goods that cost $100 in U.S. currency in 1860 had increased to

$146 by 1865. During the same period in the South, prices increased from $100 to $9,211 in Confederate dollars. It is phenomenal that the hastily formed Confederate government could fight the war as it did and sustain itself for so long with real resources on just roughly $37 million at the start. As John Kenneth Galbraith wrote, "The miracle of the Confederacy, like the miracle of Rome, was not that it fell but that it survived so long."[5]

Unlike the greenbacks that the federal government redeemed fifteen years after the war, no one could redeem the billion dollars issued by the Confederate government. Many families in the South saved their worthless Confederate money for decades after the war, but redemption never came. Because of the collapse of the money system of the Confederacy together with the destruction of its infrastructure and capital, the South, which had been the richest area in North America before the war, remained the poorest part of the nation for more than a century after the war.

The federal government emerged from the Civil War as the victor, not merely because it had defeated the South but also because it had finally managed to assert control over all of the states and over the nation's money. It had destroyed the states' power to regulate the issuance of notes through state-chartered banks; it had defeated the many banks that issued their own money around the country; and it had defeated the South militarily, politically, and economically. With the end of the Civil War, the federal dollar reigned supreme in the United States, and henceforth the federal government and federally chartered banks controlled the nation's money.

New voices rose to demand that the government issue more paper money and unlimited silver coins. In 1874 the Greenback Party formed with heavy support from the poor farmers of the West, but it fared poorly in national elections and dissolved within a decade. The People's Party of the U.S.A.—better known as the Populist Party—picked up some of the Greenbackers' demands, including a call for the government to issue fifty dollars per capita in federal currency for every citizen.[6] Although the party mobilized a large following of southern and western farmers, it too failed to win national elections and dissolved after the 1892 election.

THE CROSS OF GOLD AND THE WIZARD OF OZ

Populism had tremendous appeal in the southern states where poverty and resentment seemed the greatest. The people felt trapped between the Republican bankers of the North and the newly freed slaves, against whom they had to compete in the open labor market. Populist politicians found that they could do relatively little to control the bankers and the wealthy elite, but in the newly freed slaves they found a scapegoat for all their problems and complaints. In addition to their quest for a looser money supply, the Populists, particularly in the states of the former Confederacy, advocated a radically new system of racial segregation.

Even though they lost all national elections, the Populists managed to win control of all of the southern states and several western ones. By the 1890s the southern Populists had managed to remove all African-Americans and people of mixed racial ancestry, as well as all Republicans, from political office by severely restricting the number of nonwhites who could vote. As they took the South, the Populists segregated schools, housing, public buildings, and all modes of public transportation. They prohibited racially mixed marriages, disinherited all mixed-race children from their white parent, and classified as a Negro anyone with as little as one-sixteenth African heritage. The institutions of legal segregation that they established lasted for well over half a century, from the 1890s until the passage of the federal Civil Rights Act of 1964, long after most people had forgotten precisely how the system originated.

Even though the Populist programs had a tremendous impact on the lives of African-Americans, they had comparatively little on the bankers or on the monetary system of the country, which became even more gold-oriented. During most the remainder of the nineteenth century, different political factions fought over whether the United States should have only the gold standard or both the gold and the silver standard. Farmers usually lived in debt to banks for the mortgages of their farms and sometimes for the equipment and even the seed for planting. They borrowed in gold notes and had to repay their debts in gold notes, but the price of gold increased over the course of the century as the price of their commodities dropped. At harvesttime they received less money for their produce; yet they had to pay the bankers in gold notes, which were ever more costly. They wanted more money put in circulation, and one way to do that was by the free coinage of silver. The Populist farmers of the West and the South wanted silver as well as gold currency. With more currency around, they believed they would be less at the mercy of bankers and politicians from the cities.

Populist senator William Jennings Bryan from the farm state of Nebraska, the perennial Democratic candidate for president during a consistently Republican era, campaigned tirelessly for bimetallism, the use of both silver and gold as a monetary standard. In his famous acceptance speech after receiving the presidential nomination at the 1896 Democratic convention, Bryan aimed carefully at the bankers, financiers, Republicans, and all other goldbugs: "You came to tell us that the great cities are in favor of the gold standard; we reply that the great cities rest upon our broad and fertile plains. Burn down your cities and leave our farms, and your cities will spring up again as if by magic; but destroy our farms and the grass will grow in the city." He concluded his speech with one of the most famous lines in nineteenth-century political oratory: "You shall not press down upon the brow of labor this crown of thorns. You shall not crucify mankind upon a cross of gold." Despite the thunderous applause of his fellow Democrats, he suffered a decisive defeat by the Republican nominee, William McKinley, in 1896 and again in 1900.

Although William Jennings Bryan continued to run for office, he never won a national election. Not until after the election of Woodrow Wilson, the first Democratic president since the Civil War, did Bryan receive a prominent office when he became the secretary of state in 1913. He resigned in 1915, though, when it became clear that Wilson was leading the United States toward involvement in the war in Europe, a move that the staunch isolationist Bryan opposed almost as vehemently as the gold standard.

The most memorable work of literature to come from the debate over gold and silver in the United States was *The Wonderful Wizard of Oz*, published in 1900, by journalist L. Frank Baum, who greatly distrusted the power of the city financiers and who supported a bimetallic dollar based on both gold and silver. Taking great literary license, he summarized and satirized the monetary debate and history of the era through a charming story about a naive but good Kansas farm girl named Dorothy, who represented the average rural American citizen. Baum seems to have based her character on the Populist orator Leslie Kelsey, nicknamed "the Kansas Tornado."

After the cyclone violently rips Dorothy and her dog out of Kansas and drops them in the East, Dorothy sets out on the gold road to fairyland, which Baum calls Oz, where the wicked witches and wizards of banking operate. Along the way she meets the Scarecrow, who represents the American farmer; the Tin Woodman, who represents the American factory worker; and the Cowardly Lion, who represents William Jennings Bryan. The party's march on Oz is a re-creation of the 1894 march of Coxey's Army, a group of unemployed men led by "General" Jacob S. Coxey to demand another public issue of $500 million greenbacks and more work for common people.

Marcus Hanna, the power behind the Republican Party and the McKinley administration, was the wizard controlling the mechanisms of finance in the Emerald City. He was the Wizard of the Gold Ounce—abbreviated, of course, to Wizard of Oz—and the Munchkins were the simpleminded people of the East who did not understand how the wizard and his fellow financiers pulled the levers and strings that controlled the money, the economy, and the government.

In the Emerald City ruled by the Wizard of Oz, the people were required to wear green-colored glasses attached by a gold buckle. Beyond the city, the Wicked Witch of the West had enslaved the yellow Winkies, a reference to the imperialist aims of the Republican administration, which had captured the Philippines from Spain and refused to grant them independence.

In the end, all the good American citizens had to do was expose the wizard and his witches for the frauds they were, and all would be well in the bimetal monetary world of silver and gold. In the process, the farmer Scarecrow found out how intelligent he was, the lion found his courage, and the working Tin Man received a new source of strength in a bimetallic tool—a golden ax with a blade of silver—

and he would never rust again as long as he had his silver oil can encrusted with gold and jewels.

In the book, Dorothy's magic silver slippers got her back to Kansas, but in movie starring child actress Judy Garland, the magic slippers were ruby red, a more dramatic color on the screen than silver. By this time, however, few people realized that the book, which they now perceived as a children's story, had anything to do with U.S. monetary policy at the opening of the twentieth century. In the same year that Baum published his allegorical tale, Congress passed the Gold Standard Act of 1900, further committing the United States to a currency based on the single commodity of gold.[7]

The Populists continued to press the United States to follow a policy of bimetallism using gold and silver, but they eventually lost that struggle. The discovery of vast new deposits of gold in South Africa, Alaska, and Colorado roughly doubled the world's supply, thereby easing the currency shortage. The Populists got their inflated money without having to switch to silver, and between 1897 and 1914 prices rose nearly 50 percent in the United States and about 26 percent in Britain.[8] The United States and most of the rest of the world stayed on the gold standard, and yet there was more money for everyone.

12

The Golden Playpen of Politics

> *Money is the lifeblood of the nation.*
> —JONATHAN SWIFT

IN THE ROLLING HILLS OF NORTHERN KENTUCKY, AT a tightly guarded military base, the U.S. government stores its largest gold hoard. The Fort Knox Bullion Depository contains approximately 4,600 tons of pure gold with a market price of approximately $58 billion. This cache, along with 1,781 tons at West Point, 1,368 tons at Denver, and a little less than 1,000 tons in other parts of the Federal Reserve, gives the United States a total of some 8,000 tons of gold with a market value of approximately $100 billion.

Unlike the mints, which make coins, and the Bureau of Engraving, which prints paper money, the guardians of the gold reserves in Fort Knox entertain no visitors. Would-be tourists are not even admitted onto the military base, much less into the secured depository managed by the Treasury Department in the middle of the base. Because of this security, the very name of Fort Knox has become a synonym for wealth and security.

Because gold does not rot, rust, or deteriorate, the gold sitting in Fort Knox today may have been mined hundreds or even thousands of years ago. It could have been made into many objects and melted many times through the years. Some of it may date back to the ancient gold mines of Nubia in Africa and Lydia in Asia Minor. Almost assuredly some of it came from the booty seized from the Aztecs of Mexico by Hernán Cortés and from the Incas of Peru by Francisco Pizarro. Some of the gold may once have been Byzantine coins or part of a headdress from the ancient empire of Ghana. Some was panned from the Yukon in the nineteenth century by Irish and Scottish prospectors, and some lifted from the deep mines of South Africa by Zulu and Xhosa tribesmen. The whole history of gold on earth now rests in these chambers.

The gold is stored in bars of 1,000 ounces each. The bars need no wrapping or other protection since they do not flake or deteriorate. Aside from small amounts taken out for sale to make commemorative coins for events such as the Olympics, the gold sits and waits.

Many governments store some of their bullion in a silent vault within the bedrock of lower Manhattan Island, eighty feet below street level in the Federal Reserve Bank. It is stacked in bars, each weighing approximately 400 troy ounces and having a market price of around $160,000. The gold is divided among several different chambers, the largest of which contains a wall composed of 107,000 gold bricks stacked 10 feet high, 10 feet wide, and 18 feet deep. Deposited by many governments, the 10,000 tons of gold bars have a value of more than $125 billion. The vault contains about a quarter of all the mined gold in the world.

Many of us regard these hoards of gold as a kind of psychic security that backs up the dollars we carry in our pockets and purses. The gold at Fort Knox and in the Federal Reserve is believed to represent the American monetary system. Our government makes no effort to counter that notion, but it is merely one of the many myths that otherwise rational and well-informed people hold about money today. In truth, the gold in Fort Knox and the Federal Reserve actually has nothing to do with the American dollar. Since President Richard Nixon severed the final tie between the dollar and gold, not one ounce of gold anywhere in the world stands behind the U.S. dollar. The piles of gold are part of the wealth of the American government, as are the government storehouses filled with soybeans, nickel, and old furniture, but they are not a part of the money system. The dollar no more rests on the gold at Fort Knox than on the government stockpiles of processed cheese kept in its refrigerated warehouses.

Our dollar is neither a silver dollar nor a gold one. The government will not redeem a dollar bill for anything other than another dollar bill. The dollar is simply fiat currency. The dollar rests on the power of the government and the faith of the people who use it—faith that it will be able to buy something tomorrow, faith that the U.S. government will continue to exist and to accept dollars in payment of taxes and pay them out in expenses, and faith that other people will continue to believe in it. Aside from that faith, nothing backs up the dollar.

THE NATIONALIZATION OF GOLD

According to the act that set up the American currency system in 1792, anyone could bring gold or silver to the mint and the "bullion so brought shall be assayed and coined as speedily as may be after the receipt thereof, and that free of expense to the person or persons by whom the same shall have been brought."[1] To encourage people to turn their bullion into coins, the U.S. government did not even charge the usual seigniorage for its services. This free service was meant to encourage miners and others to convert their precious metals into coins as quickly and easily as possible, thus increasing the amount of money in circulation in the newly formed country.

The problem with a gold-based currency is that it is limited by the amount of gold in the world, and that amount fluctuates with each new find and each new development in technology. At times, newly discovered gold floods the market unexpectedly. At other times, it trickles in very slowly even though the economy may desperately need an infusion of money. Sometimes governments, banks, and even wealthy individuals can temporarily manipulate the gold market for their own benefit, but for the most part, it operates beyond the control of individuals and even nations.

The necessity of converting the money to gold on demand prevents the government from making too many loans or issuing too much money in order to satisfy a temporary political problem. As long as the citizens have the right to turn their paper money into gold, they hold a vote on how the monetary system works and how much faith they have in their politicians. As soon as they lose confidence in the paper, they can convert to gold and abandon the paper.

The United States detached its money from bullion and all other commodities through two major steps, the first one taken by President Franklin Roosevelt in 1933, the second by President Richard Nixon in 1971. Roosevelt acted in response to the stock market crash of 1929, which caused a run on the banks as depositors sought to exchange their paper money for gold, as the government had guaranteed. One of Roosevelt's first acts as president was to take the United States off the gold standard in order to stimulate the economy and increase the government's ability to borrow money to finance his economic and social policies.

By an act of March 9, 1933, "to provide relief in the existing national emergency in banking and other purposes," Congress gave Roosevelt the power to prevent the "hoarding" of gold. By Roosevelt's executive order a month later U.S. citizens and residents could no longer redeem their dollars for gold, but externally, the United States remained on the gold standard so that other countries and foreign banks could still convert their dollars into gold as they needed.

Roosevelt also nationalized gold and made it a crime punishable by arrest and imprisonment for an American citizen to hold gold bullion or coins. Banks, financial institutions, and private citizens had three weeks in which to turn in all gold coins, bullion, and even gold certificates. Each person could keep one hundred dollars in gold coins or certificates and personal jewelry, so long as the jewelry was not made of coins. Roosevelt allowed an exemption for specific industrial and artistic purposes. Also, coin collectors could keep rare gold coins, but the law limited them to only two specimens of any issue.

Refugees fleeing the rising wave of turmoil and tyranny in Europe for the freedom of America found that on arrival in the United States, they had to surrender all of the gold they brought with them. American tourists returning from abroad could no longer bring in gold coins or jewelry containing gold coins. If they did not voluntarily declare and surrender such items at the border, customs agents confiscated them. Gold bars, coins, ingots, bonds, and certificates had joined the list of controlled substances and contraband goods such as narcotics, Communist literature, and pornography, that were forbidden entry into the United States.

Those people who voluntarily surrendered their gold to the Department of the Treasury within nine months of Roosevelt's order received compensation of $20.67 per ounce in paper notes. One year after confiscating the privately owned gold, on January 31, 1934, the federal government devalued the paper money from $20.67 to $35 for each ounce of gold. Thus, everyone who had complied with the law and exchanged gold for paper lost 41 percent of the gold's value.[2] The change in the official price of gold increased the nominal value of the government's gold hoard and thus allowed it to issue an additional $3 billion in paper currency.

The Treasury melted down the gold coins and other objects to make gold bricks. Exercising the unprecedented power granted to it during the Roosevelt administration, the federal government confiscated some 5 million ounces of gold—officially worth about $1.6 billion in gold bullion—from its citizens between 1933 and 1954. Although officials of the Treasury Department kept a careful record of the weight and purity of the coins that its officials melted, they did not record the dates or designs of the coins; so it is now difficult to ascertain how much of America's earlier gold coin heritage survived.

In 1934, the year after the nationalization of gold, President Roosevelt passed another law nationalizing silver in much the same way. People could keep their jewelry and a certain amount of silver for use in art and industry, but the remainder had to be turned over to the government. Many U.S. coins at that time still contained silver, and Roosevelt could not seize them without drastically disrupting commerce, but the government later began gradually removing silver coins from circulation and replacing them with base metals. Before the law was repealed in 1963, the government acquired a total of more than 3.2 billion ounces of silver.[3]

In order to house the new reserves of precious metal collected from the American people, the Treasury constructed the massive vault at Fort Knox at a cost of $560,000. The granite building is lined with concrete on a steel frame and is composed of 16,000 cubic feet of granite, 4,200 cubic yards of concrete, 750 tons of reinforcing steel, and 670 tons of structural steel. In the marble-lined entry the legend "United States Depository" is engraved in gold, along with the gold seal of the Treasury Department. The elaborate building and its widely publicized strength serve as a symbol of the value of the U.S. currency as much as it does for actual protection of the gold warehoused in it.

Work on the depository was completed in December 1936, and from January to June of the following year, the office of the mint transferred gold to Fort Knox. Americans were not allowed to own gold coins again until December 31, 1974, according to a bill signed by President Gerald Ford. By then the dollar had no official government fixed value in gold.

With the successful invasion of Europe at Normandy by the Allied forces, victory over the Germans became certain and attention began to switch to preparations for the postwar period. Everyone agreed that the victorious Allied powers should do all they could to avoid the mistakes made at the end of the First World War, which had resulted in reparations, inflation, and finally a global depression, all of which had paved the way for yet another world conflict, even deadlier than the first.

In July 1944, one month after D day, the United States called for an Allied conference on economics to decide what kind of economic and monetary order the world should have. This conference, composed of seven hundred delegates from forty-four nations, met at a resort hotel in New Hampshire near a mountain peak ominously named Mount Deception. According to the agreement that they signed on July 22, 1946, most currencies of the world were pegged to specific values relative to the U.S. dollar, and, in turn, the United States set the value of the dollar at thirty-five dollars to an ounce of gold. The delegates also laid the groundwork for the establishment of the World Bank and the International Monetary Fund, and they prepared to begin the tariff reduction negotiations that would continue for the next fifty years. Rather than naming their agreement after the mountain on which it was signed, they chose to name it Bretton Woods, after the mailing address of the hotel where they stayed.

From February 1, 1934, until the 1960s, the governments of the United States and other nations worked together to keep the value of the dollar fixed at thirty-five dollars per ounce of gold, but by the 1960s, the increased supply of dollars and the concomitant inflation made it difficult for the central banks of the world to maintain this level.

NIXON'S FOLLY

Plagued by economic difficulties at home and with an economy severely strained by a war in Vietnam, the U.S. suffered severe inflation. President Nixon, like President Johnson, had difficulty getting Congress to appropriate sufficient money for the war in Vietnam. Congress would not raise taxes to pay for the war. Faced with an unpopular war that the American people showed no willingness to finance, Nixon and Johnson had financed it the way rulers had done for centuries—by borrowing. They borrowed billions of dollars, and as they spent it, the rapidly increasing supply of money created inflation. The United States could no longer redeem its money in gold on the world market.

To generate even more money needed for the war, Nixon devised a bold new economic policy that he had worked out with Secretary of the Treasury John Connally, a former governor of Texas. Connally's only claim to national prominence was that he happened to be sitting in the car next to President John F. Kennedy in Dallas on the fateful day of his assassination in 1963 and was himself wounded in the attack. Connally had a reputation as a hard-playing politician, a sort of minor league version of the more famous Texas politician Lyndon Johnson, but he certainly showed no talent in the realm of economics or finance. This became clear later in his life when he went bankrupt and had to hold a public auction of his belongings in his Texas home.

Under the Nixon-Connally plan, the president asked all business owners to freeze prices, wages, and rents in order to combat inflation, and he put a 10 percent surcharge on most imports to help improve the trade balance. To ensure compliance with the temporary freezes, he requested that citizens report to the federal government anyone found raising prices or rents. Almost unnoticed among all these dramatic and unprecedented political measures in a peacetime economy, Richard Nixon closed the "gold window." This meant that the dollar would no longer be pegged to a specific value in any commodity; it would float relative to all other currencies. The badly wounded U.S. dollar had become another casualty of the Vietnam war.

Of all Nixon's advisers, only Paul McCracken spoke out strongly against the price freeze.[4] Few commentators paid attention to what seemed like a quaint monetary holdover from the Victorian era that had little place in the world of atomic bombs and computers. The gold standard seemed irrelevant in the modern age where the dollar reigned as the mightiest currency in the world and where most other currencies were based on it at seemingly permanent rates. Nixon and Connally had managed to convince the American public that closing the gold window was a shrewd move against foreign speculators. This move, however, ended the era of stability and the period of greatest economic prosperity and productivity in the history of the American dollar. The dollar never regained its historical strength, nor has it since enjoyed the confidence that the world had in it prior to Nixon's move.

In March 1972, U.S. government officials devalued the dollar to $38.00 per ounce of gold. The following year they had to devalue it again to $42.22. The Swiss government said that beginning on January 24, 1973, it would no longer support the dollar with gold, and other nations quickly followed.

Between Franklin Roosevelt's decrees in 1933 and Richard Nixon's actions in 1971, the United States went from a dollar based on precious metal to one based solely on government regulation. Today's American dollar is merely fiat money, backed by the order of the government and by people's faith in that order and nothing more. The gold notes and the silver certificate dollar long ago gave way to the Federal Reserve Note. The phrase "Payable to the Bearer on Demand" has been replaced by "In God We Trust."

By severing the tie between gold and the dollar, Nixon left the price of gold free to rise and let the value of the dollar fluctuate freely relative to the English pound, the German mark, the Japanese yen, the Swiss franc, and all the other currencies of the world. And fluctuate it did. At first, it changed only moderately, but as the troughs dipped ever lower, the fluctuations began to grow steeper and the climb upward never quite reached high enough before the dollar headed downward again. Before anyone fully realized how it had happened, the dollar was on a roller coaster, but the Japanese yen and the German mark seemed to be on an ever upward track while the dollar fluctuated in the short run but fell in the long run.

The ounce of gold that had cost $35.00 in 1971 had increased to approximately $400.00 by 1995. The mark that had cost $.24 had risen to $.75, and the yen that had sold four for a penny was now worth well over a penny. While the dollar hurtled up and down the roller coaster, the currencies of poorer countries like Peru and Bolivia, which had once been pegged to the dollar, flew off the track. Still others, such as the Mexican peso, lost their wheels, and even the Canadian dollar grew weak and wobbly. Without the discipline of gold, twentieth-century money has steadily deteriorated in value. As Chaucer asked in the prologue to the *Canterbury Tales*, "if gold ruste, what shal iren do?"

Throughout the twentieth century, the power of governments to control money grew tremendously in virtually all parts of the world. This increased control allowed government authorities to print more money, to borrow, or to do whatever they wished when they needed to increase spending or adjust the economy. As governments increased their spending, they also increased their power over the economy in thousands of large and small ways. No longer constrained by the need to have a specific gold reserve for each unit of money issued, the governments simply issued more money to finance their new undertakings.

Politicians can always conjure up good reasons to tamper with the money; they often set out to combat some great evil lurking over the horizon or avert some horrific disaster looming in our children's future. When Franklin Roosevelt took the United States off the gold standard internally, it was for good reasons—to end the Depression and then to fight World War II. Then the United States had to rebuild Europe and combat communism, which encouraged more debts. Lyndon Johnson encouraged the politicians to accumulate more debt to fight the war in Vietnam and simultaneously conduct the War on Poverty at home.

Rather than reversing Johnson's policies when it became apparent that the United States was losing both wars, Richard Nixon took the dollar off the gold standard completely. With the financial freedom granted by the new easy money, politicians on both the Right and the Left could finance whatever pet projects they might support—more highways and food stamps, exploration of outer space and increased agricultural subsidies, foreign aid and urban housing, Star Wars weapons and art endowments, cancer research and fighting the narcotics trade. The country had enough money to finance the ruthless regimes of friendly dictators and to invade or pay for guerrilla wars against small countries run by unfriendly dictators. It seemed that everyone could have everything. The politicians, lobbyists, and special interests had tapped into the magic formula for generating wealth from air.

Symbolically, the growing state control over money can be seen in the changing designs used to embellish coins and notes. Early in our history, all U.S. coins bore the image of an Indian, a deity, an animal, or an allegorical figure symbolizing freedom, liberty, or some other abstract ideal. Beginning in 1909, however, the government abandoned the Indian-head penny in favor of the Lincoln penny. Thereafter, each coin in turn was changed to bear the image of an American politician. The first portraits were those of the Founding Fathers, but gradually more contemporary images began to appear. The Standing Liberty quarter became the George Washington quarter. The silver dollar with an image of crowned Liberty became the Eisenhower dollar, the buffalo nickel became the Thomas Jefferson nickel, and the Winged Mercury dime, also known as the Liberty dime, took the portrait of President Franklin Roosevelt. The Walking Liberty fifty-cent piece became the Benjamin Franklin fifty-cent piece and then the John Kennedy half-dollar.

Paper bills that had carried scenes from American history and allegorical images similar to those on the coins also switched to portraits of politicians. The largest bill ever issued by the United States was a $100,000 gold certificate that bore the portrait of President Woodrow Wilson.

With the changes in these images, the United States had moved completely away from money based on and redeemable in gold to a system of money based solely on the policies of politicians, bureaucrats, and government regulatory agencies. Money no longer had any independent value; it depended entirely on the people's confidence in their political system and leaders.

The twentieth century became the era of government-regulated currency systems around the world. Under the fashionable theories of the time, it appeared that good, wise decision-makers in the government, or in government-supported institutions protected from public opinion, could control the supply of money rationally and methodically. As a sort of impartial thermostat they could use specific methods to fine-tune the economy—by setting interest rates, for example, or by controlling how much foreign currency banks could buy and sell.

The political enthusiasm of the twentieth century also advocated government leadership in engineering everything from the elimination of poverty and racism to curing cancer and dandruff and from managing the transportation systems to regulating sexuality and birth control. Various governments took up an ideological war against their perceived enemies—communism, capitalism, fascism, Nazism, or diverse forms of fundamentalism—and they built rockets with which to conquer the moon and explore outer space.

By the end of the century it had become apparent that some national governments had assumed too many responsibilities that they could not properly meet. The Communist governments, which had assumed the greatest role, simply collapsed and became unable to perform even the most basic functions. In the more affluent democracies of the West, governments merely stumbled. They did not collapse, but it became apparent to the people that a government that had trouble delivering mail on time might also have trouble running the currency and overseeing the economy. A government that could not control the selling of cocaine and heroin might also have trouble policing the monetary system. A government that could not make its streets safe for its citizens or even keep the school grounds safe for children and teachers might also have problems keeping the nation's money supply safe and free of corruption.

Phase III

ELECTRONIC MONEY

*We invented money and we use it, yet we cannot . . . understand its
laws or control its actions. It has a life of its own.*
—LIONEL TRILLING

13
Wild Money and the Stealth Tax

If making money is a slow process, losing it is quickly done.
—SAIKAKU IHARA

TWO MEN WALKED AWKWARDLY DOWN THE STREET carrying a cardboard box of money between them. With difficulty they maneuvered the box through the doorway of a travel agency. The box was not large, but the bulk weight of so many bills made it heavy. Once inside, the men set the box on a table in front of a female clerk who summoned an assistant to bring coffee and empanadas for the two customers. Then, as the two men and the clerk watched, another assistant began emptying the box of money onto the table. The bills had been placed in the box with great care, and the clerk took them out with equal care and spread them across the marble table. Most of the bills were 10,000-peso notes. These bills had been carefully arranged in stacks of ten notes, each stack totaling 100,000 pesos and having the size and thickness of a pack of cigarettes. These wads of ten had been bundled together to make a stack of one million pesos, which was then bound carefully with rubber bands into a packet the size of a brick but heavier. The box contained eighty of these brick-sized million-peso stacks plus a few additional wads. To count the entire box would have taken a while. Instead the checker merely counted the packets of bills to make sure that each brick contained the right number of wads. If it was short a few hundred thousand pesos, no one would ever know.

Despite the shortcut in counting, it took the checker over half an hour to verify that the box contained 85 million pesos, the price of an airline ticket. As soon as the money had been counted, the checker loaded it onto the back of a motor scooter and carried it across town to the offices of Lloyd Aero Boliviano, the Bolivian airline, to pay for the ticket before the price increased again at lunchtime. To save time counting money, some checkers had learned to measure the stack of bills. Experience taught them that a stack of a certain height should contain a specific number of bills. If all the bills were of the same color, and thus the same denomination, the counter could quickly calculate the value based on the size of the stack. The less educated and often illiterate but still astute market women who operated the town markets throughout the Andes often resorted to weighing the bills to determine their value.

At the height of the Bolivian inflation in 1985, the Coffee, Sugar, and Cocoa Exchange of New York launched an advertising campaign by mailing a money clip containing a Bolivian note for one million pesos to each of two thousand commodities brokers around the United States. The accompanying letter explained that less than three years ago the bill had had a value of $5,000, but because of inflation its value had dropped to only $.55, one-thousandth of its original value. The advertisers hoped the ploy would help move more Americans out of cash and into commodities. To add further insult to the plight of Bolivia, the exchange sponsored a contest in which they offered a week's paid vacation in La Paz, Bolivia.[1]

In a market where million-peso notes eventually have the value of only a few cents and where a cup of coffee can cost 12 million pesos, notes in the denomination of mere hundreds or thousands have a value of only one-hundredth or one-thousandth of a U.S. penny, and are thus virtually worthless. Once they have lost their value as money, such bills have almost no practical use. They contain too much ink for use as scratch paper, and they are too small to use for wrapping paper. The ink makes the bills impractical as rolling paper for cigarettes, and they are too stiff for personal hygiene. People discard the old bills, which the wind blows down the street and piles up in muddy clumps in the sewage ditches beside the roads, along the banks of the river, or in the bushes of vacant lots. Even tin cans and plastic drink bottles have more utility and are more carefully guarded than recently devalued money.

COCAINE CASH

During hyperinflation, as in Bolivia in 1984 and 1985, the economy operates on a cash-only basis. No one accepts payment by check or credit card because clearance takes far too long. Consequently no one keeps money on deposit in the bank. Banks make no loans because of difficulty determining the interest rate. Credit, in the local currency, ceases to exist. Even services such as telephone and electricity, which are supplied on a monthly basis and billed at the end of the month, demand advance payment unless they are government services, in which case customers wait as long as possible to pay their bills, because a bill for fifty dollars could drop to only a few pennies within a week.

Hyperinflation follows a similar pattern wherever it strikes. Banks stop financing mortgages. Would-be home buyers and even businesses pay for their buildings as they progress. A conscientious family buys bricks or bags of cement as quickly as they acquire the money, even though they build the house slowly, over years or even decades. Because of this practice of investing in building materials, the cities and countryside seem to be filled with partially constructed houses, walls without roofs, houses without windows, and bare-brick structures without stucco, all of which gives the neighborhoods a deteriorated and sloppy appearance.

During hyperinflation, fixed incomes no longer exist. People on pensions or retirement find the value of their payments reduced to only a few dollars a month. Even though government offices adjust the checks, they are usually weeks behind the inflation rate in an economy where even one week can reduce the value of the money by 99 percent.

At the height of the Bolivian inflation, employers paid workers in stacks of bills, bundled in the familiar wads and bricks. On payday, a university professor in Sucre, for example, would expect to receive a stack of bills about half a meter or nineteen inches in length; a secretary might receive a stack of only half that. As soon as the employee received the cash, he or she would dash off to convert the money into commodities such as food, clothing, or electronic goods—anything that would maintain its value and might be used by the family or resold. Even families without electricity would eagerly buy a high-prestige item such as a CD player, since it would retain its resale value long after the wad of cash would have lost all value. Even after months or a year of use, the CD player could be resold for many times its original cost.

Peasants who came into the urban markets of Bolivia to sell their crops could not take the money home without its losing much of its value before the next market. Consequently they had to spend their money in the city immediately after acquiring it and take the goods back with them. Thus, while the city operated on a cash-only basis, villages had virtually no cash. Their citizens returned to more traditional systems of barter and exchange.

The most popular purchase of all was U.S. dollars of any denomination, since they held their value far longer than the quickly deteriorating national currency of Bolivia. The plentiful supply of dollars, particularly one-hundred-dollar bills, was due primarily to Bolivia's main export: coca paste for the manufacture of cocaine.

Bolivia had far more American hundred-dollar bills than it had tens, fives, or ones. This excess of hundred-dollar bills meant that smaller bills, which were needed to make change, could be found only at a premium. The market created an odd situation in which a stack of one hundred one-dollar bills had a greater value than a single hundred-dollar bill. Customers eagerly exchanged a hundred-dollar note for ninety-seven one-dollar bills.

The United States was battling its own inflation during this time, with the dollar losing about 3.6 percent of its value annually. The dollar was the currency against which Bolivians measured all others. The value of the Bolivian peso relative to the U.S. dollar changed twice a day, once in the morning and again in the afternoon. Calculated on an annual basis, the rate of inflation in Bolivia reached 24,000 percent, and over the course of the hyperinflation the value declined by a total of 40,000 percent. These figures carried little relevance to daily life, however. The more pressing fact was that the peso was declining at a rate of 1 to 2 percent an hour. Under such conditions, a peculiar inflation culture developed whereby the people coped with such strange circumstances.

Because of the rise in the use of plastics, Bolivia could no longer rely on its traditional export of tin, and the government had borrowed far beyond its ability to repay. In the upside-down world of the Bolivian economy in the 1980s, cocaine became the primary export and cash became the country's primary import. Because the government lacked the facilities to print its own money, Bolivia imported its own currency notes by the thousands of tons from Germany, Brazil, and Argentina. The pallets of new peso bills had to be flown into La Paz, the administrative and financial capital of Bolivia, as quickly as possible, since the people and the authorities could not wait for it to be sent by surface transport. Similarly, illegal markets imported millions of U.S. dollars by air to service the "informal economy." The narco-bankers landed their planes on private airstrips in the Beni region, from which the American bills quickly circulated around the country. By destroying the value of the peso, the managers of the nation's money had provided a gap that the narcotics traffickers quickly filled. The drug traffickers supplied American dollars while Bolivian authorities could only supply the nearly worthless pesos; the traffickers controlled the dollar supply and thereby kept a dangerous grip on the economy of the nation.

The abundance of dollars in Bolivia created an alternative currency and further weakened the peso. Whereas the peso was merely an internal money, the dollar represented an international currency and was therefore far more popular than the peso, thus further reducing the value of the peso and further exacerbating the inflation.

In such times of runaway inflation, currency speculation becomes a major business for virtually the entire adult community. Hundreds of people line the streets exchanging pesos for dollars on the illegal but tolerated black market. Currency traders walk the streets, and messengers scurry back and forth exchanging dollars for pesos and pesos for dollars. Because store transactions must be made in the national currency, shoppers arrive with dollars, which they trade for pesos on the street before entering the store. Because the shopkeeper does not want to be left with large numbers of pesos at the end of the day, when the customer leaves, he sends the newly arrived pesos to a currency trader to trade them back into dollars. Often the same traders may trade the exact same bills several times in a day, charging, of course, a small fee each time. These small fees and the high turnover make the currency trader's job much more lucrative than that of the businessmen who exchange goods.

Every business, from the large national airline to the woman selling shelled nuts on the street corner, must know the value of the peso relative to that of the dollar at all times of the day and must play a constant game of shuffling pesos, dollars, and goods. As in a game of musical chairs, everyone knows that at any moment of the day, week, or year, the rates could suddenly change, and whoever has too much of one currency and not enough of the other will lose.

Hyperinflation cannot last long because it destroys the capital markets and makes cash increasingly unwieldy. To keep up with the changing value of the currency and the large stacks of bills, people mentally lop off the zeros. In everyday market transactions, a million pesos simply becomes one and ten million pesos becomes ten. This may suffice for buying groceries and other small purchases, but for higher-priced items such as refrigerators and automobiles, people simply abandon the peso terminology entirely and discuss prices in dollars, regardless of whether payment will be made in dollars or pesos. Production and commerce gradually slow as people spend more and more of their daily lives searching for ways to escape the cost of inflation.

As pressure increases on the government to control the inflation, and as the national economy continues to deteriorate, the government must eventually issue a new currency that removes the zeroes and returns the currency to between one and ten to the dollar. Although hyperinflation is devastating for some segments of the population, others—debtors, for example—benefit from it. During inflation loans that once totaled thousands of dollars are reduced to only a few cents.

Although the neighboring countries did not all share Bolivia's unusual cocaine economy, they did face economic and social problems that resulted in similar bouts of severe inflation. As hyperinflation progressed in Peru, Brazil, and Argentina, the economies of those countries also became dollarized—that is, they remained peso economies superficially, but they were in fact becoming dollar economies. Loans, contracts, and other financial dealings, both formal and informal, were increasingly transacted in dollars rather than in the national currency.

In 1990, when Alberto Fujimori took over as president of Peru, the country had an inflation rate of 7,000 percent. The sol, the Peruvian national currency, accounted for only 15 percent of the currency in use; U.S. dollars accounted for the remaining 85 percent. As inflation subsided, however, the use of the sol climbed and use of the dollar declined.[2]

4.2 TRILLION MARKS TO THE DOLLAR

Although inflation existed in the past, particularly in the century following the introduction of the gold and silver taken from the Americas by the conquistadores, the twentieth century has proved to be its heyday, and hyperinflation seems to be unique to modern times. As long as currency retained some metallic base such as gold, silver, or even copper, hyperinflation could not occur because the amount of money in circulation depended ultimately on the number of coins that could be produced. Inflation developed only when the supply of silver or gold expanded, thereby increasing the number of coins in circulation; but ultimately the major control on the amount of money was the amount of available gold and silver.

Unlike worthless bills, even a small copper coin has some inherent value as metal. If all else fails it can be melted and used for some other purpose. With the arrival of the paper money era, governments found themselves in a whole new economic world. So long as they had access to paper, ink, and printing machines, they could print as much money as they liked. And so they did.

Governments have three primary ways of financing their expenditures: taxing, borrowing, and printing more money. If the government lacks credit and anything worth taxing, the seductive alternative is to forgo taxes and debt by unilaterally printing more money. The increase in the money supply drives down the value of the money in circulation; and the drop in value forces the government to print even more money to meet its expenses. In exceptional

circumstances such as wartime or some special strain on the economy such as Bolivia felt during the cocaine era, this minor excess by
the government grows into an uncontrollable flood and the country
is trapped in a rapidly whirling spiral of dizzying inflation.

The first of the twentieth-century countries to see its currency collapse was Russia soon after the revolution that brought the Communists to power. The Communists deliberately sabotaged their own
currency by printing as much money as everyone wanted. This soon
meant that 10,000 new rubles had the purchasing power of one
Tsarist ruble. Some of the newly powerful Communists felt that by
allowing rampant inflation, they would destroy the currency and
therefore be able to build a society without money. Once the citizens
became thoroughly disgusted with the worthless rubles, the government planned to replace money with a rationing system in which
coupons would be used to procure whatever food, housing, clothing,
and other goods seemed appropriate for each person.[3] Within only a
few years, however, it became evident to everyone that even the new
Soviet Union needed money to function, and in 1921 the government began a series of moves to institute a new currency system.

After losing the First World War, Germany and the dismembered
Austro-Hungarian Empire became the next nations to stumble into
the whirlpool of hyperinflation. The weakened Austrian currency,
the crown, began to lose value first. It fell from the prewar level of
4.9 to the dollar to 70,000 to the dollar before the Austrian government brought it under control in 1922. The Austrian inflation, however, proved to be merely a prelude to the crises in the German and
Hungarian currencies.

At the end of the war, the victorious governments of France and
Britain pressed hard to extract as much money as possible in the form
of reparations from Germany, which had to accept full blame for causing the war. Under the terms of the Treaty of Versailles, which the
U.S. Senate refused to ratify but which was accepted by all the European governments, Germany agreed to pay virtually the entire bill
for the war, which it did not receive until April 1921. Despite American objections, the Allies presented Germany with a bill for 132 billion gold marks, twice the national income of Germany and equal to

$33 billion. To meet these demands, the German government would have had to generate a surplus of $33 billion after paying for basic services for its people. Because of further treaty restrictions, Germany could not sell its goods in a fair market to meet the reparations, and as the government printed more money without any backing, the value of the paper mark began to slide in 1922. When Germany could no longer make its war payments, the French army moved in to seize the industrial area of the Ruhr, which contained Germany's major mines and most important railroads.

Within three months of receiving the full bill, prices in Germany began to rise, and by the end of the year they were thirty-five times the prewar level. By the end of 1922, prices stood at 1,475 times the prewar level, and they soon surpassed one trillion times their earlier levels. In less than two years, the cost of a German postage stamp increased from 20 pfennigs to 500 billion marks. Lenders charged interest rates of 35 percent a day. At the end of the war it had cost roughly 4 marks to buy a U.S. dollar; by July 1922 the cost had risen to 493 marks. By New Year's Day 1923 the mark had dropped to 17,792 to a dollar. By November 15, 1923, at the height of the inflation, it required 4.2 *trillion* (4,200,000,000,000) marks to buy one dollar. An American penny had the value of 42 billion (42,000,000,000) German marks. An item that could be purchased for one mark at the end of the war cost 726 billion marks by 1923. The Weimar government issued paper money so fast that it did not have time to print both sides. Delays in shipping sometimes meant that the monetary notes had become nearly worthless before they arrived at the bank; so the treasury simply stamped more zeros on them and issued them as higher denominations. Workers received their pay daily, but if any delay prevented them from arriving at the stores before closing time that same day, they could only use the bundles of paper bills as fuel in the stove because they would be worthless by the time the shops opened the next morning. Inflation raced out of the control of the government, banks, and businesses, to say nothing of the common people who were its greatest victims. To help German businesses stay afloat, the government made loans of 497 billion billion marks. German newspapers reported the outbreak of a new medical malady called "zero strokes," or "cipher strokes," caused by the difficulties of calculating such large figures; the zeros became a symbol for the collapse of the capital markets and all the other woes of inflation. Because the mark fell so low in this period relative to other world currencies, Germany became a bargain basement for anyone with dollars, pounds, or other hard currencies. The German government had to pass a law prohibiting foreigners from buying and exporting its national art treasures.

The inflation took a horrendous toll. The birth rate fell while the death rate rose, particularly the infant mortality rate, which climbed by 21 percent, and the adult suicide rate. H. G. Wells called the German inflation an "economic massacre," particularly for the middle class, professionals, and anyone living on a fixed income. Some of the most cynical observers of the time claimed that German officials had engineered the inflation as a way to arouse public sympathy and to force a decrease in the reparations forced upon their country.

The inflation ended on November 20, 1923, when the mark reached 4.2 trillion to the dollar and the government lopped off all the zeros and created the new *rentenmark*. The new mark was based on land values, and it traded at 4.2 to the dollar—the exchange rate of the imperial mark before World War I—or one trillion marks to the rentenmark. Exhausted from the ordeal, Finance Minister Rudolf Havenstein died on the same day, allowing a new minister to assume power along with the new mark. In 1924, following the recommendation of an international commission headed by Charles G. Dawes for the purpose of examining German war reparations, the United States loaned Germany $200 million in order that Germany could return to the gold standard.

More than any other factor, the economic collapse of Germany and the great financial and psychological burden that it placed on the middle class and working class probably paved the way for political extremism of the sort that brought Adolf Hitler to power within another decade.

With the dissolution of the Austro-Hungarian Empire in the aftermath of World War I, each newly formed country created its own currency, but each suffered problems similar to those of Germany. Inflation attacked all of the defeated powers as the currencies of Austria, Hungary, Czechoslovakia, Poland, Bulgaria, and Greece collapsed one after the other. This collapse, followed by the worldwide depression of the 1930s, also fostered extremist political movements on both the Left and the Right, resulting in the rise of dictators in each country.

In the presence of regional economic problems and situations, hyperinflation seems to erupt like a plague that ravages one country and then races on to another. France, Belgium, Italy, and Spain saw the value of their money drop to around one-fifth of its prewar purchasing power. The pressure on the British pound caused a threefold rise in prices that Britain curbed only by returning briefly to the gold standard in 1924–1925. The resulting depression forced Britain to leave the gold standard once again, and it has never returned.

NEW HYPERINFLATION

The 1980s produced another even more widespread and devastating round of hyperinflation, but this time it erupted in Latin America and Africa rather than in Europe. The circumstances varied from country to country, but the inflation usually followed a prolonged period of financial disorder and corruption, political instability, and excessive borrowing from Western banks. This lethal social and economic mixture produced an explosive cocktail that destroyed the national currency.

One after another, Bolivia, Peru, Brazil, Argentina, and Zaire traveled down the well-worn path to inflation by printing ever more worthless bills. When inflation rose to a rate of from one to ten million units per dollar, the governments issued new currency that renewed the cycle, until the bureaucrats in the national treasury ran out of names for their currency, whereupon they borrowed names from other languages or simply made them up. Peru fluctuated between the sol, which means "sun" in Spanish, and the inti, which means "sun" in Quechua, the language of Peru's native people. Bolivia changed from the peso to the boliviano and back to the peso. Brazil had the crucero, the crucado, and finally the real. Argentina created the austral, which meant more or less "the southern money," but after that too became worthless, the country returned to the peso.

By the 1990s the Latin American republics had managed to stabilize their currencies, and the exhausted citizens settled into the relative comfort of simple double-digit inflation. Hyperinflation continued to move on around the globe, however, this time to plague the republics of the former Soviet Union whose citizens had lived with an extremely stable, albeit neither particularly valuable nor widely accepted, currency for nearly seventy years. As soon as the Soviet Union dissolved and, along with it, the system of resource allocation and set prices, the ruble plummeted in value. The allied republics that had issued their own money but kept it pegged to the ruble found their currency falling even faster than the Russian ruble. Ukraine, which had virtually no experience as an independent nation with its own currency, suffered the most. In Ukraine during the early 1990s the politicians and bureaucrats did not even have a proper name for their currency. The so-called coupons were just poorly printed bills that lacked the luster even of play money.

THE HIDDEN TAX

Inflation need not become hyperinflation for it to be important and to provoke severe consequences. Inflation can creep along at a lower level, like walking pneumonia, unnoticed yet sapping the energy of the patient until some other germ delivers the fatal blow.

At a steady inflation rate of only 5 percent a year, money loses half of its value, and prices therefore double in only fourteen years. Thus at the 5 percent annual inflation rate, a house that cost $100,000 in 1985 would sell for $200,000 by 1999. At 10 percent annual inflation, the cost of the same house would double in seven years. Thus a house that was worth $100,000 in 1985 would cost $400,000 by 1999.

In the United States, inflation has rarely surpassed 10 percent outside of wartime, and this country has never sustained such a high rate of inflation for long—certainly not for a whole decade. Even though the currency of the United States has proved far more stable than that of any of the countries that experienced hyperinflation, the dollar has undergone a nearly constant decline in value in the twentieth century when measured against gold, certain other currencies, and the price of a home, a car, or any basket of goods.

When Congress established the dollar as a gold coin by the Coinage Act of 1792, the value of the dollar was set at $19.75 per troy ounce. In 180 years the value of the dollar dropped by nearly half relative to gold so that it stood at $35 to the ounce at the time Nixon closed the gold window. Between then and the mid-1990s, the dollar sank to roughly $400 per ounce of gold. In other words, the value declined by nearly half before 1971, but in the next twenty years it declined to less than one-tenth of what it had been in 1971.

In the United States, inflation never reached the levels of Germany or Bolivia, but some of the same inflation culture became institutionalized here. During the severe inflation of the 1970s real estate became the favorite refuge from cash for middle-class Americans. Their flight from cash meant that they were willing to take out large loans at high interest rates in order to convert what money they had into a home, which would rapidly increase in dollars while the value of the dollar was dropping precipitously.

Inflation became such a fixed part of the world landscape in the twentieth century that it resembled a natural landmark rather than one artificially created by governments. It is difficult to believe that prices actually fell throughout most of the nineteenth century and well into the twentieth. Aside from wartime and a few other unusual episodes in the nineteenth century, machines manufactured goods more cheaply; and as transportation of goods improved, prices declined because the value of the currency was fixed to gold and silver. In the twenty-five years following the Civil War in the United States, wholesale prices declined by an average of 60 percent, and in some areas such as textiles, the decline proved even steeper and more substantial. Most goods in 1900 were cheaper than they had been in 1800.[4] In only a little over twenty-five years, between 1872 and 1897, "one dollar could buy 43 percent more rice than in 1872, 35 percent more beans, 49 percent more tea, 51 percent more roasted coffee, 114 percent more sugar, 62 percent more mutton, 25 percent more fresh pork, 60 percent more lard and butter, and 42 percent more milk."[5]

The economic theme of the era of industrialization, on the one hand, was falling prices as more goods became available to more people at a lower cost. The economic theme of the twentieth century, on the other hand, was declining currencies. Measured against one another, some currencies such as the German mark and the Japanese yen performed well during the late twentieth century while others, like the Italian lira, the Mexican peso, and the Russian ruble, performed rather poorly. Despite these variations, the century witnessed a decline in value of all the world's currencies. Even the mark and the yen at the end of the century stood considerably below what they had been at the beginning. Government after government tinkered with the system and allowed the value of its currency to decline steadily in a form of hidden taxation that brought temporary benefit to the rulers in power but at a great price to the people, who were dependent on money to survive.

At the beginning of the twentieth century, exchange rates were stable enough among the European currencies that American Express printed on its traveler's checks the value of the dollar in twelve European currencies. At that time, it was difficult for travelers to conceive of going to a country without knowing in advance the exact rate of exchange. In 1919, however, when rates still had not stabilized after World War I, American Express dropped the printed rates of exchange and posted the changing rates in its offices.

In a democratic society, politicians are often unwilling to raise taxes because of the expected voter anger. For them, inflation and the devaluation of the currency serve much better because they constitute a hidden tax. The government releases more money into the system, and the politicians and bureaucrats have more money to spend on their favorite projects. The release of new money, however, makes all existing money worth a little less and thus eats away at the nation's money and commercial vitality. As William Greider, an expert on the history of the Federal Reserve, wrote, "The recurring experience of inflationary spirals strongly suggested that the underlying source of these traumas lay not in economics but in politics—the choices made by government or, more precisely, choices that the government refused to make."[6]

Initially it might seem that the inflation tax would apply equally to all people, since all people use money, or even that it might affect most those who have the most money. The inflation rate is merely a numerical index, but it is an average based on quite different life circumstances. It lumps together the billionaire and the pauper, and therein lies a great inequality.

If a billionaire loses 10 percent of her fortune, the loss amounts to $100 million; for a person earning $50,000 a year, the loss is only $5,000. The billionaire does not feel the inflation so badly, however, not merely because she is so rich, but because she does not keep the billion dollars in her dresser drawer or even in her checking account; the money is invested and will yield higher returns during inflation. Her accounts will keep up with inflation, and with any skill at all, she should be able to do much better than that. For wage earners and pensioners, however, the entire loss of buying power comes out of the family's lifestyle, not out of their investments. The loss of $5,000 represents a substantial decrease in buying power that is not recuperated through increasing investment yields.

The inflation tax constitutes the most retrogressive of all forms of taxation because it hurts the poor the most. Inflation might even be called simply a tax on poverty. The poor use more cash, and they are more likely to be living from fixed income sources such as retirement or government payments that increase only slowly and far behind the inflation rate. The sales tax, or value-added tax, another form of retrogressive taxation, taxes only what an individual actually spends. By contrast, inflation taxes all money that the middle class and particularly the poorer classes possess or anticipate receiving in the future.

The inflation tax also harms large segments of the gray, or informal, market and the illegal markets. The government has great trouble taxing drug pushers, for example, but through the device of inflation, it constantly decreases the value of the cash that forms the center of their business. Unlike legitimate businesses that can easily transfer their cash into other kinds of investments, drug sellers have great trouble protecting their money via investments or even interest-

bearing bank accounts. The walls of the middle-class financial structure keep out the drug dealers' cash and leave it constantly exposed
to the ravages of inflation.

Together with drug smuggling, the expansion of the black market,
and the general deterioration of world currencies, inflation has been
an emblem of the twentieth century. It seems ironic that the rise of
inflation has so closely followed the expansion of the world narcotics market.

Inflation caused a flight from cash in the second half of the twentieth century. As cash became increasingly less important in business,
particularly in international business, however, it maintained its importance in the drug trade and other illegal endeavors. In the final
decades of the twentieth century, the American dollar became the
preferred currency of those in the international drug market, from
opium dealers in Burma to cocaine distributors in Colombia. Because
of the illegality of its products and the limited use of checks, credit
cards, and regular banking services, the drug market has functioned
primarily on a cash basis with American dollars. The large sums of
cash needed for the international market have siphoned off billions
of cash dollars from the legitimate market.

14

The Cash Ghetto

The greatest of evils and the worst of crimes is poverty.
—GEORGE BERNARD SHAW

UNIVERSITY AVENUE RUNS SEVEN MILES FROM EAST to west, connecting the University of Minnesota in Minneapolis with the State Capitol in neighboring Saint Paul. In what was a prosperous suburb in the decades immediately following World War II, the avenue served as a thriving retail and commercial center lined with banks, automobile dealerships, restaurants, and large stores. In the 1970s, construction of a freeway parallel to and a few blocks south of University Avenue gave most commuters a faster route between the two cities and initiated a general economic decline in the area. The middle-class African-American community disappeared as those who could afford it moved to new suburbs, and those who could not were forced into new government housing developments built to replace the homes torn down by the freeway construction.

University Avenue evolved into a new type of commercial center with the changing economic situation and pressures. The family diners became fast-food franchises with drive-through windows, and the restaurants became beer taverns with dart corners, pool rooms, and large televisions tuned to the sports channel. The car dealerships gave way to used-car lots, auto repair garages, and body shops. The banks followed their customers into the newer suburbs, and their buildings along University Avenue became pawnshops and check-cashing businesses. New businesses offered tattoos, used comic books, and palm reading, and a variety of stores appeared offering Asian foods. The Faust movie theater switched from family entertainment to pornography before being demolished in 1995. Some of the nearby taverns featured exotic dancers on the bars and tables. Grocery stores, discount stores, and liquor stores continued to thrive, but other retail businesses became outlets for damaged or used clothing or offered discontinued merchandise for sale.

Discount franchises such as bulk grocery stores, convenience stores, and fast-food restaurants proliferated, but the more upscale franchises avoided the area, leaving it to the long rows of small entrepreneurial shops with hand-lettered signs and recycled decor from other business ventures. Such shops offered karate or tae kwon do lessons, used household appliances, synthetic tombstones and plastic flowers, auto parts and repair, bail bonds, and day care. Mainline religious denominations withdrew from the strip and were replaced by fringe religious movements and ad hoc institutions created by charismatic spiritual leaders from the neighborhood.

A few arts projects moved into the abandoned retail space along the strip, but they catered to people who lived outside the area and contributed little to the neighborhood economy. City and state government repeatedly united in attempts to improve the area by erecting government buildings—a library, police station, motor vehicle bureau, and an employment and retraining office—but the construction added to the decay. Each new windowless concrete building with fortresslike walls increased the number of sterile facades where even graffiti seemed to improve its appearance. The new buildings destroyed more blocks of old houses and stores and made the area look even less like a neighborhood and more like an abandoned social experiment.

A Culture of Poverty

Early in the twentieth century, French writer Anatole France noted that "It is only the poor who pay cash, and that not from virtue, but because they are refused credit."[1] In the 1950s, anthropologists who studied poor communities around the world noted the high reliance on many small monetary transactions conducted almost exclusively in cash. The high reliance on cash became an almost universal identifying characteristic of poor people. In studying the poor Indian immigrants from the countryside into Mexico City, Oscar Lewis found that they rarely bought in bulk but instead bought minute quantities.[2] Rather than shopping in a large grocery store, the Indians more frequently bought small meals or snacks such as tacos, ice cream, pineapple, or a plate of beans and rice from a local vendor. They bought cigarettes one at a time from a local vendor even though they cost twice as much as cigarettes bought by the pack or carton in a store.

Similarly, people in the poorest parts of contemporary American cities buy hamburgers or fried chicken for cash and for one meal at a time. Even in the grocery store, they buy many snack foods already packaged in small, and therefore more expensive, amounts.

In the cash ghetto, people also use pay telephones, rented furniture and televisions, and taxis or hired cars. If they buy a newspaper to look through the want ads, they are more likely to pay cash for it at a convenience store than to pay for a subscription by credit card or check, thereby paying more than the subscriber pays. They tend to pay cash to buy or rent a VCR and watch rented films instead of subscribing to cable television.

Liquor stores sell far more alcohol in one-pint and even half-pint bottles in poor neighborhoods than do liquor stores in wealthier suburbs where people can buy by the quart, gallon, or case and pay for it without cash. Even when buying illegal drugs, people in the ghetto buy smaller, more expensive quantities, or hits, than middle-class or affluent customers. Poorer users buy crack by a single dose, marijuana by the smoke, or heroin by the syringe, whereas those from more prosperous neighborhoods can afford to buy their drugs at bulk rates, by the bag, gram, ounce, pound, or kilogram.

Proportionally, the poor pay substantially more for these goods and services, whether legal or illegal, that they buy in small quantities. Even when gambling, they are more likely to use cash for a poker game, a betting pool, or lottery tickets than are middle-class people who gamble in casinos with plastic chips and cards or who use organized betting pools and bookmakers who accept checks as well as cash. Cash is not only lower class, but it is part of a much more expensive system to operate than the cash-free system of the middle and upper classes.

By the end of the twentieth century, cash in all forms, including coins and paper bills, had declined in importance around the world. Even before money lost its gold backing, it was becoming less important for the financial elite and thereby for the general society. At the same time, however, cash found correspondingly greater usage among poor people. In the modern two-class system, the poor pay with cash while middle-class consumers use plastic and checks.

With the segregation of the poor into a cash economy and the rest of the society operating in a plastic-paper-electronic one, a need has arisen for intermediary institutions to connect the two. Many poor people do not have bank accounts or credit cards, but they do receive checks from their employers or from unemployment, welfare, retirement, income tax refunds, or Social Security, and they lack a means to cash them. Some merchants, such as grocers, provide this service, but as the volume of checks received in the poorer neighborhoods increased, check-cashing businesses began to appear. Anyone with a check and proper identification can go into a check-cashing office and, for a substantial fee, turn a check into cash.

Several such check-cashing businesses line University Avenue; the largest one stands at the corner of Lexington Avenue, another major artery. Even though the store has large plate-glass windows facing the two main streets and from the outside resembles any other retail business, inside it seems more like a fortress, with all employees and cash safely ensconced behind bulletproof windows. Customers and clerks communicate awkwardly through metal mouthpieces, and they pass paper and money back and forth through curved metal drawers that prohibit any direct contact between customer and clerk.

The same businesses that turn checks into cash also transfer cash into checks for people who need to mail off a car or insurance payment, send money to a relative, or pay a debt. The check-cashing business also provides a number of related services that connect poor and working people in the cash economy with the larger middle-class paper economy. They issue money orders and wire money to other places, and some will make small loans or advances on checks that have not yet been received. They take photographs and provide identification cards for their customers, and they sell bus and subway passes. They notarize documents, photocopy and fax them, or arrange to send them out by registered mail or a private carrier service. All of these services come at fairly steep prices compared to the cost of similar services in banks, post offices, and photocopy shops.

In recognition of the ever-changing face of the poor in America, such institutions advertise their services in various languages— Spanish, Chinese, Vietnamese, and French Creole—and in some communities they offer money transfers to other countries and in various currencies. They frequently offer services twenty-four hours a day every day of the year. For even higher fees, such shops can cash foreign checks or buy gold or silver coins or small ingots that customers may have brought with them when fleeing their home country.

Many of these establishments take on the superficial appearance of a bank. They have names such as My Bank, the Un Bank, the Bank Teller, or even John's Bank. Frequently the names resemble those of the cash machines in mainstream banks: Money Express, Money Exchange, or Check-X-Change. Check-cashing services are also offered at some pawnshops, the traditional banks of the poor. They offer the additional service of changing goods into cash. Some pawnbrokers specialize in expensive items such as guns, jewelry, or even cars, while others carry a wide variety from car stereos and construction tools to computers and diamonds. Pawnshops and check-cashing businesses, then, serve as intermediaries between the cash ghetto and the larger society.

The Informal Economy

People in the cash ghetto are more likely than mainstream Americans to perform services for under-the-table cash payment, even when working outside the ghetto for legitimate businesses or as household workers in affluent homes. Much of their work is temporary pickup work. Men idle in small clumps on the sidewalk in front of the employment office or the government retraining center in the hope that someone will pull up to the curb and hire one or two of them for a temporary job loading a truck, cleaning out a lot, shoveling snow, digging up a tank, or doing anything else that will earn them a day's cash wage.

Other people offer specialty services that their neighbors call on them to perform. One knows how to fix cars; another cuts hair. One makes household repairs, and another knows how to tap into the cable television line or to install a device to unscramble the pay-per-view channel. One sells firewood and coal; another sells barbecued ribs and chicken on holiday weekends. One serves as an ad hoc taxi driver while another keeps children by the day or even by the month. Compared to the more affluent communities, poor neighborhoods have more vendors selling goods for cash on the streets or from door to door, and they have more garage sales, yard sales, flea markets, and swap meets where they sell used or stolen merchandise for cash.

Such economic systems for the exchange of goods and services operate as an informal or parallel economy, largely beyond the control and supervision of the law and outside the normal financial structures and rules. They maintain this independence and flexibility by functioning on a cash basis. They operate not so much as a black market as a gray one, and not so much against the law as simply beyond it.

Cash has become so important in the lives of poor people that the government has issued new forms of cash such as food stamps, which circulate almost exclusively as a form of poor people's money. In the cash ghetto, large grocery stores and small convenience stores compete vigorously with one another for food stamps. Merchants willing to step over the legal limit also accept food stamps for goods other than food, but of course the customer must pay more for the convenience of using this second-class cash and for the legal and financial risk the merchant takes in accepting the stamps. On the street, people illegally trade food stamps for cash at a steep discount that also results from the status of food stamps as a second-class, less desirable, and less useful form of money.

CASH VALUE

Among poor people, cash continues to function as an appropriate gift throughout life. They may present cash at a birthday, literally pass the hat for a friend in trouble, or use it in any number of ceremonies. During wedding celebrations among some peasant and working-class groups, guests publicly present cash to the bride, sometimes even stuffing it into her clothes or pinning it to her dress. Among American Indians, a blanket dance is performed at powwows for people who need money, and guests throw cash onto the blanket. In a similar practice, guests will drop money onto the drum at the end of a powwow to help cover expenses for the drum group.

When poor people save money, they often do so by investing it in goods that can be easily sold or pawned when cash is needed. In many parts of the Middle East, poorer men buy bangles and other forms of gold jewelry for their wives and the other women in their families whenever they have extra cash. These very light pieces of gold or silver jewelry are usually bought and sold by weight. By contrast these men buy relatively few precious stones because their value is much more difficult to evaluate in terms of purity, clarity, and cut. In financially difficult times or when they want to buy something more expensive such as an animal or a piece of land, they can easily sell the gold or silver (which has standardized units of purity stamped on it) by its weight in the shops of many different kinds of merchants.

When the governments of the world minted silver and gold coins, poor people used the coins as decorations. They sewed them on their clothes or attached them to earrings, necklaces, bracelets, and belts. Worn on or attached to the body, the coins were safe, and yet they were always available when needed, since they could be easily pulled off and used as payment. In the Middle East, women usually wore the family money as jewelry, but the macho gauchos of Argentina made leather belts up to a foot wide and studded them with large silver coins from Peru and other silver-producing areas of South America.

Words such as *sequin* derive from the practice of using gold and silver coins as jewelry or as decorations sewn onto cloth. The word came from *zecchino*, a coin minted in Venice in various denominations and widely used in the Ottoman Empire as money and as decoration on scarves, veils, and other women's garments. The less common English word *bezant* has a similar meaning, but refers to ornamental disks used in architecture and derives from the small gold coins of Byzantium.

As governments in the twentieth century devalued their currency and removed most of the precious metals from them, poor people used them less for ornamentation. Instead, they bought more gold and silver jewelry, which served the same purpose but retained its value no matter what government might be in power or what occupying army, religious cult, or political party might come or go.

Peasants and other poor people in many societies buy high-prestige and expensive items such as watches even if they cannot tell time, or they purchase VCRs and television sets even if they do not have electricity. Though seen as illogical purchases by outsiders, these items represent a type of investment or savings. Because the item is so high in prestige, it can be easily sold when the owner needs money. A watch or television, even if useless to the owner, may prove more stable and durable in value retention than money itself. Still, the goal is to acquire items that can be easily converted into cash or used when needed.

The economy of the ghetto, the barrio, and other poor neighborhoods from Mexico City to Milwaukee and from Seattle to Istanbul functions around cash, but this same cash that keeps the poor people's economy operating also puts up barriers against their participation in the general economy that bases its operations on checks, plastic cards, and electronic impulses. The general society has erected its own walls to keep the cash of the ghetto from penetrating the middle-class economy. Although invisible to most people in daily life, these barriers create strips like University Avenue in cities throughout the modern world.

In the United States and other Western countries, laws and business practices make it very difficult for most people to transfer large amounts of cash. Banks must report cash transactions above $10,000 to the government, although there are no such requirements for reporting much larger sums if they are handled by credit card, check, or electronic transfer. The Internal Revenue Service and the Federal Bureau of Investigation take a suspicious interest in the bank accounts of individuals or businesses that exceed what they think should be the appropriate volume for cash transactions.

Even though people who have foreign bank accounts and who transfer money electronically may move millions of dollars in a day without any government supervision, people entering the United States must declare any sum above $10,000 in cash to U.S. Customs, and they are subject to losing any money over that amount that they do not declare. It is far easier to move a billion dollars from a Tokyo bank to one in Atlanta than to drive across the border from Vancouver or to fly into Dallas with more than $10,000 in cash.

Because the people in the cash ghetto rely on cash but encounter great difficulty in transferring it into mainstream financial institutions, they sometimes accumulate large sums of illegitimate cash. In addition to the cash handled by pimps, drug dealers, bookies, and others engaged in illegal enterprises, stores and legitimate businesses often have much more cash than would comparable businesses in more affluent neighborhoods.

People who live in the cash ghetto often carry larger sums of money with them than do affluent people who have a pocketful of charge and bank cards. Men may carry wads of bills bound together by rubber bands. Women often carry cash in their purses or hidden in their clothing. Such people are more likely to keep cash hidden at home in a can at the back of the closet, in a plastic bowl in the kitchen, hidden beneath the mattress, or even in the proverbial cookie jar.

In the culture of the cash ghetto, everyone knows who is most likely to have cash. In addition to the shopkeepers and the managers of small businesses, the people with money are the ones who receive regular checks from the government—the unmarried mothers receiving welfare and the elderly receiving Social Security or retirement checks, which they turn into cash. Such people, particularly the elderly without family, often become the victims of crime.

Some elderly people leave their homes only during the day; others do not go out at all. The ones who live in government housing often fare the worst, especially if they are mixed in among released mental patients, drug addicts and alcoholics in treatment, and ex-convicts on parole. In some high-rise buildings, elderly pensioners cannot leave their apartments or ride the elevators without fear of attack and robbery by boys and girls as young as thirteen or fourteen. If such people have no relatives to help them, they must pay someone—often a middle-aged man—to cash their checks and bring them their groceries, medications, and other necessities. Trapped day and

night in their own homes, these older people literally become prisoners in the cash ghetto.

Thieves go where the money is, and much of the money, or at least
the cash, in modern cities can be found in the poorest areas. A rob-
ber can often steal as much from a local liquor store or a check-
cashing office in the ghetto as from a suburban bank. Furthermore,
robbing a bank is a federal crime that involves the FBI, whereas the
thief who robs a local liquor store or check-cashing office need fear
only the local or state police.

15
Interlude in Plastic

And forgive us our debts, as we forgive our debtors.
—Matthew 6:12

A T THIRTY DEGREES BELOW ZERO, WHETHER MEA-
sured in Fahrenheit or centigrade, exposed flesh freezes in a few
minutes, spit hardens like stone before it hits the ground, and rubber can shatter and explode like delicate crystal hitting stone. The
carbon monoxide exhaust from cars freezes into black ice along the
roads, and the lakes freeze so solid that trucks can drive across them
as though they were made of concrete. Yet no matter what the season or temperature or how solidly frozen the ground and lakes, the
air stays at an eternally spring temperature of 72°F. inside America's
largest shopping mall in Bloomington, Minnesota. Kids ride the
water chute, forty-foot palms rise up toward the glass ceiling, and
flowers bloom throughout the year.

The twisting and turning current of the water slide sprays a light
mist into the air, giving the central part of the mall a constant crisp
smell of chlorine. Each of the shops, boutiques, stores, and vending
carts scattered up and down the hallways of the mall emits a distinct
aroma—the scent of floral potpourri from the department stores,
perfume from the cosmetics store, leather from the shoe store, wicker
from the furniture store, chocolate and roasted peanuts from the
candy stand, popcorn from the theater, and musky cologne from the
men's clothing store. Each of the forty-five restaurants and take-out
stands produces its own, unique aroma—cheese and oregano from the
pizzeria; gumbo spices from the Creole restaurant; fried egg rolls from
the Asian counter; fresh bread from the sandwich stall; cinnamon

from the bake shop; french fries, ketchup, and hamburgers from the burger palace; and roasting coffee beans from the café.

On a normal workday, 100,000 customers shop in the Mall of America. On weekends and during special shopping times such as Christmas, more than 200,000 customers clamor daily through the cavernous passageways. Cars arrive at the mall early in the morning from homes throughout the the upper Midwest and central Canada. Some of the biggest spenders, however, arrive at the adjacent airport. Charter flights carrying shoppers from around the United States and Canada arrive early in the morning and leave late at night with their baggage compartments stuffed full of purchases. Special flights between Japan and Europe stop at the Minneapolis–Saint Paul airport to allow their passengers a few hours or even a few days of shopping. To accommodate the many airborne shoppers, the mall maintains constant shuttle service to the airport, and parts of the mall resemble an airport, with banks of computer screens to inform the shoppers of arriving and departing flight times and gates. Even patients from the Mayo Clinic in nearby Rochester schedule an afternoon or a day of shopping in between medical tests.

The builders erected the mall only a few miles down the highway from America's first covered shopping mall, the Southdale Center, which opened in Edina in 1956. By the mid-1990s, America had over 37,000 shopping malls, which attracted 175 million customers every month.[1]

At its 1992 opening, the Mall of America represented the pinnacle of the twentieth-century retail shopping experience. Architects designed it in the form of a large square with a major department store in each corner. Because of the quarter-mile arcades connecting the department stores with their neighbors, the halls of the mall were given street names such as Broadway. In between the large stores are some four hundred shops on three levels. Each floor of the mall has one mile of stores, and the mall has three such floors. The square surrounds a large amusement park with live trees, a roller coaster, and a water chute with a log ride, all of which is protected from the fierce Minnesota cold by a glass roof four stories above the park. Adult entertainment is provided on an additional fourth floor of the complex where customers can find restaurants, sports bars, and country-and-western dance halls along with fourteen movie theaters and a variety of game and video parlors.

Operation of the mall requires some 12,000 employees, and their combined efforts generate sales that average $2 million a day. The mall seems to be less a shopping center than a city in its own right. In addition to the usual support services such as a bank, a travel agency, and a medical center, the mall has its own police force and even its own school where students study entrepreneurship and business as well as the traditional subjects. Parents might work in the mall while their children attend school there, and they all meet at one of the stands for lunch before the student goes to an afternoon job in one of the hundreds of businesses in the mall.

The largest pools of cash in the mall seem to be the many thousands of coins thrown daily into the decorative fountains. A mother gently holds the hand of her toddler and helps him toss in a coin with great squeals of delight as the metal plops into the water. A four-year-old begs her father for a penny, races away to throw it into the pool, and then races back to ask for another. Teenage lovers jointly clutch a coin, and, facing away from the fountain, throw it over their shoulders into the pool in pursuit of a wish known only to them. As the pennies, quarters, dimes, nickels, and foreign coins accumulate through the day and night, maintenance workers use large brooms to push the thick layers of them toward the center of the pool, out of reach of anyone who might be tempted to steal them. At the end of the week, the workers drain the pool, scoop up the coins, and pour them through a money-sorting machine that packages the coins in neat paper rolls for charity.

Except for its size, the Mall of America does not differ greatly in layout or activities from the ancient markets of Sardis, Rome, Malacca, or medieval London. Retail is retail. Yet if we compare the daily activities in the Mall of America with those of the ancient markets more closely, we discern one major distinction: despite all the goods passing back and forth over the counters in the mall and despite its ringing cash registers, little actual *cash* changes hands.

Aside from throwing coins into the fountains, customers use cash only to make small purchases such as drinks, candy, and snacks and to play arcade and video games. Even the mall's amusement park has abandoned cash in favor of electronic money. To enjoy the rides and amusements in the Camp Snoopy theme park, children pay with cash-debit cards that their parents purchase in various amounts. The child need not be capable of distinguishing a quarter from a dime or of reading the different denominations on dollar bills, much less adding, subtracting, or calculating the change due from a purchase. The little child needs only to insert the card in a slot. The machine then automatically debits the appropriate amount, and the gate swings open for the child to climb on the roller coaster or log chute. When the child has exhausted the electronic cash, the card stops working, and the child, without hesitation, tosses the spent card into the trash.

For meals in the larger restaurants and for bigger purchases in the stores, most adults pay by check or electronic charge, which comes in many forms. Customers can use credit cards that increase their total debt, or checking cards that automatically deduct the purchase amount from their bank account and deposit it in the merchant's account. Customers who need cash can use the electronic cards at any of a number of money machines located throughout the bank. If a customer pays by check, the availability of adequate funds in the account or an adequate line of credit must be electronically verified. Any customer who has sufficient credit but is short of electronic cash can easily tap into more electronic money by phoning the bank or credit card company and requesting an electronic transfer of funds from one account to another or activating a line of credit.

DEMOCRATIC DEBT AND SOCIALIST RISK

At the end of World War II and just before the great changes in American banking, checking, and credit, most Americans—like virtually everyone else in the world—still used cash for buying and selling. Americans, however, proved particularly eager to switch to new forms of payment, and by 1990 some $30 trillion a year was being

transferred via check. By 1993 about $400 trillion was being trans-
ferred each year by various electronic means.[2]

Just as different banks, moneylenders, and government entities
once issued different types of paper money, today different institutions create electronic money in different ways. No single electronic
mint produces this new money, and no large electronic vault protects
it. It derives from networks as large as the Federal Reserve and as limited as the electric purchase cards used by kids as money in Camp
Snoopy.

In the cash era prior to World War II, credit remained a rich man's
prerogative around the world. Banks lent to people who had substantial property to serve as collateral or an outstanding track record
of earning money to repay debts. Aside from farmers, most middle-
and working-class people had no bank debts because no one would
lend them money.[3] They usually rented their houses, and, in the rare
instances in which they owned a home, they usually paid for it as it
was built. A merchant might allow trusted customers to pay for an
item over time in installments, or allow them to keep a running tab
at the grocery store, but such relationships remained highly personal,
and the sums involved were minor in the larger financial environ-
ment. A middle-class person in need of cash might pawn some family jewelry or an heirloom or, as a last resort, seek money from a loan
shark who extracted exorbitant interest and demanded payment
under penalty of great physical pain.

In 1928, National City Bank of New York experimented with a
radical new idea: it offered to make small loans to working-class people. The bank first entered the consumer loan program under great
pressure from the state attorney general in an effort to clamp down
on the loan sharks. In the first day of the bank's new operation, the
consumer credit department took in five hundred loan applications.
The working class of New York City proved to be a good credit risk:
the bank lost less than three dollars for every one thousand dollars
lent. With an interest rate of 12 percent and a very low rate of de-
fault among conscientious borrowers, the bank soon found consumer
loans to be a wonderful new source of profit.

During the Great Depression of the 1930s, governments around the world looked for new ways to stimulate their economies. The new policy, particularly in the United States under Franklin Roosevelt, took the form of encouraging banks and other financial institutions to lend more money for the purchase of worthy commodities such as modest homes and cars. To encourage this practice, the government backed and guaranteed low-interest loans. Following World War II, the U.S. government guaranteed home loans for veterans. Banks could still make modest profits from these loans, but the banks had very little risk since the government was accepting increasing responsibility for the risk.

Economic analyst and reporter James Grant called this process "the democratization of debt and the socialization of risk."[4] Americans soon learned to borrow money not merely for homes, cars, and education but also for televisions, kitchen appliances, boats, and vacations. Within a generation, debt became not only the norm but the expected right of virtually the entire middle and working class.

At the same time that banks galloped into new credit markets, the federal government found even more ways to encourage borrowing and to guarantee debts. By the 1970s a potential homeowner might take out a loan guaranteed by any one of a half-dozen government agencies. People who had served in the military could apply to their local banks for loans guaranteed through the Veterans Administration; farmers and rural residents could apply for loans guaranteed by the Farmers Home Loan Administration. Working-class people who were neither veterans nor farmers could apply for guaranteed low-interest loans through the Federal Housing Authority. In the 1980s and early 1990s the number and variety of such programs increased greatly under the auspices of the Department of Housing and Urban Development.

By 1989, home mortgages guaranteed by federal programs accounted for nearly 40 percent of all home mortgages in the United States, and the sum of government-subsidized and -guaranteed debt reached $1 trillion.[5] By this time, the financing of mortgages, although still done through local banks, which made a consistent profit from it, had essentially become a government business. Government involvement allowed millions of Americans to own a home when they otherwise might not have been able to afford one. The same policies, however, created the greatest inflation of residential property prices in American history and contributed to the highest rate of homelessness in the developed world. They also resulted in a financial debacle when the real estate bubble burst in the 1990s and caused the collapse of banks and savings and loan associations across the United States.

Prior to the savings and loan bankruptcies and defaults of the 1980s and 1990s, many analysts had assumed that the backing of the FDIC would be enough to protect the financial institutions from severe misfortune and most certainly from collapse. The Federal Deposit Insurance Corporation, however, was meant to serve primarily as a guarantor of public confidence in the banks and as a public relations tool rather than as a genuine safety net. Few realized that such a guarantee had encouraged savings and loan officers to take ever greater risks with ever greater sums of government-protected money. In the end, only massive government intervention with a large infusion of money saved the FDIC itself from bankruptcy.

The federal government backed loans for those wishing to pursue an education, obtain a mortgage, open a small business, or operate a farm, but it did not directly back loans for household appliances, recreational vehicles, or family vacations in Mexico. Banks that issued credit cards backed such loans, but behind the banks and their responsibilities and liabilities stood the financial force and stability of the federal government in the form of the FDIC. No matter how risky the loans, the depositors' money would be secure.

THE MAGIC CARD

Credit cards were mentioned in fiction long before they found a place in the twentieth-century economy. The concept was fully developed in 1888 in a utopian novel by journalist Edward Bellamy, a dedicated proponent of the populist philosophy of his era. In *Looking Backward: 2000–1887*, Bellamy told the tale of a man who fell asleep on May 30, 1887, and awakened 113 years and 4 months later on September 30, 2000. In America's utopian future of the twenty-first century, Bellamy described a large "industrial army" that produced everything everyone needed, but they did so merely from their desire to serve humanity and received no wages. No coins, notes, or other currency circulated, and there was neither buying nor selling. In an anachronistic holdover from the past, Americans still spoke in terms of dollars and cents, but neither coins nor notes circulated. Instead, they settled accounts by means of "pasteboard credit cards" issued to all citizens and used to obtain all needed goods at large central warehouses.

Oddly enough, in light of how the credit card actually came to be a major tool of capitalist banks and business in the twentieth century, Bellamy's fictional credit card was issued in a postcapitalist society in which the government issued all goods. Each person received a certain money ration based on the total output of the nation during the preceding year, but since all credit cards were personalized, citizens could not exchange them, use them to pay for goods not issued by the government, or use them to accumulate savings from year to year. In Bellamy's America of the twenty-first century, the credit card served as an easy accounting device in a world where people no longer bought and sold goods and where the government had replaced the market. Money no longer had value in terms of gold, silver, or any other commodity. It had become merely "an algebraical symbol for comparing the values of products with one another."[6]

In the twentieth century the automobile gave rise to the first credit cards. Cars carried people to new places where they did not have personal relationships with the merchants and where they might not always have the cash necessary for gasoline, oil, and the frequent repairs demanded by early automobiles. To solve that problem and to create customer loyalty, the oil companies began issuing their own credit cards to be used for the purchase of their products from any merchant who carried them. Soon, in imitation of the oil companies, larger store chains also began to issue their own credit cards.

In 1950, Diners Club created the first modern charge card. This credit card was accepted at twenty-seven of the country's finer restaurants and was used primarily by affluent businessmen as a convenient way to charge business-related travel and entertainment expenses. The card was designed to grant credit as part of a scheme worked out by Frank McNamara of New York's Hamilton Credit Corporation. The first Diners Club cards were merely pasteboard with the customer's name on one side and a list of member restaurants on the other. In 1955, Diners Club switched to plastic, thereby launching a whole new monetary trend in consumer culture.[7]

In 1958–1959 the American Express Company, which had already become well established as "the traveler's check company," targeted the businessmen's market by issuing its first plastic charge cards. By this time, banks recognized that they were losing control of the credit market to these new nonbank companies.

The Bank of America introduced its BankAmericard, a bank version of the credit card, in 1958, and because it had the whole state of California as its base of operation, it quickly became the nation's most widely known card. Soon other banks that were too small to have their own card joined the BankAmericard system. In 1977, the BankAmericard shortened its name to Visa. By the mid-1990s, Visa had become the largest credit card in use, with nearly 400 million cards in circulation worldwide for use at 12 million business locations.

Meanwhile, Barclay's Bank in Britain followed with its own Barclaycard in 1966, and in 1967, City Bank of New York introduced the Everything Card, a plastic credit card that allowed its elite depositors with the best financial records to charge their purchases whether or not they had enough money in the bank. Two years later this card became the MasterCharge and eventually, simply MasterCard.

The credit card expanded credit, but it also removed the personal element. For a fee, the credit card company now took on the responsibility and the risk of judging a customer's creditworthiness. The spread of credit cards that began in the 1960s provoked major changes in the shopping and paying patterns of customers. The credit card freed their money from temporary constraints by allowing people to use money they had not yet earned or received but that they expected to earn at a later date.

By drawing on anticipated income, a cardholder created money merely by purchasing something. Buying a one-hundred-dollar blouse increased the store's sales by that amount for that day, thereby adding one hundred dollars to the market. For the store, the income from the blouse sale was the same whether the customer had the money in the bank or not. The manufacturer received payment, the clerk received a commission, the government received sales tax, and the store received a profit. In essence, the purchase created money by borrowing it from tomorrow and depositing it in today's market. With a credit card valid for charges up to $5,000 or even $10,000, a consumer could choose to create any quantity of money up to that amount or choose to create none at all by not using the card.

An individual cardholder can use the card to create a few thousand dollars of what economist Joel Kurtzman calls "near-money," but the amount remains subject to the policies and the ability of the bank to support that creation. When this amount of credit is multiplied by the 18 million American Express cardholders or the 25 million credit cards held through Citibank, the amount that these institutions can create rises quickly. In total, such near-money exceeded $150 billion a year by the mid-1990s.[8]

The credit card increased purchasing and, therefore, production and services, but it did so at the cost of increased individual debt and international inflation. By the mid-1990s consumer debt in the United States surpassed $1 trillion. Only twenty years earlier the entire gross national product of the United States had just passed that amount for the first time in history. Yet within another two decades customers had managed to accumulate that much in debt, much of it through the use of credit cards. Because many cardholders purchased cars and electronic goods made in Japan and the other Pacific Rim countries, much of the money flowed out from the United States to Asia, further increasing the strain caused by America's inordinate appetite for credit.

PLATINUM PRESTIGE
Recognizing the importance of the mode of payment in the class and prestige structure of the country, the makers of plastic charge cards frequently create advertisements that emphasize prestige as an integral benefit of using their particular card. Advertisements frequently show credit cards being used by fashionably dressed people in luxu-

rious surroundings such as country clubs, fine hotels and restaurants, luxury ships, limousines, and first-class air travel, and the ads are peppered with words like *exclusive, refined, by invitation only,* and *prestige*.

Sponsors often produce several different prestige levels of a particular card: Visa regular and Visa gold or American Express green, gold, and platinum. By using the words *gold* and *platinum*, they seek to associate themselves with the prestige level of valuable metals that are no longer used to make money.

American Express devised the card class system. In 1958 they began with one category of service and a quarter of a million holders of the then purple card. To compete with the earlier prestige of Diners Club, American Express aimed its card primarily at upscale business travelers for use in making three major purchases: transportation, hotels, and restaurants. Like Diners Club, American Express maintained an illusion of membership—more like a private country club than a mere retail business.

After a few years American Express switched from purple, the color of royalty, to green, the color of American money. As the membership expanded and the range of services and merchants increased, American Express added the gold card in 1966 for its big-spending members. By the prosperous and glitzy 1980s, American Express had approximately half a million gold cardholders and needed to further refine them by class. For a time during 1984 the company tried an even more exclusive black card service, but this gave way to the platinum card in 1985. MasterCard and Visa added their own platinum cards in the mid-1990s. The credit card system of platinum, gold, and plain corresponded to the upper, middle, and working classes in the stratification of debt in America.

The whole concept of money has once again taken on a new meaning. The existence of money takes on a metaphysical tone similar to the question of whether or not a tree makes a sound if it falls in a forest where no one hears it. Credit cards, particularly when combined with electronic technology, took money to a whole new plateau of being.

MIDDLE-CLASS PERKS

By the final decade of the twentieth century, the United States had developed a multitiered money system. Poor people still use cash, primarily in the form of government printed paper dollars supplemented by food stamps, vouchers, and other forms of near-money issued by the federal government. The remainder of the population use bank-issued checks and plastic for all major money transactions.

Just as the government offered food stamps as a type of near-money for the poor, businesses developed new types of near-money geared specifically to the middle class. In the last decades of the twentieth century, one of the most popular forms of near-money arose in the form of *airline miles*. When American Airlines announced that it was giving "free travel" to its frequent fliers, the company was offering its customers a commodity—an airline ticket. Other airline companies quickly matched the offer from American Airlines. In return for flying a designated number of miles with an airline, a customer received a free round-trip ticket. The program worked well in maintaining customer loyalty. The airline industry also played on a small unexploited niche in the modern economic system. Most business travelers' tickets were paid for by their employers, yet the travelers themselves could choose the airline. More people were flying than ever before, but the frequent-flier system helped to ensure that those who traveled the most were also most likely to fly one favored airline whenever possible. Travelers paid for their tickets with their employers' funds, but in return they received "miles" that they could keep for themselves.

Because any ticket awarded under the frequent-flier program was not actual money, it could not be counted as income. Thus the tickets remained free of state and federal income tax. In some regards, this made them even better than cash awards, and this soon led to the creation of this specialized monetary niche based on frequent-flier miles rather than cash.

At first the airlines awarded one accounting mile for each mile flown, but inflation immediately set in as airline companies competed with one another to offer the most mileage. They awarded extra miles for certain flights that had not been selling as well or for flights at certain times of day, and first-class passengers received double mileage for each mile flown. To further encourage customer loyalty the airlines ranked their frequent fliers in categories such as silver, gold, or platinum based on how much they flew, then gave them weighted mileage. The silver category flier might receive 1.25 accounting miles for each mile flown while the gold flier received 1.5.

The concept of *miles* had increasingly less to do with actual miles flown. The severance of accounting miles from actual miles flown came when the airline industry connected its program to hotels and car rental companies, which began offering "air miles" to their customers. Similarly, telephone companies rewarded frequent callers with "mileage" based on the number and length of telephone calls made, and credit card companies offered their "mile" for every dollar charged on their cards. Customers could soon earn "mileage" for visiting the dentist, buying dog food, or getting a haircut, and it did not matter that much of this was in the form of yet more consumer debt.

What had begun as a simple and temporary advertising campaign and sales promotion to boost air travel had grown into a large system in which people did not have to travel at all in order to earn a large number of frequent-flier miles, which they could redeem not merely for airline tickets and family vacations but also for a great variety of goods and services that were, at least initially, tax free.

While merely trying to boost its own profits, the airline industry had inadvertently created a new form of money, an invisible commodity that they called *miles* but that could be used to purchase real services and commodities. Frequent-flier miles became for the upper middle class what Gold Bond, Greenbax, and S&H Green Stamps had been for some time for working-class housewives who did the family grocery shopping.

From credit and charge cards to frequent-flier miles, commercial institutions created new forms of money and pseudo-money during the second half of the twentieth century. Other commercial novelties and financial innovations acquired some of the characteristics of money without exactly being money. Trading stamps and flier miles represented future goods or services promised to the consumer, but the overwhelming majority of these new kinds of money represented consumer debt owed in rapidly escalating quantities to large financial institutions. The commercial innovations and new ways of incurring debt altered the way customers paid for purchases, but they were also changing the nature of money itself and people's relationship to it.

16

The Erotic Life of Electronic Money

When money stands still, it is no longer money.
—GEORG SIMMEL

E VER SINCE ANCIENT TIMES, WHEN PROSTITUTES serviced the worshipers in the temples of the Middle East in return for donations of golden coins to the gods, money has been closely associated with sex. This connection intensified greatly with the rise of capitalism. As Benjamin Franklin noted at the beginning of the capitalist era, "Money can beget money, and its offspring can beget more, and so on." Like an animate being, money has the ability to reproduce. Some Victorians, including Karl Marx and Friedrich Engels, were irritated by this uncanny facility of money to mimic sex.

In reaction to Victorian constraints, the twentieth century became a time of rebellion during which sex and money became much freer and easier. In the second half of the century, computers did for money what the birth-control pill had done for sex. The result was an era of unparalleled monetary promiscuity.

INVISIBLE MONEY

Immediately following the invention of the telegraph, people began to look for ways to move money electronically. Using the telegraph, banks could speed up certain customer services, but money transactions still had to be made in person. Not until the check and credit card era after the Second World War did banks finally catch up with the new technology. As more people paid by card and check, banks needed to find faster and better ways of moving large sums of money around.

233

In one sense, the electronic banking era opened in 1960 when the American Express Company used magnetic ink to code its traveler's checks for faster mechanized processing. Since they issued checks in only a few predetermined denominations and without small change, the processing of them electronically was much easier than for checks issued from personal bank accounts in varying amounts.

A more important step in the creation of electronic money was taken in 1972 when the Federal Reserve Bank of San Francisco experimented with electronic payments that bypassed paper checks for transactions between its main office and its Los Angeles branch. By 1978 the network had expanded to include all Federal Reserve banks and branches around the United States, but it remained primarily a way for different parts of the Federal Reserve to move funds within its own system. This process expanded again in 1980 when Congress passed the Monetary Control Act, which enlarged the electronic money network to include other financial institutions connected to the Federal Reserve.

The electronic system first touched the lives of a substantial number of Americans in 1975 when the Social Security Administration and the federal retirement system offered their recipients the option of having their money electronically deposited directly in their bank accounts. Other government retirement and payroll systems followed. The use of electronically deposited paychecks spread throughout the workforce, and the federal system was soon used for automatic payroll deductions for savings bonds, mortgages, insurance, retirement, and income tax payments.

The initial system was rather clumsy. The institutions transferred money through the system by putting large numbers of deposits and payments onto magnetic tapes, which the Federal Reserve banks sent by courier from one bank to another. These computer tapes replaced the large amounts of paper that otherwise would have been used. With the development of more sophisticated technology, the Federal Reserve could soon bypass the human unloading, transfer, and reloading of the tapes; and computers could send information to one another directly via telephone lines, thus creating a completely electronic money system by the early 1990s.

By 1992, twenty years after the creation of the federal computerized system, the network carried 67 million transfers annually with a total value of approximately 200 trillion electronic dollars. By the mid-1990s, the Federal Reserve system averaged $20 billion a day in electronic transfers in comparison to $47 billion a day in paper checks. Electronic banking remained, however, largely a behind-the-scenes and professional activity. The average consumer benefited from it through services such as paycheck deposit and the quicker movement of money.

Before learning to withdraw money from their accounts electronically, many working people gradually became accustomed to having money deposited electronically from their place of work. Germans and some other west Europeans became comfortable with such deposits in the 1970s, and in the 1980s the practice began to spread through North America. Over the years, as employees became confident that the money was *really* in their accounts, they began to transfer their money from one account to another, pay their bills automatically, and make automatic savings and retirement deposits. Aside from computer hackers and technophiles, however, relatively few people actively use electronic banking in their private accounts. The much discussed concept of the average person banking over the family computer using phone lines proved much more elusive than futurists and technophiles had anticipated. The financial institutions had difficulty in presenting technology that people liked and trusted.

The electronic money systems evolved differently in the various developed countries. Germans greatly prefer paying with debit cards and use credit cards far less frequently than Americans. Europeans never embraced the check as ardently as Americans did; many of them skipped that stage and went directly from cash to electronic cards. The Japanese, on the other hand, have a preference for paying even large sums in cash. Despite these differences, the trend in all developed nations and among the financial elites throughout the world is away from cash and toward electronic payment, processing, and recording of monetary transactions.

Public acceptance of electronic banking has proved to be quicker in many other parts of the world than in North America. By the 1990s nearly 100 percent of Japan's workers received their pay through automatic deposit, and about 90 percent of the workers in the advanced west European countries had similar services. By comparison, in the United States, the number still lagged at around one-third.[1]

In the United States during the 1990s, electronic cards gradually replaced both the government check and food stamps in some areas. Electronic deposit of welfare payments has helped prevent the theft of government checks from the recipients' mailboxes, but it has opened the way for electronic fraud by unscrupulous merchants and common street hustlers.

As various countries expanded their internal electronic nets for transferring money, the need arose for them to make such transfers between countries. In 1977 the Society for Worldwide Interbank Financial Telecommunication (SWIFT) went into operation in Brussels to coordinate the electronic movement of money across national borders. SWIFT grew into the largest international electronic network, connecting the banking systems of nearly one hundred nations.

THE VENDING MACHINE HOLDUP

The invention of money 2,500 years ago marked the beginning of the coin era. It was followed by the era of paper money, which began some five hundred years ago, after the invention of the printing press. The third great innovation in money began in 1971. In that year, a banker in Burbank, California, had an idea: why not develop a vending machine for money? An electronic bank teller could dispense cash by night and on weekends to customers who had trouble getting to the bank during office hours. With this modest innovation, the automated teller came into being. In that same year, the stock market went electronic with the creation of NASDAQ, a computerized system for buying and selling stocks; and at the same time, the Federal Reserve began to experiment with its electronic system for the automatic deposit and clearance of money without having to write out paper checks. Together these events kicked off a whole new way of dealing with money. When connected with one another, the electronic network of the Federal Reserve, the local cash machines, and the growing number of computers gave rise to a new form of electronic money.

After credit cards became well established in the 1970s, banks began to experiment with new cards using several different forms of technology and forming slightly different functions. Money cards, usually with a magnetic stripe on the back, emerged initially as a way for bank customers to withdraw their money from cash machines. Thus, the card acted primarily as an electronic check for acquiring cash. The card replaced the clerk in the bank, and for the customer, the outcome of obtaining cash remained the same.

Soon new applications were found for the money card. In an experimental program as early as 1974, the First Federal Savings and Loan of Lincoln, Nebraska, installed machines at the cash registers of the Hinky Dinky supermarket. Customers no longer had to go to a cash machine for money before going to the store to buy groceries with the cash. The grocers and bankers had eliminated the cash step. With the new machine, customers could simply swipe the card through the grocer's machine, thereby deducting the precise amount of the grocery bill from their bank account. With this step, the card had ceased being a convenient way to obtain cash and had become a substitute for cash as well as for checks. The electronic transfer made the transaction between customer and merchant much faster, since the customer no longer had to write out the check by hand and because the merchant no longer had to verify the check.

The greatest liability of the debit and cash cards was that they had to be hooked into a large telecommunications network, usually operating via telephone lines that connected computers. Each transaction had to be transmitted to a bank—or to some other central collection agency—verified, accepted, and then enacted. Such electronic hookups were quite profitable when linked to cash registers that rang up large sales in grocery or department stores or even at the gas station pumps, but they were too costly for businesses with less money turnover. The cards did little to relieve the customer or the merchant of handling vast amounts of coins and bills for small purchases such as those at vending machines and parking lots.

The greatest impediment to the wider spread of electronic money has come from the smallest of purchases such as those made in vending machines. The machine age and the labor-saving technology of the twentieth century inadvertently set back the evolution of money with the invention of vending machines. Throughout the twentieth century, the rise of vending machines created a tremendous surge in the need for coins, but the handling, transportation, and counting of the coins cost 2 to 6 percent of the value of the cash.

Even when the vending machine industry found ways for customers to pay for purchases with paper money, the handling costs remained high. A company that has to collect and transport one million paper dollars is collecting, inspecting, counting, and processing more than a ton of paper cut into a million strips. Money cards eliminated these costs.

At the same time that they began looking for ways to cut the expense of coin handling, banks sought ways to expand the use of bank cards. They immediately turned to a new kind of card with a computer chip embedded in it containing an authorized amount of money. This card could be inserted into a machine and the purchase amount debited without requiring electronic access to the central files of the bank where the older cash card information was usually stored.

The proponents of the so-called smart card hope that it will replace many of the routine cash payments that people make every day. By inserting the card—instead of coins or bills—into an electronic receptacle, the user can buy a newspaper from a machine equipped with a card reader, or buy snacks or drinks from vending machines. It can also be used to make telephone calls, to buy mass transit tickets, and to make many of the day's quick purchases.

The smart card provides exact payment, thus eliminating the need to make change. Seeking the correct combination of pennies, quarters, pfennigs, centavos, or pence for a purchase constitutes one of the small but persistent inconveniences for customers throughout the world. But what is an inconvenience to the customer becomes a great expense and burden to the merchant. Businesses must maintain a constant and varied supply of change in the cash register; vendors must constantly stock and monitor the change in their machines;

and all the heavy coins and bills must be repeatedly counted, organized, and transported—at great expense.

In the mid-1990s cash transactions amounted to more than $8 tril-
lion annually, and nearly a quarter of those were transactions of less
than $10 in value. In the United States alone, customers execute
some 300 billion cash transactions totaling $455 billion annually.
About 225 billion of these transactions—75 percent of all cash transactions—are for amounts of less than $20. This represents a lucra-
tive market for anyone who can find a way to replace bulky cash with
a form of money that is cheaper and easier to handle.

Because the smart chip card could hold a large amount of information in addition to the amount of stored money, it could have electronic coupons and shopping incentives coded in it; it could also
double as a loyalty card—the card that frequent customers obtain
from their airlines, hotels, car rental services, restaurants, and other
businesses that offer airline tickets, discounts, upgrades, and other services for customers depending on how often they use that merchant's
service.

Such a program has been developed in gambling casinos that use
loyalty cards. Each time a customer plays the slot or other gambling
machine, he inserts his loyalty card, which records all of his gambling
transactions. A player who wins with such a card then receives a
greater payout than does a player who wins without one. Even players who do not win receive a small compensation prize based on the
frequency of use of the card.

The English National Westminster Bank developed an electronic
cash payment system called Mondex that made their money cards
more like cash by allowing money to be transferred directly from one
card to another. By inserting the money card into a small but technologically sophisticated device, the user can transfer any amount of
money directly into a merchant's card. The merchant can then pass
the same electronic payment on to the next person. The electronic
blips continue to pass from person to person without having to be
constantly redeemed through a bank. The card might eventually be
usable to pay bills by telephone or to withdraw electronic money from
a banking account and have it transferred to the card via telephone

in the same way that it can be moved between accounts. Westminster Bank introduced the system in Swindon, England, in a test run in 1995 and began testing in North America the following year.[2] Visa introduced its simpler version of the money card at the 1996 Olympics in Atlanta.

ELECTRONIC CASH WARS

By the mid-1990s, a major struggle had begun for control of the newly emerging form of money. By entering the electronic age and transferring money over telecommunications networks, the banks were acting more like communications companies. Meanwhile, the communications companies had discovered that they could perform the same services and thereby function more like banks. Whichever side could win control of the system stood to earn great profits from millions of very small cash transactions. Control of the new electronic cash would endow the winning side with the power to make money itself.

The major players—computer companies, banks, credit card systems, telephone companies, cable television companies, and various retail interests—began jockeying for position in the great competition that was unfolding. With so many players entering the field, it quickly became obvious that no single contestant would emerge victorious; so they began negotiating with one another to form alliances and unite behind particular products. In the United States, most of the players came from the corporate sector.

Variations of the same struggle erupted simultaneously on several different fronts in North America, Europe, and the Pacific Rim. Technologically, the Europeans started the race somewhat ahead of the others since they were already using such cards to pay for public telephone calls and mass transit. By 1995 about 1.8 billion prepaid cards were in use in the world, representing some 14 billion money transactions. Most of these cards were in closed systems such as college campuses, amusement parks, cruise ships, vacation resorts, or gambling casinos. The volume of cards represented a vast market for any company that could build a network to unite the cards so that the same card could be used to make a telephone call, ride the subway, pay for lunch, and buy a newspaper.

Several companies formed networks to seize the cash market. Visa experimented with a unified stored-value card in Australia, Argentina, and Chile. In the United States in 1995, Visa introduced the TravelMoney card, which they marketed as a substitute for traveler's checks, although it was hoped that customers would expand its use into other purchases as well.

The movement toward electronic money was not the result of public demand by people who were dissatisfied with the old forms of money. The change has been technologically driven by businesses seeking a new way to make money. They invent devices that make money easier and safer for customers and merchants to use, and if they succeed, they increase their revenue. To succeed, however, the makers of this new money must educate and encourage people to try the system, develop confidence in it, and then substitute it for the older system. They have to make people want to use electronic money rather than the cash and checks to which they are accustomed. One way to attract these customers is to offer them security and freedom from fear. People are afraid to carry much cash with them because it can be so easily stolen. The cards, however, are useless to a thief who lacks the appropriate identification or number to use them.

Although security may be the major drawing point for new customers, it is also the greatest danger for merchants, bankers, and the other sponsors. Their products and services are vulnerable to electronic theft and fraud, which are not a danger to cash and traditional checking accounts. For the most part, cash withdrawal cards attracted small-time crooks and loners. They might wait around a cash machine and then mug a patron who had withdrawn cash. More sophisticated crooks watched the customer use the card in order to read the identification number, then by using a discarded transaction slip and the right string of numbers, the swindler could empty the customer's account.

As electronic systems became more complex for withdrawing money, moving money among accounts, and making automatic payments, more sophisticated crime organizations began to move

242   *The History of Money*

into the field of electronic money. The international nature of this new money also made transactions particularly vulnerable when initiated from poorer countries where criminals could gain access to the system through computer hookups and simple telephone lines.

Most world governments have not exhibited a decisive inclination to guide the complicated electronic process, but various government agencies have shown a tremendous interest in retaining their ability to monitor it. The tax offices, the drug and law enforcement agencies, and others recognize that the new electronic networks allow people to move money surreptitiously and quickly in new ways that are not available through traditional banking.[3]

At the opening of the twenty-first century, the competition among contenders is growing rapidly, and with the new electronic technology, more new contenders may appear in configurations that we cannot yet imagine. At this time the struggle seems to be between competing private interests, but the government may not remain a minor player much longer. The monetary powers of the German, Japanese, and U.S. governments will eventually turn their attention to the regulation of electronic money. Electronic cash now seems poised to replace traditional cash for most purposes. A great rivalry has begun among financial interests to determine which will win the consumer over to electronic money and which will give consumers the right card.

The debit cards and smart cards offer a more efficient way of transporting money; they function as faster versions of the pony express but with the computer and telephone replacing the horses. The full application of electronics to money, however, awaited the sudden popularization of the global Internet in the 1990s. The rapid spread of the international computer network created a whole new type of market for business and for new kinds of money in which to transact it.

The Internet provided the opportunity for people to order merchandise in an electronic mail-order catalog and make payment electronically by charging the bill to a traditional credit card or writing electronic checks on traditional bank accounts. Enthusiasts predicted that the cyber mall of the universe would take over much of the business of retail centers such as the Mall of America just as the malls had largely replaced the commercial district of traditional Main Street. The first burst of commercial enthusiasm for the Internet led to predictions that people would purchase their groceries, find the latest clothes, select a gift for Grandpa, and restock the wine cellar via orders made on the computer.

As the Internet matured, however, it became obvious that for many social and practical reasons, it posed only a limited threat to the retail merchants. For a minority of customers, the electronic mail-order catalogs offered opportunities for specialized tasks such as sending gifts and flowers or ordering pizza, but for the foreseeable future, they would continue to make most purchases in the traditional way. Even though customers could not download wine, jewelry, hardware, or other such goods directly into their homes via the computer, they could download a large variety of goods and services such as computer software, information, newsletters, games, article reprints, and even pornography. They could use on-line services to purchase airline tickets, reserve baseball or opera tickets, and execute other transactions that did not require the mailing of an actual piece of merchandise. Those customers who already had an affinity for using computers and the latest technology could perform many of their traditional banking services on-line such as paying bills or applying for loans. They could purchase stocks and bonds, take money in or out of a mutual fund, and check on their retirement accounts. The Internet offered an ideal way to do what computers were designed to do—to process information—and increasingly money had the characteristics of information. On the Internet, money is not something tangible; it is merely a record that a certain sum has been registered in a customer's account or moved out of it into a specific merchant's account. That information can be stored and transferred through a computer network faster and more efficiently than by any other means.

In 1995 the Mark Twain Bank and the First Bank of the Internet began operation as strictly Internet banks rather than as mere electronic branches of traditional banks. In their initial years, the cyber banks seemed to operate primarily as novelties for computer hackers because cyberspace still lacked the requisite technology, the commercial need, and the social acceptance for such radical departures from traditional ways of handling money, but they built part of the groundwork for a new generation of financial services on the Internet.

The Internet offered great promise as a financial marketplace, but it soon became obvious that the network needed a system of payment more sophisticated than merely transferring credit card and bank account numbers that could be easily intercepted, copied, and used by criminals. Computer specialists around the world sought to develop systems of encryption and ways of safeguarding payments, and almost immediately, they began seeking ways of creating totally electronic money that would be created in cyberspace and exist only in cyberspace. Customers could use traditional currency to buy these newly designed units of electronic money. They would have accounts with the cyber money deposited in it, and they could use those accounts to buy and sell in cyberspace. As the cyber economy developed, services could be performed and paid for in cyberspace using cyber money, and thus only a portion of this electronic currency needed to be converted in or out of conventional currency. The new currency would not completely replace either the older kinds of money or traditional bank accounts; it would, however, add another layer of financial transactions and another set of accounts to what people were already accustomed to using. In the near future, many people will probably maintain cyber accounts in much the same way they already hold various accounts in financial institutions such as savings and loans, banks, credit unions, stock brokerage firms, and retirement systems.

In the initial years, much of the commerce of cyberspace will be conducted by businesses and large institutions interacting with one another rather than with mass consumers, but gradually the commerce will spread into the mass marketing of goods and services. Electronic money will soon move into other areas of life and take over other social uses of money. Grandma can send an electronic birthday card with electronic dollars that will be carried straight to her grandchild's computer screen and deposited in a cyber-savings account for college or used to buy whatever the recipient wanted from cyberspace. The gambling aficionado will no longer need to travel to a casino to play the slot machines or to visit the local convenience store to buy a lottery ticket; such forms of gambling could be done over the Internet with great ease. Customers can buy lottery tickets from around the world or play in the casino of Monte Carlo or in the Turks and Caicos Islands.

As in most times of radical technological and social innovation, many plans for new types of money have been proposed and tested in the early years of the Internet. Some of the most logical proved untenable and some of the strangest proved quite adaptable to the needs of the newly developing system. In a very short time, the major technological, political, and cultural problems of using electronic money on the Internet will be solved, and the new cyber money promises to play a major role in the economy of the twenty-first century.

As it matures the new money will develop its own set of problems and crimes in addition to those of electronic theft and counterfeiting. Because cyberspace is nowhere and everywhere, people can make transaction around the world instantly. Their cyber account may be located in Switzerland or the Cayman Islands as easily as in the bank around the corner. The difficulty in ascertaining exactly where a transaction takes place will make it increasingly difficult for local governments to follow it or tax it. The same characteristics increase the difficulty in tracing money, thus blurring even further the distinctions between legitimate and illegitimate enterprises.

Each electronic transaction represents an opportunity to assess a fee. The charges will probably be much smaller than traditional transaction fees that merchants pay for using a credit card or smaller than the fees typically charged by banks for cashing checks or using automated tellers, but the anticipated volume of such transactions will generate tremendous profits. The companies that control this process will have the opportunity to make money through seigniorage, the traditional profit governments derived from minting money. Elec-

tronic seigniorage will be a key to accumulating wealth and power
in the twenty-first century, and as such, it represents a radical departure from the twentieth century when most people had become
very comfortable with a system in which the government exercised
a near monopoly on the creation and control of currency.

Behind the scenes at the interwoven markets of today, a fierce
struggle is under way for control of money. The key to future power
lies not just in controlling nations with large amounts of territory and
people, and not only in controlling multinational corporations that
stretch around the globe. Of even greater importance is the question
of who will control the creation and distribution of money itself—
the substance on which rests all the wealth of nations, the power of
corporations, and the success of individuals.

The great struggle of history has been for the control over money.
It is almost tautological to affirm that to control the production and
distribution of money is to control the wealth, resources, and people
of the world. Over time, competitors have aligned themselves into
various factions, institutions, governments, banks, guilds, corporations, religious orders, and great families; but from the minting of the
first coin until today, the struggle has never abated for more than a
brief respite of a century or two.

The money wars have sometimes been literal ones fought on great
battlefields with large armies, tanks, warships, bombers, and missiles.
At other times they have been metaphorical—but no less serious—
struggles conducted in private chambers, corporate boardrooms,
courts of law, and legislative halls as well as on the floors of the great
stock and mercantile exchanges of the world. As soon as a battle is
settled in one arena, the actors and interests switch to another where
they fight with new rules and new weapons.

Throughout history, whenever one faction or institution seemed
to have won control of money, an outside player invented another
form based on a new technology, and another struggle erupted.
Minted coins displaced the simpler forms of primitive money. Banking and paper money undermined the widespread use of coins; and
today we have begun the transition to electronic currency, the struggle over which is just now beginning as the major players jockey for

position on the playing field in what promises to be the great competition of the coming century.

BACK TO PRIMITIVE MONEY

Electronic money offers the user the choice of keeping money in dollars, marks, yen, or any combination of currencies. In the near future, financial corporations may begin to offer their own electronic money to compete with the national currencies in use today. Private currencies may be invented based on gold, on a particular mixture of commodities or currencies, or simply on the reputation and financial strength of a particular money-issuing entity. We might have Citicorp Currency, Yamamoto Yen, or Dresdener Talers, each based on the financial strength and reputation of its backer.

The electronic network allows money to become more personalized even as it makes the ties between customers and merchants less personalized.[4] Electronic money comes in far greater varieties than traditional currency—e-cash, e-money, cyber cash, DigiCash, cyberbucks, and as many other forms as people care to create and float. Market forces will push many of these currencies out of use, but rather than just reducing money to a few name brands—the way credit cards were reduced to Visa, Discover, MasterCard, and a few others—the new currencies will likely become special-purpose moneys. Consumers in the near future are likely to use several kinds of electronic money, depending on the kind of service or product they are purchasing. In addition to the live forms of electronic money on the wire, they will have several kinds of cash cards in their pockets or, at least, several kinds of accounts on a single card.

Electronic money resembles the diverse forms of primitive money—cowrie shells, animal teeth, and beads—in that it permits individuals more control over its creation and use. The new money has many sources and can be handled in many different ways. It has far more flexibility than governments and banks have allotted to metal or paper currency in the last two millennia.

The invention of new ways of producing money and near-money by private institutions means that money can become much more varied than it has been. Each technological change in money production added a new type of money and spread its use into new areas, but the changes did not eradicate the old types. Coins survived the introduction of paper money. Even today, when no one uses gold coins in daily cash interactions, there are more gold coins in bank vaults and hidden away in homes than there were at any other time in history. Paper money simply added a new form of money. Paper money altered the role of gold and silver coins but did not end their usefulness. Similarly, electronic money has added yet more types but without destroying paper or coins. We now also have more paper money in circulation around the world than at any other time in history.

Electronic money promises to expand the role of money in our society even farther than metal, paper, and plastic were able to do. People will create new uses for electronic money that we cannot even imagine and that could not have been possible with the earlier forms of money.

Mankind has used money for twenty-five centuries. Throughout this time, it has alternately grown and stagnated, been abandoned and resurrected, debased and restored, inflated and depressed. After a particularly long and successful tradition of money based on gold and silver, money mutated yet again in the twentieth century into invisible electronic impulses that, at first, seemed like nothing more than a more efficient modern form of ink with which to record numbers and information. But this new mutation has proved to be something far more flexible than any scholar, merchant, guru, or psychic predicted. Free at last from the confines of time and space, from the control of any particular government, from any collection of corporations, and even from the normal forces of the economy, money has evolved to a new level and into a totally new entity. Money will never again be what it was.

In the twentieth century, we saw money turn rapidly from paper into plastic and then into mere electronic blips generated in computers, transferred over telephone lines and through computer terminals, and without any corporal existence outside of the electronic domain. Throughout its history, money has become steadily more abstract. By moving at the speed of light, electronic money has become the most powerful financial, political, and social force in the world. Money has become even more like God: totally abstract and without corporeal body.

President Harry Truman had a famous sign on his desk that proclaimed "The buck stops here." From time to time, government officials in the Treasury Department and in the Bureau of Printing and Engraving have had their own corresponding signs claiming, "The buck starts here." Today the electronic buck neither starts nor stops; it is in constant motion.

On the Pacific island of Yap in the Western Caroline Islands, southwest of Guam, can be found the largest money in the world.[5] Their traditional money looks something like large millstones; it consists of round slabs of sandstone with square holes in the middle. Some are small enough for a child to lift, but others stand so high that they dwarf even the tallest man on the island. The ancient Yapese quarried the great slabs of sandstone several hundred miles away on the island of Belau, and they ferried the stones to Yap across open ocean on large double-hulled canoes.

The aristocratic classes of Yap owned the stone money and used it primarily for ritual purposes. In daily life, commoners used a variety of cheaper and more easily portable shells as money. Even the shells had a rank according to color, with the rarer blue-lipped shells possessing a greater value than the more common yellow-lipped variety. The lower the status of the person, the lower the status of money he or she had to use.

Although specimens of the giant stone money of Yap can now be seen in museums in various parts of the world, most of them remain in Yap, where the natives stand them on end beside the road like a large stone fence that constitutes the traditional public bank of the island. Each stone has its owner. Occasionally through the years the ownership changes, but the stones remain in the same public place.

The stones and shells of Yap still constitute an important part of traditional Yapese culture, but the people rushing past them also use American dollars or Japanese yen. They deal readily in traveler's checks, charge cards, prepaid invoices, and electronic transfers of funds. The stone money of Yap still stands, however, as a dramatic reminder of another system that used to dominate virtually every aspect of the social and cultural life of the island but now survives only as a shadow of its former power and grandeur. The monetary history of the island can be seen like the strata of an archaeologist's pit, as one system grew out of and then replaced its predecessor.

In some ways the new electronic money emerging in the world today may more closely resemble the old system of Yap than it does the system of national currencies now in place. As the system of national money controlled by governments comes to an end, a whole new market is forming in cyberspace where many different kinds of money operate simultaneously. Like the ancient people of Yap, future users of money will be confronted with a bewildering array of different kinds of money with different, and sometimes very specific, uses. Like the multicolored shells and the various-size slabs of sandstone, the money of the future will come in many sizes and shapes that will depend less on the country of origin than on the class and type of person using it.

We stand today at the end of a long historical process of development in which money changed from shells and commodities into an elaborate global system of currencies. We also stand at the beginning of what promises to be the greatest social and cultural revolution since the invention of money.

17
The Art of Currency Terror

Jesus went into the temple of God and . . .
overthrew the tables of the money changers.
—*MATTHEW 21:12*

A business that makes nothing but money is a poor kind of business.
—*HENRY FORD*

A SPECTER IS HAUNTING THE WORLD—THE SPECTER of money in its immaterial, electronic presence, possessing neither form nor figure. It prowls hungrily around the globe by day as well as by night; it knows neither national borders nor seasons of the year. This strange beast appeared so recently on the world scene that we do not even have a name for it. The specter that haunts the world is made up of the vast but invisible cloud of money-as-energy that rushes from one currency to another at the flick of an electronic switch or a programmed computer. It is as close as a credit card, telephone, or computer, and yet it is as far beyond our control as the tides. It represents a mixture of humankind's most basic desires, fears, and faith.

At the dawn of the twenty-first century we have reached a crossroads in the relationship between society and money—this seemingly animate force that humans created but seem unable to control. Money has become a global artifact and the linchpin of an economic system that dominates every part of the world. Now that nearly all world communism has collapsed of its own deadweight, the capitalist system—built on money—has triumphed around the globe. Money dominates not only the economic systems of production, ownership, labor, and consumption, but has a major influence on almost every aspect of private life. After a prelude of more than two thousand years during which humans developed elaborate forms and varieties of money and established a vast array of institutions around it, world history has entered the cyber age, which may well be the age of money.

The emergence of the global electronic money system with the free-floating currencies of the world allows millions of dollars to be transferred from one currency to another instantly at any time and on any day of the year. By 1995 this homeless electronic money had surpassed $1.3 trillion a day in transactions as traders deserted the dollar, fortified the mark, then raced to the yen or off to some other momentarily popular currency somewhere in the farthest corners of the world.

The volume of transactions measured in trillions is hard to conceptualize, but if converted to one-dollar bills, a sum of $1.3 trillion would weigh more than thirty-two steel ships the size of the *Titanic*. Yet the new money needs no fleet of ships to transport it around the world because it travels instantly.

The specter of electronic money wields far more power than the largest banks or corporations; it even has the ability to force politicians of the strongest world economies to cringe in humble submission to its erratic will and unpredictable movements. The direction of the money specter is determined by thousands of currency traders backed by millions of daily choices made by individuals—an American deciding to purchase a Japanese car, for example, or a Russian buying a Korean television set; a German using Russian natural gas or a Japanese choosing an American computer program.

At any second of the day, thousands of traders stand poised to react, and even more computers stand ready to buy and sell as soon as the numbers line up in the statistically programmed pattern. The many virtually simultaneous decisions of people throughout the world create a large supply of electronic money that moves like a carefully trained and choreographed flock of birds that take flight in a moment, all headed in the same direction and able to change course in midstream. This currency flock roams the earth by night and day, alighting here and there before taking off for another pond or field on the other side of the world.

COMPUTER KIDS

The traders who work in a typical currency-trading office alternate between bored idleness and frenzied activity. One minute they seem relaxed, with their feet up on the desk, sipping coffee, reading magazines, playing video games, listening to loud rock music on headphones, joking, and tossing a sponge-rubber ball into a tiny basket. The next minute they spring into action as though unexpectedly attacked by a swarm of bees. Their real focus is not in the room itself but rather in cyberspace, which they can perceive on the screens of the many monitors and terminals before them. Suddenly they are shouting into two or three phones at once and switching back and forth from one monitor to another. Such bouts of activity may last for a few minutes or may be prolonged for several days.

Sometimes the traders cannot stop for a meal or even break away from their screens and phones long enough to eat the sandwiches, chips, and drinks brought to their desks throughout the day. Occasionally one of them has a hand free long enough to grab the cup of cold coffee sitting on his desk in a Styrofoam cup.

The market without borders never opens or closes; it merely pulses. It does not distinguish winter from summer, and it knows neither night nor day. It never takes a vacation, a holiday, a siesta, or even a lunch break. When the banks close in Switzerland for the night, the offices are already open for business in Tokyo and Sydney. When the trading houses shut down for a national holiday in Shanghai, the offices in London and New York continue to hum. When the American traders pause for Thanksgiving dinner or the European offices close for Christmas, the sales continue to pulse in Bombay, Tel Aviv, Hong Kong, and Seoul. Individual offices open and close, and individual traders log on and off line; but the market continues to operate during every millisecond of every day. To meet the demands of such a market, the larger players on the currency market must stay active all night. Deep within the windowless but climate-controlled interiors of banks in New York, the mercantile exchange in Chicago, and brokerage houses in London, traders operate twenty-four hours a day beneath a ceiling of harsh fluorescent lights amid the constant flickering of computer screens, the piercing sounds of electronic whistles, and the whine of electronic buzzers.

The currency market is today the largest market in the world. The money exchanged on the currency market surpasses the gross national product of the world's major economies for an entire year. In a year a single trading center such as the Chicago Mercantile Exchange oversees currency trading the value of which surpasses that of the combined gross national product of the whole world.

The twentieth century opened with only a few currencies in the world, and they were all tied to gold. By the end of the century, there were nearly two hundred national currencies varying from the U.S. dollar to local currencies that had no circulation outside the area controlled by their own national governments. Each new currency provided opportunities for new speculation, but the primary currencies continued to be those of western Europe, North America, and Japan, with the others coming sporadically into and out of play.

The currency market stretches around the world in a network formation, but like any network it has some connecting nodes of particular importance such as the International Money Market pit in the Chicago Mercantile Exchange and the Philadelphia Stock Exchange, the two largest currency futures trading markets in the United States. Up to five hundred traders can gather in the tiered layers of the Chicago pit, and like traders in any market, they shout, use signals, and dress in distinctive ways in order to connect with the people with whom they hope to do business—that is, to sell currency futures. Just as they trade futures on hog bellies, soybeans, or gold, the currency traders sell the right to buy currency of a certain country at a certain rate on a certain future date. If a business orders goods worth a million yen due on a particular delivery date in one year, the ordering business does not want to take a chance that the yen might increase by as much as 15 percent in a year. To ensure that they can have a million yen at a reasonable exchange rate, they buy currency futures that guarantee them the right to buy the yen at a particular price in dollars next year. If the yen increases in value, then buying the currency future saved them money. If the yen does not go up in value, then the cost of the currency future served as their insurance policy. In a world of constantly changing currency prices, the futures market allows individual merchants to have a better idea of the range of costs and income they will receive in future international trades.

So long as currency trading served only to facilitate commerce, it took place in musty offices of functionaries at banks and other financial institutions. It operated in the back rooms where currency exchange required only basic clerical skills and little imagination; almost the only error one could make was in computation. This pacific obscurity changed on May 16, 1972, when the Chicago "money pit" opened as the first currency futures market.

Even though the currency trading pits seem to be exploding with activity when they are working, their overall part in the market of currency trading has been declining. Compared to the new behind-the-scenes market of cyberspace, the old face-to-face markets are dinosaurs in the world currency market. No matter how much electronic equipment they lug onto the floor, regardless of how meticulously they color-code their employees' jackets, they still open and close, and they spend more hours of the week closed than open. In mid-1995 currency options on the whole Philadelphia exchange averaged a pitiful $1.5 billion a day, not nearly enough to be a big player in the trillion-dollar market.[1]

With the fluctuations of currency set on an open market and with the improved technology of computers and satellite communications, no single center can dominate the currency market the way a few major centers dominate the stock markets, commodity markets, insurance markets, and banking. Today information from all of these markets reaches a German businessman in Singapore at the same moment it reaches a French stockbroker vacationing on a cruise ship in the Caribbean, an eccentric billionaire hermit in the Australian outback, and a housewives' investor club in Minneapolis.

The currency market differs from all others in another, even more fundamental way. In other markets, merchants exchange goods for money; but in the currency market, traders exchange the money of one country for the money of another, with no other goods involved in the transaction. They need only haggle about the bid and asking price. They do not need to discuss metric versus American measurements, preferred voltage, or shipping lines. The only quantity is money. The exchange, whether today or a year from now, will be made instantly by electronic transfer. The currency market is thus the purest market of all. It is all transaction and no goods. Without the need to plant, sow, harvest, ship, manufacture, or change the goods in any way, the currency market faces no delays; its transactions are instantaneous. With the speed of light, electronic impulses race around the globe, and dollars rush from Singapore to São Paulo, yen flood into the central bank of Zaire, Turkish pounds flee to Germany, and South African rands become Canadian dollars.

Even with telegraphs and telephones, it took time for an announcement of interest rate increases by the Bank of England to reach New York, Sydney, Buenos Aires, and Cape Town. If the office was closed for the night or for a holiday weekend, the news would not be registered until several days later, and it might be several additional days before the newspapers could print the information and disseminate it to the farthest corners of the land. In such a world, a few nerve centers dominated the financial life of entire regions, and one area—initially the City of London and later New York City—dominated the world economy. Interlinking networks of bankers, bureaucrats, and boards of directors would inform one another of the change through personal phone calls, but the general public had to scavenge for information at the bottom of the pond. In that world the currencies themselves changed very slowly over time and only after the ponderous process of government had made the decision to do so. Because each nation tied its currency to gold or silver, or to a stronger currency such as the American dollar, the British pound, or the French franc, the values of world currencies stayed the same not merely for years but for decades.

Much of the rapid currency movement is based on intangible moods, intuitions, and prejudices. Such moves often reflect the trust that investors have in the leaders of a country at any particular moment. They trusted Ronald Reagan to act the way Ronald Reagan acted, and consequently the dollar traded at higher levels during his presidency than the objective data would otherwise have warranted. Investors lacked that kind of confidence in George Bush and Bill Clinton, causing the dollar to fall.

Such intangible factors as these probably account for about 75 percent of the currency fluctuations, while only about 25 percent can be correlated with actual quantified economic factors and statistical indicators.[2]

The same technology that disseminates news so quickly around the globe also permits the newly informed recipients of the information to make rapid market decisions, whether the trader is sitting on the busiest trading floor in Amsterdam or calling from a cellular phone in Patagonia. Speculators can buy and sell currencies anywhere in the world by punching a few computer keys or clicking on an icon, but for those for whom even that procedure may be too slow, automatic computer programs can take away even those simple tasks. Traders set their computers so that they automatically sell dollars if the price drops below or rises above a certain figure. With each trader free to write an individual trading strategy, the computer programs take on vastly complicated forms and digest a wealth of information. The programs may calibrate the changing flux of currency values as well as the relative interest rates, the levels of government borrowing, the cost of commodities, the rise and fall of trade balances, or the changes in new home construction, corporate returns, or any other factor such as temperature and rainfall in agricultural areas or game scores of a favorite athletic team.

Bellum Omnium in Omnes

In the late 1980s and the 1990s, the international currency market offered financial institutions an opportunity to make money with far fewer employees. A bank that used traditional methods and provided the traditional range of customer services needed an army of approximately 5,000 workers to administer deposits, loans, and other holdings of $10 billion. A department of only 20 people, however, could handle the same amount of money on the currency markets, thereby saving the salary, training, and administrative costs of 4,980 employees.[3] Every three days New York City's financial institutions handle as much money as passes through all the major American corporations in an entire year. In a month they handle the monetary equivalent of double the world's annual industrial output.

By the mid-1990s, currency trading had become the quickest way
to make money. It followed a series of fads, from arbitrage and junk
bonds to inflated farmland. Some of the largest international corporations were making more money from their currency speculation
than from manufacturing or trading in their usual products. Financial institutions from large banks to county governments and community colleges were speculating in currency trading as a way to
make quick profits.[4]

Although the world currency market is, in theory, wide open to
any potential player, in actuality, the frontline players tend to be
young, single, and male. Only the young seem able to take the inor-
dinate risks involved in handling tens of millions of dollars' worth of
other people's assets. Before marriage and without the demands of
family dinners, childbirth classes, children's homework and music
recital, and car pooling for Little League, young single men have the
total attention, dedication, and stamina necessary for a round-the-
clock market.

Despite its electronic sophistication and its lack of a specific place
and hours of operation, the market is not impersonal. It responds even
more sensitively and wildly to subjective factors, opinions, fears, and
hopes than do other kinds of markets. Perhaps it is because their market is so dispersed and mechanical that many of the major players
keep in constant communication with one another over the telephone. They call their trading partners in New York, Singapore,
Geneva, Frankfurt, Sydney, and Tokyo in the hope of detecting some
small trend a few minutes before it shows up in the numbers on the
screen or is reported publicly on the international financial network.
The biggest players must know their partners and know how to in-
terpret what they say as well as what they do. Is the person on the
other end of the telephone line saying something important, relay-
ing a confidence in hope of a future favor, repaying a past favor, plot-
ting revenge, or repeating an unfounded rumor? Is he unaware of the
importance of what he is saying or just filling the airwaves with idle
thoughts as he waits for the next round of intense action?

To obtain even a small advantage over other players, each trader
must have dozens of contacts around the world and be able to judge

each of them carefully. There are no permanent teams operating in the currency market, but individual traders desperately need to interact with one another to figure out the market and to negotiate their sales. They constantly form and re-form ad hoc alliances and partnerships that may be dismantled quickly in favor of others. Today's rival becomes tomorrow's partner, and today's partner may be tonight's rival. The currency market probably comes as close to the proverbial *bellum omnium in omnes*—war of all against all—as any institution in history.

The market player scans constantly for odd bits of information, general perspectives, and vague attitudes that cannot be quantified or fed into a computer program. By painstakingly piecing together all the bits and pieces of personalized information in a constantly changing field, the players hope to remain just a few seconds ahead of the others.

Humans have rarely invented a tool that they did not use. In the process of creating this vast network of machines and programs and in enabling themselves to respond so quickly, the financial players also created their own imperative to use it constantly. No longer able to wait until Monday morning or even until daybreak, the trader must react instantly in a world market in which a few milliseconds can determine the difference between profit and loss and a few minutes can mean the difference between solvency and bankruptcy. The speed imperative of the new technology has heightened the flock mentality of the traders and increased the tendency of capital to move en masse. No longer able to digest information for a few days before acting on it, traders must make instant decisions to separate fact from rumor or to anticipate how the Japanese will react to the news of an increasing German trade balance. For any trader who is in doubt and unable to reflect adequately on the issue, the best course is to follow the herd. Rather than learning to assess the varied bits and pieces of financial information constantly flowing through the computer and telephone lines, traders learn to read the signs of the other traders. They respond not so much to corporate reports, other markets, and government announcements as to the actions of other traders.

For the currency traders, it is less important to know the real meaning of a new piece of information than to anticipate how the market will react. Even if a trader believes that the momentary drop in interest rates in France is not very important, if he thinks that other traders will think it is important, then he too must act on it as though it is important.

The herd mentality of the traders increases the mass and power of the large floating corpus of money circling the world. The increased mass and power, in turn, increases the importance of any move that the market makes. Because the traders are unable to act delicately or lightly, the decisions race around with the quiet and delicacy of a herd of wildebeests. A momentary flutter suddenly becomes a major stampede from the dollar to the Swiss franc and German mark. Each move produces financial ripples that quickly penetrate every part of the economy. As great an impact as such movements can have on the currency of large, powerful economies such as those of the United States and Japan, the effect can be absolutely crippling if the capital herd suddenly decides to abandon the Mexican peso, the New Zealand dollar, or the Italian lira, or if it finds unexpected interest in buying Russian rubles, Egyptian pounds, or Greek drachmas.

"THE AIDS OF OUR ECONOMIES"

At the summit meeting of the heads of state from the seven major powers held in Halifax, Nova Scotia, in June 1995, French president Jacques Chirac expressed a general mistrust of the currency markets when he labeled currency speculation "the AIDS of our economies."[5] What he neglected to say was that the governments themselves are the source of this economic disease.

With so many players and such large sums of money at risk, some must lose. Yet, oddly enough, it seems that the major players are all making profits at this game. Occasionally some large investing house experiences a major downturn or a bank collapses, but for the most part they all seem to be profiting from currency speculation more than from other, more conservative investments.

Rather than being a means for the market, money *became* the market. As William Greider wrote, "Money was meant to be the neutral agent of commerce. Now it had become the neurotic master."[6]

In abandoning the gold standard and in dropping the currency exchange rates set by the Bretton Woods Agreement of 1944, the governments of the world agreed to let the currency of each country find its own rate of exchange. National governments still attempt to influence the rate in the short run, but they lack the power to control it. One way they influence it is by the interest rates they pay on their bonds. For example, if the United States offers a higher return than Germany, more investors will need dollars with which to buy the American bonds and fewer investors will need marks, thus driving up the value of the dollar relative to the mark. Just as corporations sometimes buy up their own stock to decrease its availability and increase demand, thus raising its price, governments can influence the exchange rate for their currencies. Their national bank can purchase large quantities of their own currency in an effort to drive the price up, or it can sell large quantities on the international market in order to force the price down.

Despite such efforts, governments cannot hold back the tide of the market. When the bottom fell out of the Mexican peso in 1995, President Clinton rushed in with a $53 billion rescue package, but it proved too small to save the peso on the international currency market. The Mexican economy plays a relatively small role on the world stage and its currency has traditionally been a "soft" one, but the political bankers of even the largest nations fare little better. No matter how many resources they bring to bear to keep the mark or dollar at a particular value, if all the investors believe it is going to change and are awaiting that change, the government can only sandbag against market sentiment for a relatively short time. Eventually, market opinion wins.

Even when several countries have combined their efforts to control the market, they have not been able to do so. On September 22, 1985, the United States, represented by Treasury Secretary Donald Regan, and the foreign ministers of Japan, Germany, Great Britain, and France met in New York City. From the stately Plaza Hotel, they announced an agreement by all five governments to let the dollar slowly devalue. The market responded immediately to the word *devalued* and ignored the word *slowly*, plunging the dollar down to new low levels.

Large financial institutions such as Salomon Brothers, Citibank,

ING Bank (Internationale Nederlanden Groep), or Goldman, Sachs
can sometimes use similar practices to nudge the value of one currency up or to restrain it for a while. Despite these short-term influ-
ences, however, in the long run the market operates as the result of
thousands of decisions by thousands of different investors and institutions acting on their own information, their own analyses, and their
individual interests, needs, and goals. The losers in the game are
sometimes other large financial institutions. For the most part, the
losers are the taxpayers whose governments are trying to prop up a
currency when the tide is against it or to hold its value down in order
to protect exports.

Traders for private investors must be quicker and sharper. If they
consistently lose money, they will lose their customers. The national
banks operate under no such constraints; ultimately they work for the
government, and the aim of the government is not to make a profit
but to pursue a particular monetary policy for the moment—to expand or restrict the money supply, to hold the national currency up,
or to let it slide. The banker-bureaucrats then judge their performance
not on how much money they won or lost but on how well they ful-
filled the policy goal. If they lose money, the loss is blamed on the
market, not on them. The taxpayers, knowingly or not, must pay the
bill; it is part of the price of government. In this way the government
subsidizes currency trading and speculation. Without government intervention, there would be painfully little profit in such endeavors.[7]
The more the government banks struggle to control the currency
market, the more money can be made in currency speculation
since the government is virtually always trying to move against the
market.

At the end of the year when the government-sponsored institutions show their gains and losses from trading, the numbers might
make it appear that they are competing—thus winning and losing—
against other institutions when, in fact, they are only losing. The U.S.
Treasury Department and the Federal Reserve have considerably less
power to control the value of the dollar than the Italian bank has to
control the lira or the Thai government has to control the baht. The
more a currency is traded, the less power any government has over

it; the less it is traded, the more powerful and significant becomes any particular government intervention. As former currency trader Ted Fishman explained it, even if an individual trader wins, he loses as a citizen: "I'm a loser as a citizen and a taxpayer, as long as the U.S. Treasury and the Federal Reserve keep spending public funds on intervention, giving dollars to the guys with the squawk boxes and computers."[8]

Currency traders playing against bureaucrats will win virtually every time. Investors and bankers will defeat government officials and their economic advisers. Currency trading in the closing decade of the twentieth century gave new meaning and a new cynicism to Voltaire's comment that "In general, the art of government consists in taking as much money as possible from one part of the citizens to give to the other."[9]

18

The Age of Money

It's definitely new, it's revolutionary—and we should be scared as hell.
—BANKER SHOLOM ROSEN

MONEY BEGAN AS SIMPLE COMMODITIES OF COPPER, silver, shells, and gold; but today it includes coins and notes, checks and bank accounts, numbers on ledgers and imprints on plastic cards, electronic blips on computer screens and digits stored on silicon chips. Financial newspapers regularly monitor the money supply, using several different definitions of what money might be and when it should include items such as bonds, bank accounts, and other financial artifacts. Monetary experts seem confused about how to define modern money, much less measure it.

Since the invention of money some three thousand years ago, people have quarreled over it and struggled to obtain as much of it as possible in whatever form it happened to take: gold bars, silver slugs, copper coins, paper notes, or cowrie shells. Money was never a quiet, passive tool, and it never stayed long in the same place or in the same hands. For centuries, Western mythology and literature have chronicled the joys and sufferings of people in the process of gaining or losing great amounts of money, but buried beneath those stories lies another and even more important story of the endless struggle between great nations, large institutions, and powerful personalities to control the production and distribution of money itself—to determine even the definition of what constitutes money. Throughout the course of history, various factions and institutions have controlled the production and regulation of money—the state and its various subdivisions, the church or specific religious orders, merchant leagues and craftsmen's guilds, banking families and private industrialists, national banks and currency traders—and each had a particular role to play at a given historical moment. Humans have fought over money, not merely because it provides wealth and luxury but, more importantly, because it confers power on its masters. It is the magic key to raising armies and moving mountains; to building castles and cities; to controlling the land, the water, and the air; to building canals and launching navies; and to gaining and losing power of all sorts over other humans.

The modern world commercial system began with the voyages of Christopher Columbus to the New World and Vasco da Gama to India. For the first time in history, ships crisscrossed the high seas and called at ports on almost every continent in a global network of trade. The voyages of Columbus and da Gama opened the great mercantile age of international commerce. The way to power and wealth in the mercantile age lay in shipping and trade.

After two centuries of global trade, the routes became firmly established, and many competitors fought to convey the spices and silks from Asia to Europe, slaves from Africa to America, and silver and sugar from America to Europe. Control of the trade passed from Portugal and Spain to England, Holland, and other European nations. Gradually in the second half of the eighteenth century, a new route to wealth arose through the development of industrialized production in England. The focus of activity and the greatest source of profits changed from trade to production, a focus that endured almost to the end of the twentieth century.

Wealth passed from the merchants to the industrialists who manufactured a sequence of goods beginning with textiles but quickly proceeding to steel and other metals. In the words of Karl Marx, the great critic of industrial capitalism, power and wealth were in the hands of those who owned the "means of production"—the factory owners. During the twentieth century, production centered on consumer goods, from cars at the beginning of the century to computers at the end, as well as on the constant supply of armaments for the frequent wars that dominated the century.

Just as the Portuguese and Spaniards could not maintain their mo-

266

The History of Money

nopolies on the global trade in the centuries after Columbus and da Gama, the industrialized countries could not maintain their monopoly on production, which quickly spread to North America and Japan and soon to the rest of the world as well. Manufacturing passed from being an economic novelty to being a given. Soon Brazil and India could outproduce their former colonial masters. Computers and textiles could be manufactured more cheaply in Malaysia and Mexico than in Germany or the United States.

By the final decades of the twentieth century, it became clear that production no longer controlled the economy the way it had in the preceding century. The owners of the means of production were only rarely single individuals or families, and they certainly no longer constituted a specific class; the companies belonged to millions of shareholders—from retirees living on a limited, fixed income to billionaires who owned stock in hundreds of corporations.

In the emerging system, power flows under the control of a new class of financiers who sometimes own or sometimes only control massive amounts of money through brokerage houses, banks, pension plans, insurance agencies, or mutual fund management. They do not move spices, silks, or slaves around the world any more than they control the production of missiles, VCRs, or coffeemakers. They control the flow of money or, more accurately, the *form* of money. As money changes from metal and paper to plastic and computer chips, these financiers control its movement out of one national currency and into another, from stocks into municipal bonds, from certificates of deposit into purchase options, from mortgages into mutual funds, or from currency futures into junk bonds.

As money grows in importance, a new struggle is beginning for the control of it in the coming century. We are likely to see a prolonged era of competition during which many kinds of money will appear, proliferate, and disappear in rapidly crashing waves. In the quest to control the new money, many contenders are struggling to become the primary money institution of the new era.

History has shown repeatedly that neither the government nor the market, by itself, is capable of regulating money. From Nero to Nixon, government officials and financiers have exploited their power to regulate money for their own short-term benefit. Roman emperors reduced the silver content of coins in order to pay the cost of a growing army and bureaucracy; and French bankers and financiers issued worthless paper money and stock to the unsuspecting public. From the Roman denarius during the reign of Nero to the French assignat during the time of the Duke of Arkansas, politicians and financiers created novel monetary systems that initially improved the economic situation, but eventually—when the intoxication wore off, the bills came due, and reality returned—the system of debased money collapsed.

Money, like the calendar and the system of measurements, is a cultural construct that may have arbitrary aspects, but to function properly it needs stability and predictability. A society can base its calendar on the sun, on the moon, or even on a combination of the two, but the calendar must have an anchor somewhere in the real world. The important issue is that the calendar functions as part of a system that is stable and that all people understand. Similarly, so long as money is stable, it can be based on shells and beads, gold and silver, or plastic and electrons, but it needs to be practical and predictable.

Over the past few centuries governments have provided that stability by regulating their currency or by controlling the banks that regulated it. National currencies are now losing their importance, and we face a whole new system. We are now entering a transitional period in which there will be many competing systems of money and value with no single one dominating.

In some regards, the new system will look like the primitive systems in which many different types of money and valuable goods operated at once. We now have parallel and overlapping systems of money.

Even though national currencies such as the dollar and the yen may continue to exist, electronic technology is producing money in so many forms that, at least for a while, the state will not be able to control them. Once free from state control, money will play an even more important role in our lives than it has in the past.

From its initial appearance in world history, money created new

institutions and ways of life at the same time that it corroded and replaced earlier systems. Each technological and social change in the
form of money further expanded money's role in our lives. Through
the centuries, money has become the defining variable not merely
of commercial relations but increasingly of all types of relations from
religious and political to sexual and familial.

In the global economy that is still emerging, the power of money
and the institutions built on it will supersede that of any nation, combination of nations, or international organization now in existence.
Propelled and protected by the power of electronic technology, a new
global elite is emerging—an elite without loyalty to any particular
country. But history has already shown that the people who make
monetary revolutions are not always the ones who benefit from them
in the end. The current electronic revolution in money promises to
increase even more the role of money in our public and private lives,
surpassing kinship, religion, occupation, and citizenship as the defining element of social life. We stand now at the dawn of the Age of
Money.

Homo oeconomicus *is not behind us, but before us*.
                                        —MARCEL MAUSS

ENDNOTES

Introduction: The World Market
1. Saikaku Ihara, *The Japanese Family Storehouse or the Millionaires' Gospel Modernized*, Book 1, trans. G. W. Sargent (London: Cambridge University Press, 1959).

1. Cannibals, Chocolate, and Cash
1. Time estimates by Francis Robicsek, quoted in Frances F. Berdan, *The Aztecs of Central Mexico: An Imperial Society* (New York: Holt, Rinehart and Winston, 1982), p. 114.
2. Inga Clendinnen, *Aztecs: An Interpretation* (Cambridge, England: Cambridge University Press, 1991), p. 137.
3. An excellent discussion of the complicated economic systems of Mesoamerica and whether or not they should be called a market system can be found in Pedro Carrasco, "Some Theoretical Considerations about the Role of the Market in Ancient Mexico," and Frances E. Berdan, "The Reconstruction of Ancient Economies," in *Economic Anthropology: Topics and Theories*, ed. Sutti Ortiz (Lanham, Md.: University Press of America, 1983), pp. 67–82.
4. For a fuller discussion of the money and economic system of the Aztecs, see Berdan, *The Aztecs* (cited in note 1, above).
5. Paul Einzig, *Primitive Money*, 2d ed. (London: Pergamon Press, 1966), p. 15.
6. A. M. Hocart, *The Life-Giving Myth* (London: Methuen, 1952).

2. The Fifth Element
1. Glyn Davies, *A History of Money: From Ancient Times to the Present Day* (Cardiff: University of Wales, 1994), p. 63.
2. Georg Simmel, *The Philosophy of Money* (Routledge and Kegan Paul, 1978.) p. 152.
3. Ibid., p. 311.
4. Quoted in William Camden, *Remains Concerning Britain, 1586*, and in Kevin Jackson, ed., *The Oxford Book of Money* (Oxford: University of Oxford Press, 1995), p. 35.

3. The Premature Death of Money
1. H. G. Wells, *Outline of History* (New York: Macmillan, 1920), pp. 497–98.
2. Joseph Tainter, *The Collapse of Complex Societies* (Cambridge, England: Cambridge University Press, 1990), p. 129.
3. Norman Angell, *The Story of Money* (Garden City, N.Y.: Garden City Publishing, 1929), p. 118.

4. Arnold Hugh Marlin Jones, *The Roman Economy* (Totowa, N.J.: Rowman and Littlefield, 1974), p. 191.
5. Ibid., p. 164.
6. Tainter, p. 69.
7. Jones, p. 82.
8. Tainter, p. 132.

4. Knights of Commerce
1. Malcolm Barber, *The Trial of the Templars* (Cambridge, England: Cambridge University Press, 1978), p. 45.
2. Paul Einzig, *The History of Foreign Exchange*, 2d ed. (New York: Macmillan, 1970), p. 67.
3. Simon Schama, *The Embarrassment of Riches: An Interpretation of Dutch Culture in the Golden Age* (New York: Knopf, 1987), p. 330.

5. The Renaissance: New Money for Old Art
1. René Taton, ed., *The Beginnings of Modern Science*, trans. A. J. Pomerans (New York: Basic Books, 1964), p. 15.
2. J. D. Bernal, *Science in History* (New York: Cameron Associates, 1954), p. 445.
3. Ibid., p. 400.
4. Simmel, *Philosophy*, p. 277.
5. Quoted in John Garraty and Peter Gay, *The Columbia History of the World* (New York: Harper & Row, 1972), p. 510.
6. Pico della Mirandola, "The Dignity of Man," in *The Portable Renaissance Reader*, ed. James Bruce Rosi and Mary Martin McLaughlin (New York: Viking Press, 1952), pp. 476–79.

6. The Golden Curse
1. Quoted in James Bruce Ross and Mary Martin McLaughlin, eds., *Renaissance Reader* (New York: Viking, 1953), p. 232.
2. Eric R. Wolf, *Europe and the People without History* (Berkeley: University of California Press, 1982), p. 237.
3. Ward Barrett, "World Bullion Flows, 1450–1800," in *The Rise of Merchant Empires*, ed. James D. Tracy (Cambridge, London: Cambridge University Press, 1990).
4. Ibid., p. 228.
5. Carla Rahn Phillips, "The Growth and Composition of Trade in the Iberian Empires, 1450–1750," in Tracy, p. 65.
6. John A. Crow, *The Epic of Latin America*, 3d ed. (Berkeley: University of California Press, 1980), p. 395.
7. Adam Smith, *An Inquiry into the Nature and Causes of the Wealth of Nations* (reprint, Oxford: Oxford University Press, 1993), p. 39.

8. Quoted in John Huxtable Elliot, *Imperial Spain 1469–1716* (New York: St. Martin's, 1964), p. 183.

9. Quoted in Antonio Domínguez Ortiz, *The Golden Age of Spain: 1516–1659*, trans. James Casey (New York: Basic Books, 1971), p. 299.

10. Voltaire, "Money," in *Philosophical Dictionary*, vol. 12 of *The Works of Voltaire*, trans. William F. Fleming (Paris: DuMont, 1901), p. 8.

11. John Kenneth Galbraith, *Money: Whence It Came, Where It Went* (Boston: Houghton Mifflin, 1975), p. 12.

7. The Birth of the Dollar

1. Arthur Nussbaum, *A History of the Dollar* (New York: Columbia University Press, 1957), p. 55.

8. The Devil's Mint

1. Lien-chêng Yang, *Money and Credit in China* (Cambridge, Mass.: Harvard University Press, 1952).

2. John F. Chown, *A History of Money From AD 800* (London: Routledge, 1994), p. 207.

3. Quoted in Jackson, *Oxford Book*, p. 440.

4. Galbraith, *Money*, p. 45.

5. Chown, *History*, p. 219.

6. Quoted in Jackson, *Oxford Book*, p. 421.

7. Gerald T. Dunne, *Monetary Decisions of the Supreme Court* (New Brunswick, N.J.: Rutgers University Press, 1960), pp. 10–22.

8. *Faust*, ll. 6057–62. Many English translations of *Faust* are abridged and do not include the financial and political scenes in which Faust and the devil appear before the emperor. The full English text from which these quotes are taken may be found in *Faust*, trans. Stuart Atkins, vol. 2 of *Goethe's Collected Works* (Cambridge, Mass.: Suhrkamp/Insel, 1984).

9. *Faust*, ll. 6083–85.

10. Hans Christoph Binswanger, *Money and Magic* (Chicago: University of Chicago Press, 1994), p. 30.

11. Robert Ellis Dye, "The Easter Cantata and the Idea of Mediation in Goethe's *Faust*," in *Publication of the Modern Language Association of America* 92, no. 5 (1977): pp. 963–76.

9. Metric Money

1. William Hallock and Herbert T. Wade, *The Evolution of Weights and Measures* (New York: Macmillan, 1906), p. 85.

2. Bernal, *Science in History*, p. 353.

10. The Gold Bug
1. Galbraith, *Money*, p. 30.
2. This story was related by Cyril Asquith in recounting a conversation with J. M. Keynes. Cited in Jackson, *Oxford Book*, p. 46.
3. Quoted in Angell, *Story of Money*, p. 235.
4. Ibid., p. 236.
5. H. G. Wells, *The Work, Wealth, and Happiness of Mankind*, vol. 1 (New York: Doubleday, 1931), p. 390.
6. Oswald Spengler, *Decline of the West*, trans: Charles F. Atkinson (Oxford: Oxford University Press, 1991), p. 414.

11. The Yellow Brick Road
1. Alexis de Tocqueville, *Democracy in America*, vol. I, chapt. 3, 1835. (Reprint, New York: Vintage Books, 1945), p. 53.
2. This research is available in a series of articles by Arthur J. Rolnick and Warren Weber: "New Evidence on the Free Banking Era," *American Economic Review*, December 1983, pp. 1080–91; "The Causes of Free Bank Failures," *Journal of Monetary Economics* 14 (1984): 267–91; "Explaining the Demand for Free Notes," *Journal of Monetary Economics* 21 (1988): 47–71.
3. Chown, *History of Money*, pp. 246–55.
4. Dunne, *Monetary Decisions of the Supreme Court*, p. 106.
5. Galbraith, *Money*, p. 95.
6. Milton Friedman and Anna Jacobson Schwartz, *A Monetary History of the United States: 1867–1960* (Princeton, N.J.: Princeton University Press, 1963), p. 116.
7. Hugh Rockoff, "The Wizard of Oz as a Monetary Allegory," *Journal of Political Economy* 98, no. 4 (1990).
8. Friedman and Schwartz, *Monetary History*, p. 135.

12. The Golden Playpen of Politics
1. Quoted in Milton Friedman, *Money Mischief* (New York: Harcourt Brace, 1992), p. 53.
2. Friedman and Schwartz, *Monetary History*, p. 463.
3. Ibid., p. 485.
4. Galbraith, *Money*, p. 288.

13. Wild Money and the Stealth Tax
1. James Grant, *Money of the Mind: Borrowing and Lending in America* (New York: Farrar, Straus and Giroux, 1992), p. 368.
2. Matt Moffett, "Peru Seems Set to Stick with Fujimori," *Wall Street Journal*, April 7, 1995.

3. Wells, *The Outline*, pp. 1147–50.

4. Marvin Harris, *America Now: The Anthropology of a Changing Culture* (New York: Simon and Schuster, 1981), p. 61.

5. Harvey A. Levenstein, *Revolution at the Table: The Transformation of the American Diet* (Oxford: Oxford University Press, 1988), p. 32.

6. William Greider, *Secrets of the Temple: How the Federal Reserve Runs the Country* (New York: Simon and Schuster, 1987), p. 99.

14. The Cash Ghetto

1. Anatole France quote from *Quotations*, ed. Fran Alexander, (London: Bloomsbury, 1994), p. 173.

2. Oscar Lewis, *Five Families* (New York: Basic Books, 1959), and *The Children of Sanchez* (New York: Random House, 1961).

15. Interlude in Plastic

1. George Ritzer, *The McDonaldization of Society* (Thousand Oaks, Calif.: Pine Forge Press, 1993), p. 29.

2. Kenneth M. Morris and Alan M. Siegel, *Guide to Understanding Money and Investing* (New York: Lightbulb Press, 1993), p. 12.

3. Grant, *Money of the Mind*, pp. 91–110.

4. Ibid., p. 76.

5. Ibid., p. 352.

6. Edward Bellamy, *Looking Backward: 2000–1887* (1888; reprint, Cambridge, Mass.: Harvard University Press, 1967), p. 147.

7. Carl H. Moore and Alvin E. Russell, *Money: Its Origin, Development and Modern Use* (Jefferson, N.C.: McFarland, 1987), p. 74.

8. Joel Kurtzman, *The Death of Money* (Boston: Little, Brown, 1993), p. 83.

16. The Erotic Life of Electronic Money

1. "Automatic Clearing Houses," in the reference series *Fedpoints* 31, Federal Reserve Bank of New York, March 1993, p. 2.

2. Kelly Holland and Amy Cortese, "The Future of Money," *Business Week*, June 12, 1995, pp. 66–78; and Nicholas Bray, "Future Shop: No Cash Accepted," *Wall Street Journal*, July 13, 1995.

3. I. Orlin Grabbe, "The End of Money," *Liberty* 8, no. 6 (July 1995).

4. "E-Cash," *Business Week*, June 12, 1995, p. 67.

5. Cora Lee C. Gillilland, *The Stone Money of Yap: A Numismatic Survey*, Smithsonian Studies in History and Technology, no. 23 (Washington, D.C.: Smithsonian Institution Press, 1975).

17. The Art of Currency Terror

1. Suzanne McGee, "Why Are Currency Futures Languishing?," *Wall Street Journal*, April 10, 1995.

2. Ted Fishman, "Our Currency in Cyberspace," *Harper's*, December 1995, p. 57.

3. Kurtzman, *Death of Money*, p. 29.

4. Gregory J. Millman, *The Vandals' Crown: How Rebel Currency Traders Overthrew the World's Central Banks* (New York: Free Press, 1995), pp. 157–88.

5. Quoted in George Melloan, "Japanese Bubble, Mexican Bubble—Who's Next?," *Wall Street Journal*, June 19, 1995.

6. William Greider, *Secrets*, p. 688.

7. Michael Moffitt, *The World's Money: International Banking from Bretton Woods to the Brink of Insolvency* (New York: Simon and Schuster, 1983), p. 163.

8. Fishman, "Our Currency," p. 61.

9. Voltaire, "Money," p. 13.

BIBLIOGRAPHY

Abu-Lughod, Janet L. *Before European Hegemony: The World System* A.D. 1250–1350. New York: Oxford University Press, 1989.

Adams, Charles. *For Good and Evil: The Impact of Taxes on Civilization*. Lanham, Md.: Madison Books, 1993.

Angell, Norman. *The Story of Money*. Garden City, N.Y.: Garden City Publishing, 1929.

Barber, Malcolm. *The New Knighthood: A History of the Order of the Temple*. Cambridge, England: Cambridge University Press, 1994.

———. *The Trial of the Templars*. Cambridge, England: Cambridge University Press, 1978.

Barrett, Ward. "World Bullion Flows, 1450–1800." In *The Rise of Merchant Empires*, edited by James D. Tracy. Cambridge, England: Cambridge University Press, 1990.

Baum, L. Frank. *The Wonderful Wizard of Oz*. 1900. Reprint, New York: Dover Publications, 1960.

Bellamy, Edward. *Looking Backward: 2000–1887*. 1888. Reprint, Cambridge, Mass.: Harvard University Press, 1967.

Benedict, Burton. *Money: Tokens of Value from Around the World*. Berkeley, Calif.: Lowie Museum of Anthropology, 1991.

Benedict, Ruth. "Configurations of Culture in North America," *American Anthropologist*, 1934.

———. *Patterns of Culture*. Boston: Houghton Mifflin, 1934.

Berdan, Frances F. *The Aztecs of Central Mexico: An Imperial Society*. New York: Holt, Rinehart and Winston, 1982.

Beresiner, Yasha, and Colin Narbeth. *The Story of Paper Money*. New York: Arco, 1973.

Bernal, J. D. *Science in History*. New York: Cameron Associates, 1954.

Bethell, Tom. "Inflation, Confiscation, and Gold." *American Spectator*, September 1994.

Binswanger, Hans Christoph. *Money and Magic: A Critique of the Modern Economy in the Light of Goethe's Faust*, translated by J. E. Harrison. Chicago: University of Chicago Press, 1994.

Bohannan, Paul J. "The Impact of Money on an African Subsistence Economy." *Journal of Economic History* 19 (December 1959).

Burnett, Andrew. *Coins: Interpreting the Past*. Berkeley, Calif.: University of California Press, 1991.

Cameron, Rondo. *A Concise Economic History of the World*, 2d ed. Oxford: Oxford University Press, 1993.

Carlson, Katherine. "Reciprocity in the Marketplace: Tipping in an Urban Nightclub."

In *Conformity and Conflict*, 3d ed., edited by James Spradley and David McCurdy. Boston: Little, Brown, 1977.

Champ, Bruce, Neil Wallace, and Warren E. Weber. "Interest Rates under the U.S. National Banking System," *Journal of Monetary Economics* 34 (1994).

Chown, John F. *A History of Money From AD 800*. London: Routledge, 1994.

Clarke, William M. *How the City of London Works: An Introduction to Its Financial Markets*, 3d ed. London: Waterlow, 1991.

Clendinnen, Inga. *Aztecs: An Interpretation*. Cambridge, England: Cambridge University Press, 1991.

Coblentz, Stanton A. *Avarice: A History*. Washington, D.C.: Public Affairs Press, 1965.

Cribb, Joe. *Money*. London: Dorling Kindersley, 1991.

Cribb, Joe, Barrie Cook, and Ian Carradice. *The Coin Atlas*. London: Macdonald Illustrated, 1990.

Crow, John A. *The Epic of Latin America*, 3d ed. Berkeley: University of California Press, 1980.

Crump, Thomas. *The Phenomenon of Money*. London: Routledge and Kegan Paul, 1981.

Davies, Glyn. *A History of Money: From Ancient Times to the Present Day*. Cardiff: University of Wales Press, 1994.

Deutschman, Alan. "Money Wants to Be Anonymous." *Worth* 4, no. 8 (October 1995).

Domínguez Ortiz, Antonio. *The Golden Age of Spain: 1516–1659*, translated by James Casey. New York: Basic Books, 1971.

Doyle, Kenneth, ed. *The Meanings of Money*. Newbury Park, Calif.: Sage, 1992.

Dunne, Gerald T. *Monetary Decisions of the Supreme Court*. New Brunswick, N.J.: Rutgers University Press, 1960.

Dye, Robert Ellis. "The Easter Cantata and the Idea of Mediation in Goethe's *Faust*." *Publications of the Modern Language Association of America* 92, no. 5 (1977).

Einzig, Paul. *Primitive Money*, 2d ed. London: Pergamon Press, 1966.

———. *The History of Foreign Exchange*, 2d ed. New York: Macmillan, 1970.

Elliot, John Huxtable. *Imperial Spain 1469–1716*. New York: St. Martin's, 1964.

Evans-Pritchard, E. E. *The Nuer*. Oxford: Oxford University Press, 1940.

Ferraro, Gary P. *The Cultural Dimension of International Business*, 2d ed. Englewood Cliffs, N.J.: Prentice-Hall, 1994.

Firth, Raymond, ed. *Themes in Economic Anthropology*. London: Travistock, 1967.

Fishman, Ted. "Our Currency in Cyberspace." *Harper's*, December 1994.

Frängsmyr, Tore, J. L. Heilbron, and Robin E. Rider, eds. *The Quantifying Spirit in the 18th Century*. Berkeley: University of California Press, 1990.

Frank, Andre Gunder, and Barry K. Gills, eds. *The World System: Five Hundred Years or Five Thousand?* New York: Routledge, 1993.

Frank, Tenney. *An Economic History of Rome*. New York: Cooper Square Press, 1920.

Friedman, Milton. *Money Mischief*. New York: Harcourt Brace, 1992.

Friedman, Milton, and Anna Jacobson Schwartz. *A Monetary History of the United States: 1867–1960*. Princeton, N.J.: Princeton University Press, 1963.

Galbraith, John Kenneth. *Money: Whence It Came, Where It Went*. Boston: Houghton Mifflin, 1975.

Garraty, John, and Peter Gay. *The Columbia History of the World*. New York: Harper and Row, 1972.

Gilliland, Cora Lee C. *The Stone Money of Yap: A Numismatic Survey*. Smithsonian Studies in History and Technology, no. 23. Washington, D.C.: Smithsonian Institution Press, 1975.

Gonen, Amiram, ed. *The Encyclopedia of the Peoples of the World*. New York: Henry Holt, 1993.

Goux, Jean-Joseph. "Primitive Money, Modern Money." In *Understanding Origins*, edited by Francisco J. Varela and Jean-Pierre Dupuy. Dordrecht, Netherlands: Kluwer, 1992.

Grabbe, J. Orlin. "The End of Money." *Liberty* 8, no. 6 (July 1995).

Gragg. F. A., ed. *Latin Writings of the Italian Humanists*. New York: Scribner's, 1927.

Grant, James. *Money of the Mind: Borrowing and Lending in America*. New York: Farrar, Straus and Giroux, 1992.

Greider, William. *Secrets of the Temple: How the Federal Reserve Runs the Country*. New York: Simon and Schuster, 1987.

Gudeman, Stephen. *The Demise of a Rural Economy: From Subsistence to Capitalism in a Latin American Village*. London: Routledge and Kegan Paul, 1978.

———. *Economics as Culture*. London: Routledge and Kegan Paul, 1986.

Hallock, William, and Herbert T. Wade. *The Evolution of Weights and Measures*. New York: Macmillan, 1906.

Hamilton, Earl J. *American Treasure and the Price Revolution in Spain, 1501–1650*. New York: Octagon, 1965.

Harris, Marvin. *America Now: The Anthropology of a Changing Culture*. New York: Simon and Schuster, 1981.

Hart, Keith. "Heads or Tails?" *Man* 21 (December 1986).

Hassig, Ross. *Trade, Tribute, and Transportation: The Sixteenth-Century Political Economy of the Valley of Mexico*. Norman: University of Oklahoma Press, 1985.

Herodotus. *The Histories*, translated by Aubrey de Selincourt. London: Penguin, 1954.

Herskovits, Melville J. *Economic Anthropology: The Economic Life of Primitive People*. New York: Norton, 1952.

Hewitt, Virginia. *Beauty and the Banknote: Images of Women on Paper Money*. London: British Museum Press, 1994.

Hibbert, Christopher. *The House of Medici*. New York: Morrow, 1980.

Hicks, John. *A Theory of Economic History*. Oxford: Oxford University Press, 1969.

Hocart, A. M. *The Life-Giving Myth*. London: Methuen, 1952.

Hodge, Mary G., and Michael E. Smith, eds. *Economies and Polities in the Aztec Realm*. Vol. 6 of *Studies on Culture and Society*. Albany, N.Y.: Institute for Mesoamerican Studies, State University of New York at Albany, 1994.

Hughes, Robert. *The Fatal Shore: The Epic of Australia's Founding*. New York: Random House, 1986.

Ihara, Saikaku. *The Japanese Family Storehouse or the Millionaires' Gospel Modernized*, translated by G. W. Sargent. Cambridge, England: Cambridge University Press, 1959.

Jackson, Kevin, ed. *The Oxford Book of Money*. Oxford: Oxford University Press, 1995.

Jennings, Francis. *The Founders of America*. New York: Norton, 1993.

Jones, Arnold Hugh Marlin. *The Roman Economy*. Totowa, N.J.: Rowman and Littlefield, 1974.

Junge, Ewald. *The Seaby Coin Encyclopaedia*. London: Seaby, 1992.

Kadletz, Edward M. "Preface—A Banker's Call to Action." *Strategies, American Bankers
Association* 3 (Winter 1995).

Kennedy, Paul. *The Rise and Fall of the Great Powers: Economic Change and Military Conflict from 1500 to 2000*. New York: Random House, 1987.

Kitto, H. D. F. *The Greeks*. Harmondsworth, Middlesex, England: Penguin, 1957.

Koran, Jan, ed. *Sborník pro Dejiny Prírodních ved a Techniky Acta Historiae Rerum Natu-
ralium nec non Technicarum: 450 let Jáchymovskych dolu*. Prague: Ceskolovenská
Akademie Ved, 1967.

Kurtzman, Joel. *The Death of Money*. Boston: Little, Brown, 1993.

Lapham, Lewis. *Money and Class in America: Notes and Observations on Our Civil Religion*. New York: Weidenfeld and Nicolson, 1988.

LeClair, Edward E., Jr., and Harold K. Schneider, eds. *Economic Anthropology: Readings
in Theory and Analysis*. New York: Holt, Rinehart and Winston, 1968.

Levenstein, Harvey A. *Revolution at the Table: The Transformation of the American Diet*.
Oxford: Oxford University Press, 1988.

Levy, Steven. "The End of Money?" *Newsweek*, October 30, 1995.

Lewis, Oscar. *Five Families*. New York: Basic Books, 1959.

———. *The Children of Sanchez*. New York: Random House, 1961.

Lottman, Herbert R. *The French Rothschilds: The Great Banking Dynasty through Two Tur-
bulent Centuries*. New York: Crown, 1995.

Lytton, Bulwer Edward. "On the Management of Money." In *Caxtoniana: A Series of Essays on Life, Literature, and Manners*. New York: Harper and Brothers, 1864.

Marx, Karl, and Friedrich Engels. *The Communist Manifesto*, translated by David McLel-
lan. Oxford: Oxford University Press, 1992.

Mauss, Marcel. *The Gift: Forms and Functions of Change in Archaic Society*, translated by
Ian Cunniso. New York: Free Press, 1954.

McCurdy, David. "Savings on Loans in a Peasant Society." In *Conformity and Conflict*,
4th ed., edited by James Spradley and David McCurdy. Boston: Little, Brown, 1980.

Millman, Gregory J. *The Vandals' Crown: How Rebel Currency Traders Overthrew the
World's Central Banks*. New York: Free Press, 1995.

Mirandola, Picco della. "The Dignity of Man." *The Portable Renaissance Reader*, edited
by James Bruce Ross and Mary Martin McLaughlin. New York: Viking Press, 1953.

Moffitt, Michael. *The World's Money: International Banking from Bretton Woods to the Brink
of Insolvency*. New York: Simon and Schuster, 1983.

Moore, Alexander. *Cultural Anthropology: The Field Study of Human Beings*. San Diego:
Collegiate Press, 1992.

Moore, Carl H., and Alvin E. Russell. *Money: Its Origin, Development and Modern Use*.
Jefferson, N.C.: McFarland, 1987.

Morris, Kenneth M., and Alan M. Siegel. *Guide to Understanding Money and Investing*.
New York: Lightbulb Press, 1993.

Neal, Larry. "The Dutch and English East Indian Companies Compared." In *The Rise of Merchant Empires*, edited by James D. Tracy. Cambridge, England: Cambridge University Press, 1990.

Norris, Floyd. "After Eleven Years, It's Payday." *New York Times*, July 1, 1995.

Nussbaum, Arthur. *A History of the Dollar*. New York: Columbia University Press, 1957.

O'Hanlon, Michael. *Paradise: Portraying the New Guinea Highlands*. London: British Museum Press, 1993.

Ohnuki-Tierney, Emiko. *Rice as Self: Japanese Identities through Time*. Princeton, N.J.: Princeton University Press, 1993.

Ortiz, Sutti, ed. *Economic Anthropology: Topics and Theories*. Lanham, Md.: University Press of America, 1983.

Pareto, Vilfredo. *The Rise and Fall of Elites*. Totowa, N.J.: Bedminster Press, 1968.

Phillips, Carla Rahn. "The Growth and Composition of Trade in the Iberian Empires, 1450–1750." In *The Rise of Merchant Empires*, edited by James D. Tracy. Cambridge, England: Cambridge University Press, 1990.

Polanyi, Karl. *The Great Transformation: The Political and Economic Origins of Our Time*. Boston: Beacon Press, 1944.

———. *Primitive, Archaic and Modern Economies*. Boston: Beacon Press, 1968.

Polanyi, Karl, Conrad Arensberg, and Harry W. Pearson, eds. *Trade and Market in the Early Empires: Economies in History and Theory*. New York: Free Press, 1967.

Pospisil, Leopold. *The Kapauku Papuans of West New Guinea*. New York: Holt, Rinehart and Winston, 1963.

Radford, A. R. "The Economic Organization of a P.O.W. Camp." *Economica*, November 1945.

Richards, Gertrude R. B. *Florentine Merchants in the Age of the Medici*. Cambridge, Mass.: Harvard University Press, 1932.

Richards, John, ed. *Precious Metals in Later Medieval and Early Modern Worlds*. Durham, N. C.: Duke University Press, 1983.

Ritzer, George. *The McDonaldization of Society*. Thousand Oaks, Calif.: Pine Forge Press, 1993.

Rockoff, Hugh. "The Wizard of Oz as a Monetary Allegory." *Journal of Political Economy* 98, no. 4 (1990).

Rolnick, Arthur J., and Warren Weber. "New Evidence on the Free Banking Era." *American Economic Review*, December 1983.

———. "The Causes of Free Bank Failures." *Journal of Monetary Economics* 14 (1984).

———. "Explaining the Demand for Free Notes." *Journal of Monetary Economics* 21 (1988).

Roover, Raymond de. *The Rise and Decline of the Medici Bank: 1397–1494*. Cambridge, Mass.: Harvard University Press, 1963.

Ross, James Bruce, and Mary Martin McLaughlin, eds. *Renaissance Reader*. New York: Viking, 1953.

Sahlins, Marshall. *Stone Age Economics*. Chicago: Aldine, 1972.

Schama, Simon. *The Embarrassment of Riches: An Interpretation of Dutch Culture in the Golden Age*. New York: Knopf, 1987.

Shelton, Judy. *Money Meltdown: Restoring Order to the Global Currency System*. New York: Free Press, 1994.

Simmel, Georg. *The Philosophy of Money*, translated by Tom Bottomore and David Frisby. London: Routledge and Kegan Paul, 1978.

Smith, Adam. *An Inquiry into the Nature and Causes of the Wealth of Nations*. 1776. Reprint, Oxford: Oxford University Press, 1993.

Smith, Adam [George Goodman]. *Paper Money*. New York: Summit Books, 1981.

Smith, Carol A. "Regional Analysis in World-System Perspective." In *Economic Anthropology*, edited by S. Ortiz. Lanham, Md.: University Press of America, 1983.

Spengler, Oswald. *The Decline of the West*, translated by Charles F. Atkinson. Oxford: Oxford University Press, 1991.

Stack, Carol. *All Our Kin*. New York: Harper and Row, 1974.

Strauss, Leo. *Xenophon's Socratic Discourse: An Interpretation of the Oeconomicus*. Ithaca, N.Y.: Cornell University Press, 1970.

Swartz, Marc J., and David K. Jordan. *Anthropology: Perspective on Humanity*. New York: Wiley, 1976.

Tainter, Joseph. *The Collapse of Complex Societies*. Cambridge, England: Cambridge University Press, 1990.

Taton, René, ed. *The Beginnings of Modern Science*, translated by A. J. Pomerans. New York: Basic Books, 1964.

Tocqueville, Alexis de. *Democracy in America*. 1835. Reprint, New York: Vintage Books, 1945.

Tracy, James D., ed. *The Rise of Merchant Empires*. Cambridge, England: Cambridge University Press, 1990.

Trilling, Lionel. *The Liberal Imagination*. New York: Viking, 1950.

Tweddell, Colin E., and Linda A. Kimball. *Introduction to the Peoples and Cultures of Asia*. Englewood Cliffs, N.J.: Prentice-Hall, 1985.

Voltaire. "Money." In *Philosophical Dictionary*, vol. 12 of *The Works of Voltaire*, translated by William F. Fleming. Paris: DuMont, 1901.

Waateringe, W. Groenman van. "The Disastrous Effects of the Roman Occupation." In *Roman and Native in the Low Countries*, edited by Roel Brandt and Jan Slofstra. *British Archaeological Reports International Series 184*.

Wallerstein, Immanuel. *The Modern World-System: Capitalist Agriculture and the Origins of the European World-Economy in the Sixteenth Century*. New York: Academic Press, 1974.

Weber, Max. *The Protestant Ethic and the Spirit of Capitalism*, translated by Talcott Parsons. London: Unwin University Books, 1930.

———. *The Theory of Social and Economic Organization*, translated by A. M. Henderson and Talcott Parsons. New York: Free Press, 1947.

Wells, H. G. *Outline of History*, rev. ed. Garden City, N.J.: Garden City Publishing, 1931.

———. *The Work, Wealth and Happiness of Mankind*. 1931. Reprint (2 vols), New York: Greenwood, 1938.

White, Jenny. *Money Makes Us Relatives: Women's Labor in Urban Turkey*. Austin: University of Texas Press, 1994.

White, Lawrence H. *Competition and Currency: Essays of Free Banking and Money*. New York: New York University Press, 1989.

White, Peter T. "The Power of Money." *National Geographic*, January 1993.

Wittfogel, Karl A. *Oriental Despotism: A Comparative Study of Total Power*. New York: Random House, 1957.

Wolf, Eric R. *Europe and the People without History*. Berkeley: University of California Press, 1982.

Yang, Lien-chêng. *Money and Credit in China*. Cambridge, Mass.: Harvard University Press, 1952.

Zelizer, Viviana A. *The Social Meaning of Money*. New York: Basic Books, 1994.

INDEX

abacus, elimination of, 85
accounting, double-entry bookkeeping, 78, 87
Africa:
  cultural focus in, 8–11
  currency in, 122
  gold mines in, 162, 177, 178, 179
  hyperinflation in, 203
  marketplace in, 1–2, 3–4
  slave market in, 108
airline miles, as near-money, 230–31
Alaska, gold mines in, 177
Alexander the Great, 35, 44
algebra, origin of term, 87
algorithm, origin of term, 87
American Express Company, 227, 229, 234
Americas:
  mines of, 93–102, 104–5, 106, 107
  wars against natives in, 163
  wealth of, 95–100, 107, 108, 131
animals, 9–11, 21
Aristotle, 42
Asia:
  electronic money in, 235–36
  European trade with, 56–57, 99, 108
  money flowing to, 228
  trade dollars and, 120–21
Australia, gold mines in, 162
Aztecs, 17–20, 23, 178

bank, origin of term, 73
BankAmericard/Visa, 227, 229
banking:
  bills of exchange in, 74–78
  and brokers, 107
  and cash-only economy, 195–98
  central, 159–60, 166–67, 184, 261, 262
  and commerce, 77
  and communication, 240
  electronic, 235–41
  and FDIC, 225
  and Great Depression, 181
  international, 76–77, 82–84, 257–60
  on Internet, 243–44
  Italian families in, 72–74, 76–79, 82–84, 89–90
  and lending, 223–25
  loans vs. contracts in, 73–74
  and mathematics, 88–92
  and money machines, 222, 236–40
  Templars' system of, 64, 65, 66–67, 72
  in U.S., 169–70
Barclaycard, 227
barter, 3, 4, 19, 107
Baum, L. Frank, 175–77
Behn, Aphra, 11, 12
Benedict, Ruth, 8
bills of exchange, 74–78

Bolivia:
  inflation in, 193–98, 200
  mines in, 93–95, 96
bookkeeping, double-entry, 78, 87
Brazil, Portuguese colony in, 100–101
Bretton Woods Conference, 183–84, 261
Bryan, William Jennings, 175, 176
buck, origin of term, 23

cacao beans, 17–20
calculation, and numbers, 85–88
California, gold in, 162
calpixque (tribute collectors), 18
Canada, currency of, 120
capital:
  mass movement of, 259–60
  origin of term, 22
capitalism:
  money as basis of, 251–52
  in New York City, 168–69
  roots of, 22
  Russian elimination of, 165
  and wealth, 161
cash:
  and crime, 217–18, 241
  decline of, 208, 211–12
  economy based on, 195–98, 212, 213–14
  from money machines, 222, 236–40
  in multitiered money system, 230
  and poverty, 210–18, 230
  in shopping malls, 221–22
  transfers of, 216–17
  and vending machines, 238–39
  see also coins; paper money
cash-debit cards, 222, 237, 242
Charles VIII, king of France, 84
chattel, origin of term, 22
checking cards, 222
checks:
  cashing of, 212–13
  direct deposit of, 234
  elimination of, 236–37
  introduction of, 78
  money transferred by, 222–23, 233–34
  travel, 234
Chicago Mercantile Exchange, 254–55
China:
  currency of, 121, 125–28
  on silver standard, 159
Chirac, Jacques, 260
chocolate, as medium of exchange, 17–20, 22
Christianity:
  birth of, 54–55
  growth of, 44–45
  and persecution, 47, 59–61